The Sociology of Education

The Sociology of Education

P. W. MUSGRAVE

METHUEN & CO LTD
11 NEW FETTER LANE LONDON EC4

First published in 1965
© 1965 by P. W. Musgrave
Reprinted twice 1966
Reprinted twice 1967
Reprinted 1968
Printed in Great Britain by
Cox and Wyman Ltd, Fakenham, Norfolk
SBN 416 28300 4
1.6

Contents

Acknowledgements

A book of this kind naturally owes much to a great many people, but I wish particularly to thank the following:

My teachers at the Institute of Education, the University of London, Dr G. Baron and Mrs J. E. Floud (now of Nuffield College, Oxford).

My students on the postgraduate and certificate courses at Homerton College, Cambridge during 1962–4, who left little unquestioned.

My colleagues at Homerton, who gave much assistance, often without knowing it, and particularly Dr N. K. Willson, who gave a great deal of her time to read and comment on the final draft.

My wife, for the typing of this book and much else besides.

ABERDEEN, 1965   P.W.M.

I

Introduction

Sociology is a social science. This implies that sociology is an attempt to build up a set of logical and consistent theories about the society in which we live. Its subject matter includes the institutions which mark our society; such are the family, the class system and the economy. One important institution in a modern society is the educational system. The increasing concern with education has led to a specialism within the larger field of sociology which deals with the sociology of education. In this branch of the subject a study is made of the relationship between education and society as a whole. This book is an introduction to this specialized field and, since it is intended for British readers, it will mainly be concerned with conditions in this country, though comparative examples from other countries are useful for indicating more clearly what is happening here.

A science should contain no prejudice. Therefore a sociology of education must give a neutral analysis. Politics must be avoided, though very often decisions on educational policy are the very stuff of politics. On the whole we shall be concerned with means and not ends, but sometimes we shall be brought to the point beyond which a sociologist can no longer go without taking up a philosophic position. This must and will be made clear. All teachers should realize when they are arguing from evidence and when their position is based on political or other beliefs.

There are two parts to our subject – society and education. To understand the sociology of education the student must learn something both of sociology itself and of education. Sociology often, but not always, demands statistics to demonstrate a truth, to indicate an order of magnitude, to make a point clear. These figures are not to be learnt parrotwise nor are they to be feared. They are only used where essential to the argument. Footnotes have also been kept to a minimum.

After each chapter there is a reading list to which references are made
in the text by adding the date of publication to the author's name.[1]
Whenever a book exists in the Penguin or Pelican editions, this has been
indicated.

The book is divided into three parts. The first concentrates on the
relationship between children and certain parts of society. Three important social institutions are taken, namely the family, the social class
system and the economy. Each is examined in turn with the object of
teaching some of the basic sociology upon which a sound sociology of
education can be built. The chapter analysing the institution is followed
in each case by a chapter outlining the implications of this analysis for
the education of children.

The second part examines the relationship of the contemporary British
educational system with other social institutions. The main concern
here is with the schools, though higher education and other forms of
education are mentioned. The functions of education in relation to certain important fields are analysed. An attempt is made to answer four
questions. What part does education play in the balance between
stability and change, in maintaining a democratic political system, in
ensuring the full use of the talented people in our society and, finally, in
supplying trained manpower to the economic system?

In the final part the position of teachers in the schools is considered on
the grounds that teachers who have thoroughly examined the forces at
work on themselves will be more effective in their vocation. Four facets
of the teacher's position are examined. A teacher is a member of a
profession. He serves in a school where he is at the centre of a complex
web of forces which act upon him both from outside and from inside
the school. Next the individual teacher's position in the classroom is
examined; here he is the representative to the children of the aims
implicit in the British educational system, and he is part of a definite
social system together with the children in his class. Finally, an attempt
is made to answer the fascinating question, what does teaching do to the
teacher?

Particularly in the second and third parts of this book there are areas
where the research that the topics warrant has not been done. An
introductory textbook should avoid controversy and, therefore, an

[1] If a fuller bibliography of the field is needed, the reader may refer to
Current Sociology, VII, No. 3, 1958, 'The Sociology of Education', J. E. Floud
and A. H. Halsey.

indication is given where facts are sparse. But a reasonably uncontroversial narrative has always been provided on the grounds that it is of overriding importance to give teachers and all others interested in education the analytical framework within which to view children, schools and teachers.

PART I

*Education and
the Social Framework*

2

The Family

In the first part of this chapter the family will be considered as a social institution. The analysis will be of a qualitative rather than a quantitative nature. An attempt will be made to answer three questions, namely what purposes does the family serve, in what ways have sociologists looked at families and what is family life like in Britain today. In the second part of the chapter certain demographic trends that influence the family will be examined; examples are changes in the size of the family and in the age of marriage. The family is an important social institution and has close connections with education, which will be examined in the next chapter, but here it is intended to give a fairly complete introduction to the sociology of the family, whilst at the same time not over emphasizing material that will be irrelevant elsewhere in this book.

A. The Family as a Social Institution

How can we define the word 'family'? To a sociologist the family is one of the many small face-to-face groups that he calls 'primary groups'. It has certain peculiar characteristics that differentiate it from other common primary groups such as groups that work together or meet together regularly for some leisure pursuit. Firstly, it gives special recognition to the relationship between one male and one or more females or between one female and one or more males. The former case covers the common Western European or American family; the latter covers the case found in Tibet where one woman and a group of brothers form the family unit. This definition is influenced by the findings of anthropologists among primitive peoples, but it serves to remind us that the typical family pattern found in Britain is not the only one nor even the universal one in this country. The purposes that the family serves can be fulfilled in several ways. Temporary liaisons and men with several spouses, more

B

frequently in succession than at the same time, are found in all social classes in the so-called civilized countries. These forms of family will give their offspring an upbringing of a quality very different from that given to children born into families of the more usual Western European pattern.

Anthropologists have found that some pattern of family organization is a common social institution even amongst peoples who do not understand the connection between the sex act and the birth of children. The theory held quite commonly in the nineteenth century that sexual communism was to be found amongst lower civilizations has not been substantiated. Even amongst those peoples who are ignorant of the significance of the sex act, there is a strong feeling between mother and child. The position of the father is less definite, as the part of father in the family may be played by a 'social' father rather than by the biological father. However, here can be seen the second peculiar characteristic of the family, namely the stress given to kinship in the way that the family is organized.

1. *The Functions of the Family*

One of the main ways in which sociologists analyse any institution is by asking what are the functions that it is fulfilling. The first question that must be answered here is, therefore, what are the chief functions of the family? Traditionally answers to this question have been given under three headings. Consideration has been given to the way that the family first fulfils the satisfaction of sex needs, secondly acts as an economic unit, and thirdly cares for the young and the old. Each of these functions will be examined in turn, though it is to the way that the family cares for the young that most attention will be given because of its more direct relevance to education.

(i) *Sex needs.* There are very powerful impulses to sexual behaviour in most humans, and any organized society will wish to place this area of conduct under control. Whatever family system is chosen, sex needs can be met in some way within the family. Today amongst the more civilized peoples this function of the family has become more complex. In a modern industrial society marked by many impersonal contacts the individual could feel isolated and develop a personality insufficient to meet his problems, if he had not some secure base from which to venture forth and to which he may return. The family provides this security, giving the individual the affection and interest which is needed to sustain him in the many brief and temporary contacts with the world at large.

A person can often manage his psychological tensions if he can take his troubles home.

The institution of marriage has changed greatly over the last century: it is coming to be viewed today more as a partnership of equals than, as was the case, as a relationship between a dominant male and an almost servile female. The family has ceased to provide all the meals and most of the clothes, since many meals and clothes are now bought outside the family. The family has come to be used as a very specialized agency for providing the affection that helps to ensure the emotional stability needed if men and women are to manage their lives successfully under modern conditions.

(ii) *Economic*. The primitive family was a subsistence unit that organized the raising and getting of food. The family held and farmed the land. In countries where hunting and fishing were important means of food supply the family organized the labour for these purposes. Today production of most goods and services is carried out in factories or out-side the household, and members of the family are employed as individuals, not as one unit. Rewards in the form of money wages are paid to individuals who are often adolescents. Work and home or family have become separated. Different codes of values may rule in both, with the result that there is a loss of emotional unity within the family.

There is a further economic function that the family used to fulfil. Before the industrial revolution it was normal for the child, whether boy or girl, to learn his future occupation within the family; son usually followed father. This continuity is now no longer common, though in some of the professions there is evidence that this 'self-recruitment' of occupations still occurs.[1] The case may be cited of the sons of doctors following their fathers. Today the child does not learn the technical skills of the job from his father, but picks up the social skills and the background to the job. Again, in areas where one industry is pre-dominant, such as in a mining village, the possibility that a son can do other than follow his father is remote. But the majority of children live today in urban areas that contain a diversity of industries and occupations. In these conditions the family cannot fulfil its former function. Most parents can give neither the specialized training necessary nor the advice that a child needs if he is to match his abilities and aptitudes to the local opportunities for employment in the best possible way.

[1] R. K. Kelsall, 'Self-recruitment in Four Professions', in D. V. Glass (ed.), *Social Mobility in Britain*, London, 1954.

(iii) *Socialization.* All groups have at least one problem in common. New recruits must be taught the accepted ways of behaviour within the group. This is as true of a family as it is of society. It is, in fact, mainly through the family that society at large does initiate its new recruits, and it is to this process that the name 'socialization' is given. It will be noticed that no consideration is here being given to one part of the third function of the family, namely the care of the old. This is of no less importance in itself, but the socialization of the young has a more direct relevance to education. Therefore in the context of this book socialization must be given the main emphasis.

Although any group must initiate its recruits, the family socializes its young in a different way because of its peculiar structure. This ensures that there is a difference in age between the older members – the parents, and the new recruits – the children. In addition in the vast majority of cases families are bound to be of two sexes, unlike such groups as men's clubs. Exceptions can occur if one parent has left the family or has died. The family provides not only physical care but also teaches the ways of the society and, perhaps of more importance, it is within the family that the child's personality is developed in the early and formative years.

The family is not a necessary social institution from the biological point of view, since reproduction of the species does not demand such an organization. But within the limits set by hereditary potentiality the personality is formed, and this development takes place best through the socialization of the young within a small group such as the family (T. Parsons, 1956). The child learns the patterns of behaviour needed to exist in his environment. The young learn not just how to subsist but how to exist socially. Boys learn what to wear and how to treat other boys and girls. They learn what behaviour to expect from other children of the same and the other sex. They notice how their parents behave, often internalizing these patterns through their play, as, for example, when children dress up to play at weddings. These behaviour patterns are called 'roles' and it is important to note the complementary nature of any role, since the pattern includes both the expected behaviour of that role and also the behaviour expected in others towards that role. It is only by knowing each other's roles that we can co-operate with each other.

Children may play at roles like actors in the theatre, but ultimately they become these roles. The girl playing at mother takes on the characteristics of personality associated with women in that society; the personality expected in an American woman is different from that expected in an English woman. In their earliest years children are egocentric, but as they grow older they gradually achieve the capacity to put themselves in the positions of others. This process takes place mainly within the family. For example, the child comes to know that his mother may be too busy to attend to his immediate needs. In sociological terms he has begun to appreciate that roles are complementary. The child learns that age governs behaviour as he watches his mother and father. He comes to a wider view of adult roles as he makes visits with his parents and observes other adults. He also learns from his parents and other adults the many occupational and leisure roles that are current in his environment.

As the child grows older the process becomes more complex. The older child or adolescent comes into contact at school or at work with values that may be very different from those held within his own family. His parents, as members of an older generation, may not change their values as quickly as the younger generation. There can, therefore, be discontinuities between the values of the family and its young. This becomes more possible after the adolescent has left school, as he meets an even wider range of values. The young worker can have encountered three different and conflicting codes of honesty, that of the home, of the school and that of the factory. Thus it is that the process of socialization often ends in conflict and sometimes in rebellion by the adolescent. The educational problems that are inherent in this situation will be discussed in the next chapter.

2. *Family Systems*

Anthropologists have described many primitive societies which have very complex family structures so as to carry out the above functions. Some family units combine closely more than two generations, namely of adults and children stretching vertically over three or more generations. These families may also cover several degrees of kinship, stretching horizontally to include cousins and in-laws. The technical term given to this system of organization is 'the extended family'. A form of this system was found in Britain before the industrial revolution, but under the impact of industrialization the extended family has gradually changed in character. Today in most industrial countries the family is thought of as a small unit consisting of parents and perhaps two children. To such a unit the name of 'the nuclear family' has been given.

Many advertisements show the nuclear family of 'mum, dad, and the kids'. This type of family has come to be considered as the norm by many, particularly perhaps among the middle-class occupations which include teachers and social workers. Yet, as will be seen later in this chapter, larger families are more common amongst the working class and, more important, there is still a tendency for a modified form of the extended family to persist amongst the working class in large urban areas. Hence much of what is implied in the organization of the modern family and assumed to be a usual part of family life by many teachers may be peculiar to the middle class. A good example of this tendency is the value placed on the exclusive mother–child relationship, which is considered to have almost the universality of a biological law, but which may well be a local and temporary pattern. Those brought up in a nuclear family must beware of the parochialism that considers the extended family as a deviation from the norm.

Bott (1957) has pointed out that when considering the modern urban family the whole network of social relationships maintained by the family must be taken into account. She lays down the hypothesis that the closeness of the relationship between the husband and wife varies with the closeness of the tie between the family and its own social network. As a concrete case one may think of the working-class husband who goes out to the pub and leaves his wife at home with her relations. Here there is separation in the family of marriage directly offset by a close relationship by both husband and wife with the surrounding environment. But Bott points out that such a situation is not purely a matter of social class. In professional families also the relationship between husband and wife may be marked by distance. Though close-knit family systems are more likely in the social conditions under which the working class live, they are not universal or peculiar to those conditions.

Industrial societies allow various types of family system. Within Britain several ways of organizing the family have been reported, varying according to such factors as whether the environment is rural or urban, in Scotland or England, and what the prevailing local industry is.[1] However, the nuclear family has some advantages in an industrialized society. Movement, both of a geographical nature and up or down the social class system, is probably easier for a small family with few local

[1] Compare W. M. Williams, *The Sociology of an English Village: Gosforth*, London, 1956 (rural); W. Littlejohn, *Westrigg*, London, 1963 (Scottish rural); N. Dennis, F. Henriques, and C. Slaughter, *Coal is Our Life*, London, 1956 (a one-industry town). Also see the next section of this chapter.

connections than for members of an extended family. These two types of movement, known as geographical and social mobility, are very necessary in the rapidly changing conditions of a modern industrial society.

We have taken the view of Talcott Parsons and his followers that the family is one particular type of small group. Parsons (1956) has gone a stage further and proposed a general theory of the family applicable to all family structures and covering all the local differences found by anthropologists. Briefly the theory is that the father's role is especially concerned with tasks and can be termed 'instrumental', whilst the mother's role is considered to be centred on the emotions and can be termed 'expressive'. A good example may be seen in the setting of an industrial community where the father is out at work, whilst the mother looks after the young children at home. The theory covers such cases which are common in Britain or America, but seems to be contradicted by anthropological evidence of peoples amongst whom the mother plays the roles more usually attributed to the father. In such societies descent is through the female, but it has been reported that another male, often the mother's brother, performs the roles played by the husband in our society, where both the nuclear family and the descent group are one. It would therefore seem that the general theory fits here, since the uncle and mother play the roles associated with the mother and father in our form of the nuclear family. Parsons's general theory notes that the family has sub-systems; such are the relationship between father and mother, child and child, mother and daughter, father and son, and so on. The relationships in some of these sub-systems will be of use later in this book. Any complete general theory of the family would have to cover all such sub-systems.

Parsons's theory gives a useful unity and provides tools for the analysis of the family, but social scientists offer also the concept of limiting cases. This section has indicated two such extreme cases, the nuclear and the extended family. We must now discover whether these types are found commonly in Britain today or whether the usual pattern of family organization is located in the continuum between the two limiting cases.

3. *The Facts*

Since 1945 there have been several investigations in Britain that have examined the family either as a main topic or as an important facet of the study. Here evidence will be cited from two famous studies, both of which contain corroboratory evidence from other British investigations and the results of which may, therefore, be taken as fairly representative descriptions of family life in Britain today. Young and Willmott (1957) described a predominantly working-class situation in Bethnal Green and also examined what happened to families moved from this environment to a new housing estate in Essex. They subsequently studied family structure in the North London suburb of Woodford (Willmott and Young, 1960). This latter area is mainly middle class and provided an admirable comparison with their first study.

In Bethnal Green the extended family system was found still to be very much a reality. Families may be smaller now and the marriage partnership may be closer, but isolated nuclear families were not normal. Though nuclear families appeared to live in separate flats or houses, the actual organization was found to be in units of three or even four generations with wide contacts between near relations. 'Mum' was the centre of a complex network of kin who maintained a very close relationship through constant visiting and meetings in the street, both of which were made easy by the confined physical space within which kin lived. More particularly there was a very close relationship between mothers and daughters. The sub-units of these extended families often merged to provide such services as meals or baby-minding, thereby enabling women to do part- or full-time work and to cope with illness more easily. There were even some cases of sons following fathers into the same occupation as, for instance, on the docks. In this 'village' in the midst of a city many people knew many others. The individual was given a position in the community because his kin were known, not because he had achieved status. Kin was the link between the individual and the community.

Amongst those on the housing estate there was much less visiting of kin because Bethnal Green was almost twenty miles away. The neighbours were not so well known. Mutual services became impossible, and this caused difficulties in times of illness or childbirth that in Bethnal Green the extended family could easily have taken in its stride. Husbands spent more time at home in the evenings and at the week-end. This meant a different quality of married life and a new relationship between father and children. The family became more home centred. One result of this tendency was that position in the community came to be judged by the way the house was kept and furnished rather than by who one's kin were. Style of life came to be more important than in Bethnal Green.

The nuclear family came to matter more than kin, though contact with kin was maintained by regular visits to Bethnal Green.

It was expected that in Woodford, an area predominantly middle class, family organization would have moved even further towards the pattern of the nuclear family. This was not entirely true. Perhaps kinship mattered less and friendship more, yet there were similarities with working-class Bethnal Green. Old parents came to live with or near their children at retirement or on bereavement. In Bethnal Green the generations were together throughout life; in Woodford nearness depended upon the stage of the life cycle. The tie between mother and daughter, though not as close as in Bethnal Green, persisted. There was much friendliness, perhaps even more than on the housing estate, though it seemed to be of a different quality. There was less spontaneous friendship and more stress on conformity to social norms. An individual was not taken for granted because his kin were known; he had to prove himself.

4. *Conclusion*

It can be seen that for a very large proportion of the population it is still safe to use the extended family as a framework for analysis. Yet the nuclear family is growing in importance and is a useful tool for considering the process of socialization. It is this last function of the family that is of most interest when looking at the relationship between education and the family. At the simplest level before the child starts his formal education he has already learnt much in the family that the school takes for granted. Even when the child is at school he spends more time in the family than with his teachers. It is for these reasons that knowledge of the family is important to the teacher, especially if the teacher's experience is of a different type of family structure from that of his pupils. After examining the main demographic trends that affect the family the inter-relations between family and school must be taken up in the next chapter.

B. Demographic Trends

Demography is the social science that deals with population. It has a wide field, covering such topics as the rates of change of populations of whole countries and, on a smaller compass, the differential birth rates of the social classes or religious denominations within one country. These trends are much more easily represented in numerical terms than the qualitative material with which the first part of this chapter dealt. Five important statistical measures will be discussed here – the birth rate, the average size of the family, the average age at marriage, the divorce rate and the percentage of women in the labour force.

1. The Birth Rate

It is generally known that in the late part of the nineteenth century the high birth rate prevailing in this country began to fall. This decline continued until the mid-1930's, by which time the birth rate was so low that the population was barely reproducing itself. The titles of two books published at the time show the concern felt by social scientists. These were *The Parents' Revolt* and *The Economics of a Declining Population*.[1] The exact size of the drop in the birth rate can be seen from the following figures. In 1870–72 the birth rate was 35·0 live births per 1,000 population per year; the figure for 1900–02 was 28·6 and for 1939 had fallen to 15·2. Since the war there has been a reversal of the trend, and the rate has risen. In the years immediately after the war certain once and for all conditions operated; thus the demobilization of the armed forces was bound to add to the crop of births and in 1947 the birth rate reached 20·7. By 1955 the rate had dropped back to 15·4 as the smaller numbers of those born in the 1930's reached the age of marriage, but since then the birth rate has consistently risen and in 1962 stood at 18·3.

These are gross figures which could be examined in more close detail. For instance it could be shown that the birth rate for the Roman Catholic part of the population is higher than for the rest or that there is a difference between the birth rate of each of the social classes. The drop in the birth rate that began in the upper and middle classes in the 1870's came to the working class some years later, and this lag has remained to this day.[2] The working class still has the highest birth rate, though there are some indications that the rate of the upper classes may be rising again.

2. Family Size

A fall in the birth rate need not necessarily bring a smaller average size of family, but in Britain the two measures have moved together. In the 1870's the average size of completed families was around six; by the

---

[1] Respectively by R. M. Titmuss, London, 1939 and W. B. Reddaway, London, 1942.

[2] See J. A. Banks, *Parenthood and Prosperity*, London, 1954.

1900's it had dropped to three and by the 1920's to two (R. Fletcher, 1962). As may be expected these rates varied between the social classes; this can be seen from the following table:

Family Size for Women Married in:	1900–09	1920–24
Non-manual husbands	2·81	1·90
Manual husbands	3·96	2·72
Average	3·53	2·42

The last column represents the size of families that must be complete since the women concerned are now past childbearing age. These figures clearly show both the decline in family size and the differential rate between the social classes. The figure for non-manual families for 1920–24 also hints at the move towards a population that was not re-placing itself.

3. *The Age of Marriage*
Throughout the nineteenth century the proportion of women in the population who married remained fairly constant in the range of 86 to 88 per cent. By 1951–5 the proportion had risen to 94·5 per cent. This increase must have been due to the increased proportion of women in the total population as much as to any change in social habits. However, it has been accompanied by one major social change in that the age of marriage for both men and women has fallen greatly. The age of marriage rose through the late nineteenth century up to 1911 when a steady fall began which was only broken during the depressed period of the inter-war years. Again there was a social class differential since brides of professional and managerial status were estimated to be on average one and a half to two years older than their working-class con-temporaries (O. R. McGregor and G. Rowntree, 1962). By the 1950's the situation was as follows:

Percentage of brides marrying

	All Classes	Non-Manual	Skilled Manual	Other Manual
Before 20th Birthday	20·0	11·0	22·8	25·3
Before 25th Birthday	73·0	61·5	79·9	76·1

Though bridegrooms were slightly older the same tendencies were at work; they were younger than in years past, and a social class differential existed.[1]

This tendency to earlier marriage is often ascribed to a fall in the moral standard of the young today. It is argued that this change in the moral climate leads to more premarital intercourse and conception, which in turn forces earlier marriages. This may be so in the 1960's, a period so recent that it is not yet possible to establish a statistical trend. But in the 1950's the percentage of all teenage brides who were pregnant was about 27 per cent as it was in 1939; for brides between twenty and twenty-four the figure was also the same as in 1939, namely about 15 per cent. These figures do not indicate that it is a lowering of moral standards that has caused the move towards earlier marriage.

4. The Divorce Rate

In 1938 there were 6,092 divorces in England and Wales. The comparable figure for 1947 was 58,444, but by 1962 the yearly number of divorces was running at a fairly constant figure of around 26,000. It would seem that about 10 per cent of those marriages made during the 1939–45 war ended in divorce, but that the rate for those married since the war will eventually settle to about 5 per cent. These marriages naturally include the increasing number of teenage marriages. About 60 per cent of all divorces are of marriages that have lasted ten years or more. This in itself gives further evidence that marriage today is not usually begun in any spirit of irresponsibility. From our point of view the incidence of divorce on children is of importance. About a third of all divorces in 1957 involved no children and a further third ended marriages with one child.

Certain changes in the legal system have made the process of divorce very much easier. Legal changes that were made in the inter-war years widened the grounds upon which divorce was possible. The introduction in 1950 of free legal aid has enabled the working class to substitute divorce for separation. This had often been unofficial rather than sanctioned by legal process. Divorce is no longer an upper-class privilege. There now seems to be no differential divorce rate between the social classes (O. R. McGregor and G. Rowntree, 1962).

[1] R. M. Pierce, 'Marriage in the Fifties', *Sociological Review*, July 1963; for this and the next paragraph see G. Rowntree, 'New Facts on Teenage Marriages', *New Society*, 4 October 1962.

Despite these explanations of the higher divorce rate some writers still make a convincing case that the high divorce rate is an index of the additional strain that the nuclear family has to bear in modern industrial urban communities. Furthermore, as the proportion of the population marrying rises, there is a greater chance that more couples will marry who are not suited for marriage on either physical or psychological grounds. Hence the risk of divorce is increased. However, it is of importance to note that most of those who are involved in divorces do re-marry. The family still seems to be considered by them a worth-while social institution.

5 Women at Work

Industrialization offers women jobs outside the home. With smaller families and earlier marriage it has become more possible for women in their forties to end their responsibilities as mothers, whilst they still have before them a life expectation of some thirty or so years. To older women in this situation a job is a welcome interest. In addition despite the rise in the standard of child care which is now normally expected, many younger women, mothers of young children, go out to work. These two facts have brought changes to the age and proportion of the women in the labour force. Whereas in 1911 one in four of occupied women were in the age range of 35–64, by 1951 the proportion was four in nine. In 1911 those under twenty-five made up half of the women in the labour force, but in 1951 they were a little more than a third. Further, though the proportion of women in the total labour force had stayed around a quarter from 1881 to 1921, since then it has risen so that by 1962 it stood at 29·5 per cent.

Changes of an economic nature, partly in the structure of industry, have caused a shift in the occupations in which women work. There has been a move from domestic service into light industry and clerical work, though those in part-time work still tend to be found in occupations of a domestic nature such as office cleaners or canteen workers (S. S. Yudkin and A. Holme, 1963). Another change in the type of woman worker required is due to the establishment of the Welfare State and to the improvement of other social services in Britain in recent years. This has increased the demand for well-trained women, particularly in the minor professions. It is this that has brought about the shortages of teachers, nurses, librarians and other social workers.

Investigations[1] into why women go out to work have shown that the decision depends upon a complicated set of factors, but that the actual reason seems more important for the effect on the quality of family life than the fact that the woman goes out to work at all. The woman who stays at home with her children, but who suffers severe frustration because she cannot go to work, may well do more harm to her family than if she went out to work. The wish to earn money in addition to the husband's wage is common, but some reasonably adequate arrangement is usually made to care for the children. Very often the grandmother looks after a child, further evidence that the extended family system is still alive in our urban areas. Paradoxically it is often today's younger grandmothers who wish to go out to work now that their own children are off their hands at a time when they themselves are still relatively young. What has to be examined is how much influence a mother at work has on her child at school. In the next chapter this and the other demographic trends outlined above must each be considered in turn to see how they influence education.

BIBLIOGRAPHY

E. Bott, *Family and Social Network*, London, 1957.

R. Fletcher, *The Family and Marriage*, London, 1962 (Penguin).

T. Parsons, *Family, Socialization and Interaction Process*, London, 1956.

O. R. McGregor and G. Rowntree, 'The Family' in A. T. Welford and others (ed.) *Society*, London, 1962.

P. Willmott and M. Young, *Family and Class in a London Suburb*, London, 1960.

M. Young and P. Willmott, *Family and Kinship in East London*, London, 1957 (Pelican).

S. S. Yudkin and A. Holme, *Working Mothers and Their Children*, London, 1963.

[1] See, for example, *Woman, Wife and Worker*, (DSIR), London, 1960 for evidence from Bermondsey, and 'Married Women who work in Early Motherhood', B. Thompson and A. Finlayson, *British Journal of Sociology*, June 1963, for Aberdeen.

3

The Family and Education

A. Implications of the Analysis of the Family

Not all the analysis and information contained in the last chapter has direct implications for education. Some is essential background and some will be used in later parts of this book. If we consider the three functions of the family from the standpoint of the educational system, the first, the sex function, has little direct relevance, though when the implications of the trend to earlier marriages is considered we shall find this function is relevant. The economic function is of some importance though still in an indirect way. Since the nuclear family has lost this function in its pre-industrial form, some other social institution has had to take over. The teaching of the basic skills necessary to earn a living in a modern community has been handed to the educational system. Literacy is one such skill. In the same way schools can undertake much of the vocational guidance that is essential to steer a child into the job for which he is most suited. This task is unnecessary in a primitive village. These educational problems will be covered more fully later, particularly in the second part of this book. There remains the process of socialization. It is to this third function that most attention will be given here, since this is the part of family life which has most impact upon the young child and has the most direct connection with education. The inter-relation between education and socialization will be discussed under three headings – early socialization, personality development and the control of the adolescent.

1. *Early Socialization*
The patterns of behaviour that a society has to pass on to its new recruits are referred to as its 'culture'. It must be stressed that this term will

always be used in this its anthropological sense and never with any aesthetic connotation. In a primitive society the transmission of the culture was a major part of education. One of the most famous of contemporary anthropologists, Margaret Mead, studied the way children grew up in Samoa (Mead, 1928) and in New Guinea (Mead, 1930). Her accounts are based on life in one form of extended family and describe how the children of these peoples were given what we should call their primary education in the family without ever entering a school. The extended family did not need to hive off part of its function of socializing the child to a special educational institution. In our culture there are many patterns of living that are passed on in the same way, but the traditional peoples that Margaret Mead was describing did not yet have to cope with the rapidly changing culture that our children must do. The nuclear family can teach a child when to shake hands or how to eat a meal, but it cannot easily teach the child how to read or do equations, particularly if both parents go out to earn a living.

Two problems are at once raised. At what age should education outside the family begin and what alternatives should be available both at the start and later ? These are administrative decisions and here the important point is that by the age of five or six when children in most European countries start at school the family has already done a great deal of an educational nature. Much of the culture has by this age been transmitted. Also during the next few years when the majority of children are very malleable the school works alongside the family which still has a very potent influence. There is the possibility of a partnership or of a clash between the two institutions that are socializing the child. The danger of conflict is probably lessened by the fact that the school tends to stress the learning needed for future life in a complex industrial community, whilst the family on the whole stresses the development of the personality and emotions. However, certainly in Britain, the schools have come to consider that they have a pastoral care for their pupils. Therefore the values that the school tries to inculcate may be at odds with those that the family attempts to teach to the child. For example, stealing may be thought very wrong by the teacher, but no one may stop a country child from taking apples from an orchard or a city child from taking fruit from a lorry moving through his playground, the streets (J. B. Mays, 1951).

The children in Samoa and New Guinea whose upbringing was

described by Margaret Mead could learn all the roles that they had to play from the education that they received as they were socialized within the extended family system. But the roles that an adult in contemporary Britain needs to learn cannot all be taught within the nuclear family. A very simple example will show this to be true. A nuclear family is of one social class and mainly meets members of the same or almost the same social class. In industry, however, a manager or a workman must meet all social classes and know how he is expected to behave in each different social situation. The school can provide experience of a wider range of adult roles in a less emotional frame of reference than the family. This opening of the world to the child is one important function of the school that is often forgotten by teachers in their stress on sheer knowledge and on the inculcation of moral virtues.

Yet though the family cannot do everything and may clash with the school it does much more than teachers are sometimes prepared to admit. Children come to learn what is expected of them and of others. 'You're a big boy now, you mustn't cry.' 'You don't do that to smaller children, do you?' They begin to learn how their family views adults of other social classes that impinge on them; the middle-class child who imitates his mother's telephone voice when she orders from the local grocer has begun to learn something of the social class system. Vocational aspirations may be mainly of the fantasy type in very young children. 'I want to be a fireman.' But, when the child is older and reaches the stage of reality, the family has been found to have a very strong influence on occupational choice, and often this power is exercised without the more precise knowledge that the school could give. Sex roles are learnt, as are views on modesty, the latter often in the process of toilet training. The nursery rhymes that are sung, first at home and then at infant school, begin to stress the moral virtues. Bo Peep found the lost sheep and the Knave of Hearts was punished for stealing the tarts. In the type of single-class environment common in suburbia or on housing estates, differences in cultures between social classes are reinforced, since the children's playgroups are homogeneous. 'I wouldn't play with that Tommy if I were you, he's not a nice boy', or 'he's stuck up'. The family teaches the child a great deal, both consciously and unconsciously, during the first few years. Later the school takes over part of the task, but few teachers come to influence a child as deeply as his parents do. This deep influence does not only extend to the transmission of the outward signs of the culture. It has already been pointed out that the child becomes the

C

roles that he plays. The connection between the family and personality therefore requires examination.[1]

2. Personality

There are inherited determinants of personality which put limits on the moulding that society can do. These, if anything, form the core of individuality in a person. But how is it that individuals show their singularity against a basic personality that is common to their own culture and different from other cultures? Why is it that a Cockney or a Scot is credited with a certain type of personality? (J. Klein, 1965.)

Anthropologists have reported some of the most significant cases of such differences. Margaret Mead described two tribes in New Guinea who lived in relatively close physical proximity, but who did not meet due to the impenetrable nature of the intervening country. In one tribe the men cared for the children, whilst the women did the hunting and the food gathering. Each sex had the personality characteristics that one would associate with the tasks allocated to it. In the neighbouring tribe the pattern of tasks and of personalities was more akin to that in our own culture. As in these two cases, each society ensures that its members have a substantial degree of conformity in this respect, so that individual personalities fall within the permitted range. In this process the link between the community and the personality is the family.

There is a basic psychological need for the child to attach himself to others, especially to adults. The nature of such attachments is very general. The child loves its mother, not any of her specific acts. The loved adult becomes a model that the child will imitate. He will attempt to imitate all the different roles that the adult plays. These roles are structured differently in each individual, and the emphasis put on different parts of the role structure are different from that in other individuals. The child internalizes these systems of roles to lay the foundation of his own personality. Personalities come to differ because of varying inherited potentialities and because the experiences that are met even in early life are not common to all members of society. But the traits of personality that are common to any one country can be understood to have their beginnings within the family. It is worth adding here that evidence will be produced in Chapter 5 to show that such inter-cultural

---

[1] For a fascinating account by a novelist of how easily the effects of early socialization may be sloughed off under certain conditions see W. Golding, *Lord of the Flies*, London, 1954 (Penguin).

differences in personality exist between social classes as well as between nationalities.

Although personality development is a process that continues throughout life, the foundations are laid before the child goes to school. By the age of five or six the child has begun to learn within the family how to cope with the many tensions and frustrations that are inescapable in life with others, how, for example, to control his anger or how to postpone his immediate desires. After the child goes to school, his teacher may become the model that is imitated and hence a potent influence upon the development of the child's personality. In this respect teachers and the school once again can reinforce or conflict with the foundations laid in the family. Under modern conditions, however, there is one particular way in which the educational system can be of great assistance in the development of personality.

Smaller families and the physical isolation inherent in living in some flats and semi-detached houses can cut children off from other adults and more particularly from an ample experience of other children. This can result in an exclusive and over-intense relationship between the adults in the nuclear family, especially the mother, and the children, who may develop overdependent personalities. This tendency can be corrected by sending the children to nursery schools, where they must learn to live with other children who conflict with them. Today in Britain the supply of nursery schools does not meet the demand for them. The contemporary demand appears to have two sources. There are middle-class parents who realize that they cannot give their children the best environment in which to develop their personalities. Secondly, there is a demand from the working class for a place to leave their children when the mother goes out to work. In as much as this demand is met the mothers are unconsciously allowing their children a fuller chance of developing the personality through coming into contact with the wider range of children who attend the nursery school.[1]

3. *Control of the Adolescent*
The nuclear family offers enough scope for the young child, but as he grows older he needs to go outside this narrow circle, not just to learn the social skills that he will need as an adult but to fulfil the psycho-

---

[1] For some doubts as to whether children who go to kindergarten ultimately have any advantage over those who do not see J. W. B. Douglas and J. M. Ross, 'The Later Educational Progress and Emotional Adjustment of Children who went to Nursery Schools or Classes', *Educational Research*, November 1964.

logical needs that come with adolescence. The most obvious need is to experiment with sexual roles amongst those of the same age. By convention this is impossible within the family. However, as soon as the child becomes attached to a group of his own age outside the family, his conduct, which was relatively easy to determine within the family, becomes far less capable of control. Such groups of adolescents have or rapidly evolve codes of values and of behaviour of their own which will in all probability be very different from those of either the family or the school. This makes for conflict, but when social change is rapid there is a further cause of difficulty. The code of values evolved in the group may not only be at odds with the home and the school, but will also almost certainly differ from the code that was common amongst the adolescent groups of twenty-five years ago, when the parents and teachers of today's adolescents were young. There are various reasons for this gap in values. The major causes are that there have been big changes in the generally held moral code over the last generation and that there are very different ways open to the young today to spend their spare time in our wealthier society.

One of the most important attitudes involved in this problem is that towards authority. A fully developed adult personality will be able to obey those in authority, co-operate easily with his equals and, if necessary, assume some authority. To a certain extent these three abilities can be learnt within the family, though the stress put on each will change as the child grows older. The ready obedience expected from a five-year-old cannot be exacted from a fourteen-year-old. Schools are supposedly arranged to achieve this same purpose as the chances of assuming authority rise as the child nears leaving age. In the past there were social institutions organized so that there was a smooth transition in this respect from childhood to full adult status. The training to become a medieval knight or the apprenticeship system in pre-industrial days are good examples.

Where the transition is not smooth from family to school, or from either of these social institutions to work or to adult life, a discontinuity is said to exist and there is the possibility of conflict. Where this occurs, possibly because the family or school does not fully meet the needs of the adolescent, children will create or find the spontaneous type of youth group that is often called 'a gang'. Youth organizations, such as Youth Clubs, may be started by educational authorities or by adults interested in the welfare of youth, such as religious bodies, but they are often rejected by the adolescents for whom they are intended because of their connection with adults and authority (S. N. Eisenstadt, 1956).

Discontinuities can be built into the process of socialization. It is probable that authority is wielded in a working-class family in a very different way from that in a middle-class family. The working-class parent will often make his child do what he wants more by a gesture than by a verbal command backed by the reason for the order argued at the child's level of understanding. Punishment in the working-class home is probably more often based on the consequence of the wrong done rather than on the intent of the action.[1] The child who is brought up with a working-class notion of authority will note great discontinuity when he enters the world of school which tends to be governed by middle-class attitudes. The more formal the atmosphere of the school becomes, more particularly when he reaches secondary school, the greater will the discontinuity become between the idea of authority learnt at home and that which he meets at school. The child can react in a number of defensive ways. Wrong-doing may be automatically denied. Feelings of guilt may in these circumstances become dissociated from many anti-social acts. This can be true particularly if the adolescent in his gang comes to feel that 'we' have gained over 'them' – the adults in authority. Many of the roots of the contemporary youth culture with its stress on gangs may be usefully analysed in these terms.

One of the results of such an analysis is that the problems of authority and discipline in the secondary modern school must be reassessed in sociological terms, though it still has to be said that the solution of these problems is very complex. The problems found in a grammar school are less dramatic. There is, however, discontinuity here. Older boys and girls now have come to feel that, when they reach the sixth form, to be treated as older children is not the way they ought to be treated at that age. There is evidence that in some areas these adolescents leave the grammar school to complete their education at local technical colleges, where they know that they will be treated as young adults.

This latter tendency raises a problem inherent in the notion of the continuity of socialization. Continuity implies that the roles of the growing child are fairly rigidly defined at each stage and that this knowledge is widely known. In the primitive tribes described by the anthropologists there was no doubt about this, as the movement from stage to stage was

---

[1] B. Bernstein, 'Social Class and Psycho-Therapy', *British Journal of Sociology*, March 1963, especially pp. 58–63.

marked by 'rites of passage', such as initiation ceremonies. In contemporary Britain no one is clear when a child becomes an adolescent. Even the word 'teenager' does not mean what it would seem to indicate. There is no clear universal agreement as to what the rights and privileges of an adolescent are. In different families, social classes and schools, and at different times, childhood has had a different duration. This lack of clarity in defining the role of the adolescent is bound to lead to conflict both within the family and at school as the child grows up. Sex will often be the centre of this conflict because of the strength of the biological forces involved, though to the family the difficulty may seem to be the hour at which the child must return home or to the school how much homework is to be done.

The spirit of rebellion implicit here can have the result that these spontaneous gangs become totally dissociated from school and even feel themselves to be against all that school stands for. Under these conditions culture transmission in the school is very difficult. One of the more serious effects may be that the rebellion is expressed in actual crime. The peak rate for juvenile delinquency amongst boys is in the last year at school, and the incidence is far greater amongst boys than girls. At the age of fourteen the number of crimes excluding motoring and other non-indictable offences is double that committed by those between seventeen and twenty-one and almost three times that for those between twenty-one and thirty. Whilst this problem must not be minimized, it can be seen as a passing phase of adolescence.

That this problem of discontinuity in the process of socialization is peculiar to contemporary urban communities can be seen clearly by comparing a rural community. In Gosforth,[1] an isolated village in Cumberland, the young, especially if brought up on a farm, are members of families that provide for their psychological needs as they grow older. There is no great discontinuity. The children gradually learn more of their future adult roles; in the school holidays and the long summer evenings there are plenty of interesting odd jobs around the farm to hold their attention and at the same time prepare them for adult life. The result is that, though there are groups of youths who meet together, there is nothing equivalent to the urban youth culture. The same point was shown to be true in Israel in an investigation that is about as near to laboratory conditions as the social scientist is likely to come. In Israel there are two types of co-operative farm, both of which have approxi-

[1] W. M. Williams, op. cit.

mately the same school system, but which have very different family organizations. In the Moshavim the family is the basic unit of production, whilst in the Kibbutzim this is not so and living is on a more communal basis. The very different family systems seem to be the reason for the comparative lack of youth activity in the Moshavim and the intense youth activity in the Kibbutzim.[1]

4. Conclusion

From the individual's point of view the way that the family is organized and the direction in which the family system is changing are important. The family moulds the personality of the child before he goes to school and is a potent influence on the child throughout his school life. Culture is transmitted within the family, and this helps to form national character within the limits imposed by biological inheritance. From the point of view of the State and the school one of the most important functions of the family is to assist in taking the child through the stage of adolescence with the minimum possible anti-social behaviour and yet in such a way that the child's personality is not warped by any undue repression.

B. The Implications of the Demographic Trends

1. The Birth Rate

Changes in the birth rate alter the number of children coming forward to the educational system. A rise means that more children will need places in primary schools some four to five years ahead, in secondary schools in about ten years' time, and eventually there will be a greater need for places at universities and other institutions of higher learning. For example, it can be said with a fair degree of certainty that in 1972 there will be about 4,895,000 children between five and nine, 4,390,000 between ten and fourteen, and 3,877,000 between fifteen and nineteen. Allowing for changes due to death and the balance of immigration and emigration the number of the children born this year will provide a firm basis for forecasting the number of places needed in the educational system over the years that they are of school age. Between the ages of fifteen and twenty-one the figures become less certain since the trend towards staying on longer at school may become more or less pronounced.

The wave-like movements in the birthrate that have occurred since

[1] S. N. Eisenstadt, 'Youth, Culture, and Social Structure in Israel', *British Journal of Sociology*, June 1951.

the war make the provision of educational facilities very difficult, as the intensity with which the schools will be used varies over quite short periods of time. There are, in addition, other changes that could make forecasting difficult. For example, a change in the attitude of industry towards Day Release could increase the demand for places and hence for teachers in institutions for Further Education.

The ability to give relatively firm answers to the question of how many children will need education at a given number of years ahead should give the Government and local authorities the knowledge with which to make future plans for school building and for recruitment of teachers at each stage of education. There may even be regional differences that can be observed, and here such geographical movements as the shift of population to the South-East or the building of new towns must be taken into account. So far in Britain it would not seem that the Government has been fully able to grasp this opportunity for forward educational planning.

2. *Size of Family*

Demographic trends are sometimes inter-related and the birth rate is strongly connected with the size of the family. Larger families are more common in the working class, and one obvious possibility is that children in these families may suffer from poverty. An extreme example of this was the case of the family in Liverpool where the children in a family of nine had to take it in turns to be late for school, as there were not enough plates to go round at breakfast. In a recent survey J. W. B. Douglas (1964) found that the standards of infant care, of infant management and the use of the medical services were substantially worse amongst the manual working class as compared with the middle class and that in both social classes the bigger the family the worse the care. The children from larger families were found in the lower streams of primary schools more often than would have been expected statistically. Amongst the older children of large families it has been found that there is a high rate of juvenile delinquency. After a rigorous examination of the evidence from several British investigations Lady Wootton concluded that on the whole delinquents came from larger than average-sized families.[1] Another very obvious effect of large families in the working class is that living conditions may be overcrowded more often than in more pros-

[1] B. Wootton, *Social Science and Social Pathology*, London, 1959, pp. 85–87.

perous middle-class families. Under such conditions homework becomes very difficult, especially where it is impossible to escape the television set. One of the cures for such overcrowding has been the building of the housing estates that appear to loosen the structure of the extended family. This has one particular adverse effect from the schools' point of view. Illness and childbirth could more easily be met within the extended family. For families on housing estates this is not so easy and older children, especially girls, may be kept off school to care for sick parents.

There are, however, more subtle forces at work. Several large-scale and thorough investigations have shown that measured intelligence (I Q) varies directly with the size of the family. This tendency operates at each social class level. In 1947 a survey was made of all children born in Scotland in 1936, out of which a smaller and representative sample was chosen containing the 7,380 children born in the first three days of each of the twelve months in the year. The evidence from this survey showed the connection between family size and I Q at all class levels very clearly, as can be seen from the following table:[1]

Mean test score by occupational class by size of family

Occupation	Size of Family				
	1	2	3	4	5
Professional and Large Employers	52·5	52·3	53·7	51·3	43·1
Skilled Manual Workers	41·7	40·7	39·4	35·8	33·4
Unskilled Manual Workers	34·6	36·1	33·1	32·8	29·4

(Maximum score possible = 76)

More recently Douglas's work (1964) has given evidence of the same trend. His sample consisted of 5,362 children living in England, Scotland and Wales born in the first week of March 1946. As in the Scottish survey he found that there was not a dramatic fall in I Q in middle-class families until the family contained four or more children, but there was no group of middle-class families where size did not have some influence on the I Q score of the children.

There has been much speculation as to the exact reason for this connection between size of family and I Q. The argument has usually run that parents of low I Q have large families and that, since there is a

[1] From *Social Implications of the 1947 Scottish Mental Survey*, London, 1953, p. 49, Table XXIV.

correlation (of about 0·5) between the I Q of parent and child, the children of these larger families will tend to have a low I Q. Yet this does not account for the incidence of this effect at all social class levels. Recently it has been argued that the causation runs in the opposite direction. The large family results in the low I Q, mainly because the younger infants in a large family in which the children are closely spaced in age are not given sufficient time and attention so that their inherited intellectual capabilities can be developed to the full.

There is some evidence to back this view. In the Scottish Mental Survey the 974 pairs of twins were found to have an I Q on average five points lower than that of only children. A French investigation has shown that the I Q of children in families whose ages are well spaced is on average higher than in closely spaced families. A recent English investigation also supports the view. This stressed the I Q of children in different positions in the family rather than the average I Q of whole families of a certain size. The school population in a small city and in a Midland borough were examined, and it was found that not only did the eldest child in a family have a higher I Q than the youngest, but that those in these positions were of higher I Q than any intermediate children. It was held that the position in the family encouraged different attitudes, preferences and aptitudes which were reflected in the different ways that the children benefited from school.[1] It would seem that, whatever the cause, the quality of life in large families does influence measured intelligence and perhaps even attitudes towards school. These tendencies in their turn will have a vital bearing on success at school, more especially in the process of selection for secondary education.

3. Early Marriage

As the age of marriage falls and the legal minimum school-leaving age is raised, the gap in time between school and marriage lessens. This is particularly the case for girls who marry at an earlier age than young men. It may be that by the early 1970's engaged or even married young women will be present in our schools. If the schools are to help parents in pre-

---

[1] For an account of this problem see J. McV. Hunt, *Intelligence and Experience*, New York, 1961, pp. 337-43. For the English investigation see J. P. Lees and A. H. Stewart, 'Family and Sibship Position and Scholastic Ability', *Sociological Review*, July and December 1957. For Scottish evidence see J. Nisbet, 'Family Enviroment and Intelligence', in A. H. Halsey, J. E. Floud and C. A. Anderson, *Education, Economy and Society*, New York, 1961.

paring their children to leave their family of birth and move towards founding their own family of marriage, the question must be asked, what responsibility have the schools to young people who will marry soon after leaving school.

Girls' secondary schools have traditionally made provision in their curriculum for teaching their pupils domestic science, and this may be said to meet some of the material needs of earlier marriage. How much help is given to meet the psychological and moral problems soon to be encountered is not known. It may be that little is done because many middle-class teachers disapprove of this tendency towards earlier marriage. Nor does the idea of education for the role of husband seem yet to be a recognized need. So far it is social workers rather than teachers who have given their attention to the necessity of educating our adolescents for earlier marriage.

Since the tendency to earlier marriage is less pronounced in the middle than the working class, it is only to be expected that fewer children of parents both of whom were at private or selective secondary schools marry in their teens. It appears that the mother's education has a greater influence here than that of the husband. It is therefore not surprising to find that the rate of teenage marriage among brides who had been to selective secondary schools was far lower than amongst those from non-selective schools. This could perhaps be held to justify the omission of any preparation for marriage from the curricula of selective schools. Yet these young people are also marrying early, some whilst still at university. In this last case the whole problem of grants to married students is raised. Earlier marriage can add to the costs of providing education as well as change its content.

Many girls who pass through selective secondary education go to training colleges with the ambition to become teachers. The proportion of those that marry soon after completing their training and teach only a short time before starting a family has grown. This is one of the main causes of the present shortage of teachers. Many undoubtedly will return to teaching when their family responsibilities permit it, but the crisis due to this shortage has led to experiments in methods of staffing schools, as part-time teachers have been introduced. Attitudes have not always been flexible enough to allow successful experiment. In addition older teachers, particularly women, are critical of the lack of vocation of young women teachers. Yet a changed view is inevitable when early marriage or the hope of it is the normal expectation.

4. Divorce
Divorce can lead to a broken home. The children of divorced couples have often been through a period of great disturbance which can leave them with feelings of insecurity. A parent may disappear or a new 'parent' appear. More is known of a related problem, the connection between broken homes and delinquency. The majority of those who have investigated this field agree that there is a high rate of delinquency amongst children who come from broken homes. Both these problems are hard to study because of the difficulty of adequately defining the term 'broken home'. In the light of the definite connection between broken homes, a proportion of which are caused by divorce, and delinquency, it would seem that the suspected connection between divorce and bad conduct at school may well also exist.

Divorce can lead to maternal deprivation which may have serious psychological effects on a child. Yet this lack of love by the mother for her child is possible in a masked form in an apparently normal family. (J. Bowlby, 1951 and World Health Organization, 1962). Where there is divorce or where the family breaks up for some other reason, the children are sometimes placed in an institution. In this case the effects of maternal deprivation can sometimes be found in their most extreme form. In a widely reported investigation Goldfarb in the U S A examined the differences in two groups of children of similar heredity, but who had been brought up under very different conditions. The first group had been in an institution up to the age of three and a half and then were brought up in foster homes, whereas the second group were in foster homes almost from birth. At the age of about seven the children reared in the institution were found to score lower in tests of social maturity and of abstract thinking. They also had below average powers of speech. This may be considered an extreme case, but broken homes can cause less severe harm, that nevertheless affects the child emotionally and perhaps intellectually, so that his performance at school can be affected.

5. Women Working
Working mothers have often been condemned on the grounds that their going out to work has a very detrimental effect on their children. Magistrates have blamed working mothers in tones of moral fervour for much juvenile delinquency. Various studies have compared the differences in the rates of delinquency, in personality and school-attendance

record of children whose mothers are at work and of those whose mothers stay at home. No big or consistent differences have been found. Nor would one necessarily expect a difference where the extended family system can care for the child or where the mother can arrange an adequate substitute. Anthropologists do not comment on the damage to the personalities of children in primitive tribes because their mothers go out fishing or food gathering.

Yet two points must be noted. The working mother will not have so good a chance of developing the sensitive and loving relationship with her children that is considered a vital part of the contemporary nuclear family. The reverse of this is that the child will probably still need to make a close relationship with someone and the mother must not be surprised if the child develops a strong feeling for the mother substitute who may be kin or not. Relationships within a family can become strained in the evening when the young child is weary and when his parents, who are in a way strangers to the child, return home exhausted by a day's work.

As has been indicated nursery schools may more than offset the ill-effects of a mother working. Once again the parents must understand that the child is being socialized at an early and impressionable age outside their control. As a result the child may become a more independent and assertive child than they themselves would wish.

There are in addition several obvious problems for the schools created by the fact that mothers are at work. School holidays take up about one quarter of the year; who will look after the child during this time? If the mother has to go out to her job in the morning before the child must leave for school and does not return from work in the evening until after the child has come home from school, who will care for the child? It is this type of child who has been called 'the latchkey child'. Who will nurse the child when he is sick and, perhaps of more direct importance to the teacher, will the child who is not really ill, but nevertheless ought not to be at school, still be pushed off to school, so that mother does not lose a day at work? Education authorities have themselves undertaken to answer some of these problems by opening play-centres in the holidays or by organizing activities at school after 4 p.m.

The increased proportion of women in the labour force in itself raises the whole issue of how women should be educated. It has been pointed out above that education for marriage may today have increased in importance. Likewise it would seem that women as much as men should be given preparation during their education for a life in the labour force as well as in the home. This raises two further points. Many more women are needed today who have undergone the basic education which will enable them to work at a professional or near professional level. Because of the earlier age of marriage it becomes important that this education shall be directed as much to providing flexibility as to teaching knowledge of immediate value, so that women can return easily to their chosen vocation when their family responsibilities have lessened. By this time the knowledge and skills needed in their particular job will undoubtedly be different from those that they learnt at the start of their careers.

6. *Conclusion*

During the first part of this chapter the process of socializing the child was at the centre of the argument. The connection was between two social institutions, the family and the educational system. This analysis was vital for the education of the child, but perhaps not always of immediate and obvious relevance to the school. It was the educational process as a whole rather than the school alone which was given the main attention. In the latter part of this chapter five demographic trends have been considered and in each case implications for the schools have been traced. Changes in the birth rate determine the number of school places and teachers that must be provided. Size of family is linked with the measure of intelligence that the child brings into the classroom. The move to earlier marriage raises the question of what shall be taught. Divorces may be connected with bad behaviour at school. Finally, the increasing proportion of mothers who go out to work has forced some local education authorities to make some provision for children throughout the year and not just during term time. These measures of demographic change which are of a quantitative nature have implications for education as important as those raised by the qualitative considerations that were examined earlier.

BIBLIOGRAPHY

J. Bowlby, *Child Care and the Growth of Love*, London, 1951 (Pelican)
J. W. B. Douglas, *The Home and the School*, London, 1964.
S. N. Eisenstadt, *From Generation to Generation*, London, 1956.
J. Klein, *Samples from English Cultures*, London, 1965.
J. B. Mays, *Growing Up in a City*, Liverpool, 1951.

M. Mead, *Coming of Age in Samoa*, 1928 (Pelican).

M. Mead, *Growing Up in New Guinea*, 1930 (Pelican).

World Health Organization, *Deprivation of Maternal Care. A Reassessment*, Geneva, 1962.

S. S. Yudkin and A. Holme, *Working Mothers and Their Children*, London, 1963.

4

Social Class

A. Social Differentiation

In any society there are two main types of differences between its members. Firstly, there are biological differences which may be physical, for example, varying heights and weights; or psychological, for example, the differing inborn limits to intellectual capacity and to personality development. Secondly, there are the purely social differences such as those of occupation or prestige. One teaches; another is a bricklayer. One is a politician who is well known locally; another is a nationally famous sportsman. Many of these differences are essential for the survival of a complex social system. A modern economy demands that its labour force work at thousands of separate occupations. Decisions must be taken at many different levels and therefore in each sphere of society, whether political or economic or artistic, there must be leaders.

In the armed forces or in industry it is usual for there to be a recognized chain of command. At each level there is some degree of authority, the most at the top and the least at the bottom. Parallel to this structure of authority there is a system of ranking. Each layer of this system carries prestige to a varying degree. These layers can be viewed in the same way as geological strata and in this connection sociologists speak of social stratification. The word 'hierarchy' is also used. This is interesting in view of the derivation of this word which has Greek roots, meaning 'rule of the priesthood'. Historically, one of the earliest strata to separate out from the ordinary members of a society was that consisting of the priests, and five thousand years ago there were priestly hierarchies in Egypt and Mesopotamia (K. B. Mayer, 1955).

Certain conditions must exist before the social differences inherent in stratification can become more or less persistent. Positions of power, such as chief priest or chieftain, must be recognized as social institutions that are permanent. Before this is possible the community must have a large enough economic surplus to release members from its labour force to do what is apparently non-productive work. The leader or priest can no longer dig the fields, but must be provided for. One of the most important social institutions for maintaining social stratification is the family. It is most often through birth into a family that social position is first gained. If an individual is able to raise his social position, he hands it on to the members of his own family. It can be seen that social differentiation in the form of stratification is both a common and an old social institution.

B. Types of Stratification

Three main types of social stratification will be considered here. All have importance for analytical purposes today. The first in order of historical occurrence is the caste system. The criterion of membership in this system is birth. An individual must be born into a caste to be a member of it and can never either move out of it nor enter another caste. The clearest example is the caste system associated with the Hindu religion in India. There are four main divisions or castes, though within each there are innumerable sub-divisions. At the top is the priestly or Brahmin caste and at the bottom are the untouchables or Sudras. A formidable array of rules and restrictions with strong religious sanctions governs each of the Hindu castes and thereby sets the framework within which millions of Indians live.

The key to preserving all caste systems is the means whereby the divisions are closed to members of other castes. One of the most important devices for ensuring such 'closure' is the marriage system. It is essential to stop intermarriage between castes so that movement is prevented. It has been said that what little success Christian missionaries have had in India may be attributed in part to the desire of the untouchables to escape from the caste system. To change his religion is the only way open to the untouchable to overcome the restrictions that his birth have brought upon him. In modern Western society the clearest examples of caste-like systems are to be found in the USA and the Republic of South Africa, where the black and white races are held apart by birth. There is no movement between the castes here. Intermarriage is socially impossible in the USA and illegal in South Africa.

D

In medieval Europe a system of stratification evolved known to historians as the feudal system. This was originally based on the ownership of land. The different strata were given the name of 'estates'. There were originally three estates, the nobles, the clergy and the peasants. The rights and privileges of each estate were laid down by law. On the whole closure existed, though there was a little movement between the estates. But with the growth of towns and the increasing importance of commerce and trade the system grew more complex and looser. It came to be based more on cash and less on the ownership of land. However, to this day owners of much land still have a special aura of prestige in Britain and other countries; the successful man of business often buys land in an attempt to be considered a member of the landed class, thereby putting a stamp on his social ascent.

The growth of trade and, particularly since the middle of the eighteenth century, of industry has, however, almost destroyed the last traces of the estates system in Britain. Stratification is now on the basis of the class system.[1] Members of a community are arranged in order of social merit from the upper through the middle to the lower class. The latter is sometimes called the working class. The criterion is no longer birth or some legal right. It will be seen in this chapter that a mixture of the social differences between individuals are used to assign others to their social class, though primarily the criterion is economic. Wealth, occupation and income are vital here, though many other considerations are also important; for example, in this country ancestry, education and accent are all used. This system is less closely defined and hence closure is more difficult. Therefore the boundaries between the social classes are less easy to trace clearly as was the case with castes or estates.

When assigning an individual to a social class, stress has come to be put on what he has achieved rather than the position to which he was ascribed by birth into his family. Naturally his family will influence what he achieves, but the vital difference between the class system and other modes of stratification is that relatively greater movement is possible between the strata. This movement between social classes is termed 'social mobility' and can be in either an upward or a downward direction. The analysis of social mobility has come to be one of the central problems of sociology. Theoretically it is a useful concept in

---

[1] In this book the full term 'social class' will be used in this connection except where the context is clear in order to avoid any confusion with the educational term, 'the school class', i.e. a group of children taught together.

studying the formation of social classes. In the context of this book social mobility assumes great importance since under modern conditions it is through education that movement up the social class system is mainly possible. In general it is difficult today to be considered a member of the middle class unless one has an occupation for which a relatively high level of education is the prerequisite.

The more movement between the social classes there is, the more socially mobile that society is said to be. Comparisons are made between social mobility in, for instance, the USA and Britain. The generally held beliefs about these two societies are opposite ones. The American system is reputed to provide ample opportunity for upward mobility, whereas in Britain it is supposed to be difficult to 'get on'. However, recent authoritative work (S. M. Lipset and R. Bendix, 1959) shows that between 1900 and 1939 social mobility, measured by movement across the line dividing manual from non-manual occupations, seems to have been as great in Britain and several other Western European countries as in the USA. Certainly it is part of the contemporary democratic ideal that there should be as much social mobility as possible. Today in Britain a large measure of equality has been gained in many fields, for example between the sexes or before the law. Yet, though it is probably true that over the last century upward social mobility has become more possible for the lower classes, it will be shown that for various reasons there are not equal chances to gain political power or access to occupations carrying the higher incomes. One of the root causes of this inequality is to be found in the way that the educational system works.

The accurate measurement of social mobility is difficult. It is not sufficient merely to know how many individuals move up and down the social class system. For a true picture the changes in the numbers of the positions at each class level must be known. For instance, it has been said that there is a permanent tendency to upward social mobility under contemporary conditions, since in a modern economy there is a growing number of managerial and administrative positions that carry high social status and whose occupants are considered middle class. As these new middle-class positions are filled, it may be said that upward social mobility has increased. But before a true account can be given as to whether the chances of social mobility have become greater or less than at some former date, allowance must be made for those changes in the occupational structure of a country that alter the relative numbers of the available positions at each social class level.

For women one possible avenue of upward social mobility is to marry a husband of a higher social class than themselves. The role of a woman in our contemporary society contains skills that are very 'portable'. Such are the skills of housekeeping and childrearing. The role of a man is more heavily weighted towards occupational skill and upward social mobility must usually be achieved through success in a man's occupation. It has been shown that women do marry 'above themselves' significantly more often than men.[1] This fact must be remembered when mothers' attitudes towards their children's education are discussed.

Another important concept is that of 'social distance'. This refers to the imagined distance between the social classes. It is generally held that over the last century the classes have moved much closer together. Greater wealth has been distributed somewhat more evenly. Many material possessions which even twenty years ago were symbols of status are now too common to bring the prestige associated with scarcity. A good example is the spread in ownership of cars. Again the clothes worn by all classes are now much more uniform and do not provide a reliable guide to membership of social class unless one has a very detailed and up-to-date knowledge of fashion.

Taken together these two tendencies, the lessening in social distance and the increase in social mobility, can combine to bring a heightened awareness of social class. The upper strata see themselves more threatened by the lower classes and feel the need to defend their social position. Since the change in the chances of upward social mobility are in the main due to the increase in provision of education and to the more egalitarian ways of entry to secondary education, middle-class defensiveness can take the form of opposition to educational reform. This was certainly the case in Germany around 1900, as in that country then there was a very strong sense particularly among the middle class of 'Stand', which can roughly be translated as social position.

C. Determinants of Social Class

1. *Criteria*

Many attempts have been made to discover what proportions of the population are in the different social classes. In any such investigation criteria must be defined. Several have been used. Firstly, the investigator may ask a question of the following type, 'To what social class do you

[1] D. V. Glass (ed.), op. cit., p. 327.

belong?' The answer will be purely subjective. Answers to such questions vary according to the wording of the question. Thus a higher proportion of respondents will say that they are members of 'the working class' than will admit to belonging to 'the lower class'. The timing of the question also seems to influence the answers. An American survey conducted immediately after the accession to power of the British Labour Party in 1945 found that a higher proportion claimed to be working class than in a strictly comparable survey a few months earlier. Again, to ask a person's friends to what social class he belongs may bring a number of different answers. In a somewhat similar way townsmen think of countrymen as almost all of one social class, whereas countrymen divide themselves into gentleman farmers, working farmers and farmers.[1] Even the countrymen themselves may disagree as to the boundaries between the three groups and place each other in different categories.

When people ascribe others to social classes they take account of many imponderable details typical of which is accent. In different parts of this country varying weight will be placed upon whether a person speaks with or without an accent. It is probably true to say that in the South of England someone with a well-educated Scottish accent will be put into a higher social class than with a person with a well-educated Yorkshire or Lancashire accent.

Because of the obvious difficulties in attempts based on subjective measures of social class sociologists have tended to use objective criteria more frequently, particularly where statistical work is necessary. Since social class rests primarily on economic foundations, the objective criteria most often used are of an economic nature. Occupation is perhaps the commonest, though there are problems even here. Children can be included with their parents. The retired may be allocated to the occupation that they followed last, though this may not have been their life career. But the thorniest problem is how to allocate women, many of whom work at occupations which are of a lower social class than that to which they clearly belong. In fact, wives are often included in their husband's class regardless of their own occupations; the position of spinsters is, however, difficult to solve. Another possible objective criterion is income; the problem here is to decide whether it is individual or family income that is the more important determinant of social class.

---

[1] J. Littlejohn, op. cit., p. 80. This work and the other social surveys already referred to contain a wealth of information on regional differences in social class (see, for instance, Williams, Willmott and Young, Young and Willmott).

A criterion that is rarely used is the pattern of consumption. How is the income spent? Many people earn £1,000, but they may spend it in very different ways. To be specific, some dockers and some teachers earn the same income, but their expenditure follows different patterns, and these consumption patterns are the outward signs of their different social class position. Each individual expresses the pattern of values that he holds in the way that he spends his money. The teacher may be buying his house and spending considerably on his children's education, whilst the docker lives in a council house and owns a car. These different patterns of values are vital in determining social class. Aggregates of individuals with the same or nearly the same income are clearly not necessarily of the same social class, though it must also be stressed that even groups consisting of individuals who hold the same values are not a class until they are conscious of having important common values and interests. Class consciousness makes a mere aggregate into a social class.

The ownership of wealth plays an important part in determining social class, since an unequal distribution of wealth leads to the unequal incomes that make it possible to give children a more advantageous start in life. Despite the very high rates at which death duties are now levied, there are still big inequalities of inherited wealth. However, income does seem to be less unevenly distributed than fifty years ago, although this is an area of investigation in which economists are far from reaching complete agreement. A policy aimed at achieving a fairer distribution of incomes has been pursued over recent decades through measures affecting the extremes of the income structure. High incomes have been taxed heavily and part of the proceeds transferred to the lower income groups often in the form of social services and welfare benefits. By 1939 this had levelled out some inequality (J. R. Hicks, 1960). During the 1939–45 war there seems to have been a rise in the proportion of the national income that went to wage earners as opposed to salary earners and those living on unearned income. In the years since the war the real income (the amount of goods and services that the money income will buy) of the working class has undoubtedly risen, but the proportion of the national income that they earn seems to have been stationary through the 1950's and has perhaps declined slightly in the 1960's.[1]

[1] See D. Seers, *The Levelling of Incomes since 1938*, London, 1951, and Salaries', *The Economist*, 23 May and 30 May 1964.

2. Children and Social Class

Wealth can be inherited and, despite death duties, some inequality of income perpetuated. A high income enables parents to give to their children the advantages that money can buy. It is a great help to a child to live in pleasant surroundings, to be provided with educational toys, to go to a private school with a low staffing ratio, to receive stimulating experiences, such as foreign travel in adolescence, and to have the entry into 'the right circle'. In the words of the German sociologist, Max Weber, such children are receiving better 'life chances' than the children of poorer parents. The family not only transmits these material benefits to its offspring but also passes on some of the more indefinable and immaterial aspects of social class. The child undergoes social experiences of power and prestige upon which his ideas of class are built. The way in which his parents treat others and are treated by them give him the cues as to how he must later deal with his superiors and inferiors in class position.

Children of primary school age seem to mix very freely with children who to adults appear to be obviously of another social class. In rather the same way they ignore such adult caste boundaries as colour in choosing their playmates. In both cases, however, it appears that they recognize that there are differences but do not know the social customs associated with these differences. An interesting experiment was carried out with 179 children between six and ten years of age in Glasgow.[1] Drawings were prepared that showed adults of obviously different social classes in incongruous circumstances. The children usually spotted this. For instance, when a picture of a workman wearing overalls and shaking hands with a man in a suit carrying a briefcase was shown to a child he commented that men dressed in that way do not shake each other's hands.

A study[2] has also been made of the views of British adolescents on social class. This survey was carried out in the early 1950's amongst boys from both grammar and secondary modern schools. When asked if they knew what social class meant, 60 per cent (49 per cent grammar, 73 per cent secondary modern school) said that they did not know, but it was found that they had already acquired a thorough understanding of

[1] G. Jahoda, 'Development of the Perception of Social Differences in Children from Six to Ten', British Journal of Psychology, May 1959.

[2] H. T. Himmelweit, A. H. Halsey and A. N. Oppenheim, 'The Views of Adolescents on Some Aspects of the Social Class Structure', British Journal of Sociology, June 1952.

our social class system. Their views were very like those of adults and had been picked up unconsciously in their ordinary, day-to-day life. Amongst those who understood the term 'social class' the usual frame of reference was wealth or consumption pattern, unlike adults for almost three-quarters of whom the frame of reference seems to be occupation.[1] A third of these boys were aware of the importance of status symbols; they appreciated that a man may be judged by how he dresses or by his accent. They also had an understanding of the idea of social mobility; 60 per cent considered that upward mobility was associated with achievement, intelligence and personality, though those middle-class boys who were in secondary modern schools laid more stress on manners, dress and speech. Adults of all classes stressed education much more and manners hardly at all.[2] Boys of below average intelligence spoke just as easily about social class. It would seem that a knowledge of class is gained through the process of socialization, one more indication of the important social role played by the family.

3. *Marx and Social Class*
It is impossible to discuss the class system or the determinants of social class without at least mentioning Marx's views. Marx never gave a systematic account of his theory of class; it has to be deduced from the many references scattered throughout his works. Briefly he believed that in all societies except the most primitive there are the ruling class and the ruled. The position of the ruling class is based on the ownership of the instruments of economic production. The actual social system varies through time as the economic system changes. A system based on slavery corresponded to the ancient mode of production, serfdom to the feudal system and wage labour to the capitalist system. Change in the social class system comes through class conflict and the direction of the change is influenced by the course of economic development. Marx examined one society in detail, nineteenth-century Britain. From this analysis he foresaw that the future of the capitalist system would be marked by an increasing division between the ruling and the ruled classes. The rich would grow richer and the poor poorer. Ultimately there would be a revolution in which the working class would be victorious and would begin the creation of a classless society (T. B. Bottomore, 1964).

In his theory Marx was trying to explain social change and social

[1] F. M. Martin in D. V. Glass (ed.), op. cit., pp. 59–61.
[2] F. M. Martin, op. cit., p. 74.

conflict. Therefore his idea of class was conceived for the purpose of analysing these problems. His prophecies have proved wrong. In brief, he failed to foresee the great growth of a middle class between his two poles of the working and the ruling classes, and he did not notice the tendency to a spread in the ownership of wealth that had begun even in his own time mainly because of the growing popularity of the joint stock system of financing industry and commerce. Yet Marx's was the first general theory of its type and though poor in predictive value drew attention to the importance of the economic foundations of the social class system.

D. The Definition of Class

The careful reader will have noticed that as yet no definition of 'social class' has been made. Throughout the discussion of class a number of interlocking strands have been traced. To summarize briefly the first of these is economic. Occupation is vital here, mainly in that it yields an income, though wealth can also provide this. Different sizes of income lead to differences in life chances. The second strand is that of status, which measures the prestige accorded to an individual. Status tends to vary with economic criteria such as occupation or income, but this is not always the case. The status of a professional footballer or a popular singer may not be measured directly by his income. Thirdly, there is the underlying strand of power, which can be defined as the ability to control the behaviour of others. This usually varies directly with economic criteria, but there are again awkward exceptions; top civil servants or the leaders of trade unions have much greater power as defined above than their incomes might lead one to expect.

It is, therefore, very difficult to know just what is meant by the term 'social class'. It would perhaps be best to use the term 'class' only in the strict Marxian sense, that is to refer to social conflict and to analyse both the groups involved in such conflict and the attendant social change. Today in Britain the conflict between these groups is not over property ownership nor economic conditions as Marx assumed, but is rather over the exercise of power. As pointed out above these groups only become social classes when they realize that they hold interests in common. Thus the working class has come to acknowledge a common set of interests and values and works for power so as to preserve and extend these values through such institutions as the Labour Party and the trade unions. In this sense 'class' remains, as with Marx, a tool for the analysis of social change (R. Dahrendorf, 1959).

However, for convenience we continue to talk about the upper, the middle and the working classes (and even of sub-divisions within these classes) in contexts other than the Marxian one. Very often we really intend to speak of categories that are more truly socio-economic in character. In the early 1950's a socio-economic scale was evolved for Britain (C. A. Moser and J. R. Hall in D. V. Glass (ed.), 1954). Two samples of 1,389 in total ranked thirty occupations (an economic criterion) by their prestige (a sociological criterion). There was a very substantial measure of agreement in the ranking. The result was the sevenfold socio-economic scale given below; examples of the occupations within each of the categories are quoted in each case.

1. Professional High Administrative (Company Director, Chartered Accountant).
2. Managerial and Executive (Works Manager, Civil Servant – Executive Branch).
3. Inspectorial, Supervisory and other Non-manual, Higher Grade (Elementary School Teacher, Commercial Traveller).
4. Inspectorial, Supervisory and other Non-manual, Lower Grade (Insurance Agent, Chef).
5. Skilled Manual, and other routine grades of Non-manual (Fitter, Routine Clerk).
6. Semi-skilled Manual (Coal Hewer, Agricultural Labourer).
7. Unskilled Manual (Barman, Dock Labourer).

This scale has been used much in sociological work, though it is often necessary due to difficulties of placing occupations or to the small size of a sample to amalgamate the categories into three or four groups. It can be compared with the social class divisions used by the Government's decennial Census of Population. The five broad categories (I to V) are also socio-economic in character and may be termed I – Managerial, II – Intermediate, III – Skilled, IV – Semi-skilled and V – Unskilled. Using these two scales it is possible to give a very rough indication of the distribution of the population by socio-economic status or, to speak less accurately, by social class:

Socio-Economic Category		Social Class by Census	
(*Males, G.B., 1949 Sample*)		(*Heads of Households, G.B., 1951*)	
1. (Professional)	2·9%	I (Managerial)	3·3%
2. (Managerial)	4·5%		
3. (Supervisory: Higher)	9·8%	II (Intermediate)	18·3%
4. (Supervisory: Lower)	12·7%		
5. Skilled	41·2%	III (Skilled)	49·5%
6. Semi-skilled	16·5%	IV (Semi-skilled)	16·5%
7. Unskilled	12·4%	V (Unskilled)	12·4%
	100·0%		100·0%

(D. V. Glass (ed.), op. cit., p. 93 and G. D. H. Cole, 1955, p. 153.)

Scales based on socio-economic status are more relevant to the analysis of this book since under contemporary British conditions there is a very strong connection between occupation and education. Therefore, though it must be realized that the term 'social class' should strictly be kept for the analysis of social class conflict and the ensuing change, here it will be used in a socio-economic sense covering broad bands of occupations. It would seem that this is the normal use of the term in common speech today.

E. Contemporary Trends

The combination of a growing national income and its somewhat more equal distribution has enabled the British working class to lead a more affluent way of life in recent years. Some writers have held that this has brought a change in attitudes towards social class. It is said that the worker now considers himself to be middle class. This trend has been called the 'embourgeoisement' of the worker. The main basis upon which this analysis has rested is economic. Statistics can be quoted to show that many members of the working class must own expensive pieces of household equipment. Thus by the middle of 1962 eight out of every ten households in Britain had a television set, three out of five a vacuum cleaner, and two out of five a washing machine. In 1961 there were about six million private cars on the roads, a fair proportion of which must have been owned by members of the working class. The Government report that gave these figures was entitled *Social Changes in Britain*. It concluded that this country could not lapse back into the working-class poverty of the 1930's and that the average man had made a great investment in his future 'as a middle-class citizen'.[1]

It has been convincingly argued (J. H. Goldthorpe and D. Lockwood, 1963)[2] that this is not in fact a true picture of what has taken place. The economic fact of greater wealth cannot be disputed and a more even distribution of incomes can be accepted. But interpretations of these developments can differ. The teacher and the docker may earn the same income and perhaps own the same household equipment, but the teacher has a higher degree of security of employment and a much greater chance of promotion during his career. A study through time of the pattern of a typical middle-class career would yield a very different picture from that of a member of the working class. The member of the working class usually reaches his maximum income early and, despite changes in his job, will rarely raise his real income after the age of twenty-one. This is a very different picture from the normal step-like progression of the member of the middle class. In fact the chances of rising above the supervisory level, for example above the job of foreman, are actually declining in contemporary British industry and, if upward social mobility through the educational system increases, the traditional 'hard way up' is bound to assume less importance, since the more able members of the working class will have already achieved middle-class status through the educational system.

However, the main criticism of the thesis of the embourgeoisement of the worker is not on economic grounds. If the worker has become middle class, he should have taken on the norms or the pattern of values and beliefs of the middle class. The type of evidence used to indicate that this has happened is drawn from the social surveys already quoted. For example, it is said that in moving from Bethnal Green to Endsleigh the worker has left the sociability of the pub and corner shop for the loneliness and status-seeking of the housing estate. The move has been from a community-centred to a home-centred life and is therefore seen as a move from a life typical of the working class to one more usually associated with the middle class. Yet the same social surveys provide evidence of almost the opposite point of view; the home in Bethnal Green was always a private place into which only the closest kin ever penetrated; in addition there was status amongst the working class

[1] This report was never published officially, but is reproduced in *New Society*, 27 December 1962.
[2] The authors have published a shortened version of this article, entitled 'Not So Bourgeois After All' in *New Society*, 18 October 1962.

in Gosforth where there were 'respected' and 'rough' sections of the lower class; even in Woodford where the working class seemed to imitate their middle-class neighbours they did not go as far as joining clubs or holding parties at home to the same extent that the middle class did.

It would therefore appear a more valid interpretation of the evidence to say that certain parts of the existing working-class culture have come to be given more emphasis under contemporary social and economic conditions. To summarize, it seems doubtful that the working class have in fact assumed middle-class attitudes. Statistical evidence of the poll type has also been brought forward to back the thesis; between 10 and 40 per cent of manual workers in various recent studies have claimed themselves to be middle class. It has been indicated above that there is great difficulty in accepting such subjective estimates of social class position. However, evidence from a very carefully designed survey of the poll type made in 1961-2 has been used to back Goldthorpe and Lockwood's refutation of the thesis of embourgeoisement.[1] In this investigation an examination was made of the type of definition given to the term 'middle class' by the 33 per cent of the men or their wives in manual occupations who claimed to be middle class. It was found that, though the majority may have been conscious of being in some sense different from the traditional working class, yet their definitions of middle class seemed to show no definite sense of belonging to the non-manual category of occupations, here termed middle class.

There is a further point to consider. Even if the working class has taken over middle-class norms, has the middle class accepted these new recruits to their own social class? It has already been suggested that a lessening of social distance has led to an increase in middle-class defensiveness. Certainly there has been great difficulty in creating socially mixed communities on new housing estates. The middle class will not remain in predominantly working-class communities. This same tendency can be seen more clearly in industry; the status distinctions between managers and workers are as rigid as any in contemporary Britain and are institutionalized by separate canteens, as many as four of descending status in some large-scale factories. Yet it must be pointed out that there are also changes amongst the middle class. The professional part of the middle class seem to have left the individualistic stance

[1] W. G. Runciman, 'Embourgeoisement: Self-Rated Class and Party Preference', *The Sociological Review*, July 1964.

usually associated with this class in Britain and to be readier than formerly to use co-operative action almost of a trade-union type.

It is this last point that leads us to a truer interpretation of what may be happening. The two classes are changing independently under the impact of the same social and economic forces. At a time of full employment the working class may have become more individualistic, whilst the growth in the size of industrial units may have made the middle-class professional man more co-operative. The result may ultimately be a convergence into a new class. Both classes are changing. It is not a true picture to concentrate only on the changes that affect one class, the working class.

F. Conclusion

Social class is a topic to which sociologists have given much attention. Yet to define the term is very difficult and for our purposes here the important concept is that of the socio-economic group. This is closely linked with class, particularly in the Marxian sense, since Marx's whole theory was firmly based on economic grounds. The transmission of social class from generation to generation is in the main through the family. In this way both social class position and the cultures associated with each stratum are passed on. This latter process will be central to much of the analysis of the next chapter.

The key to the class system in comparison with other systems of social differentiation is the relative ease of social mobility between the various levels. Such mobility in Britain today takes place mainly through the educational system. This must be the case in an industrial community with a strong egalitarian tradition. This democratic philosophy together with certain economic developments has helped to temper capitalism in a way that Marx could not foresee. Class conflict is less obvious in a world where the thesis of embourgeoisement of the worker can be seriously considered.

BIBLIOGRAPHY

T. B. Bottomore, *Elites and Society*, London, 1964 (especially Chapter II).
G. D. H. Cole, *Studies in Class Structure*, London, 1955.
R. Dahrendorf, *Class and Class Conflict in an Industrial Society*, London, 1959.

D. V. Glass (ed.), *Social Mobility in Britain*, London, 1954.

J. H. Goldthorpe and D. Lockwood, 'Affluence and the British Class Structure', *The Sociological Review*, July 1963.

J. R. Hicks, *The Social Framework*, Oxford (3rd Edition), 1960 (especially Chapter XVII).

S. M. Lipset and R. Bendix, *Social Mobility in Industrial Society*, London, 1959.

K. B. Mayer, *Class and Society*, New York, 1955.

5

Social Class and Education

Each social class has its own particular way of life. Many examples could be given of the differences between the middle and the working classes. What is considered right behaviour varies; for example, each social class treats its womenfolk in a different way. Table manners and what is eaten and drunk vary greatly. It is possible to view each class as having a culture of its own. Strictly these ways of life are sub-cultures of the overall British culture. Each sub-culture will entail a separate pattern of socialization very different in some respects from that undergone by the children in the families of another social class. These sub-cultures are characterized most obviously by the differing outward behaviour, such as the drinking of tea at the evening meal instead of water or the watching of a game of soccer instead of the playing of a game of golf. But it will be shown in this chapter that at a deeper level there are differences even in the basic personality patterns and modes of thought found in the social classes. The transmission of all these differences is a special case of the process of socialization described earlier in this book, but in view of its importance and the interest that it has raised it has come to be analysed separately and has been given the name of 'social class learning'. In the first part of this chapter this process and its implications for education will be examined.

As might be expected social class learning leads to a differential ability to benefit from formal education. This is less so amongst really able children, but becomes more the case as one considers children of lower measured intelligence. Likewise this differential tendency becomes of more importance the higher up the educational system one goes, and is therefore more pronounced at university level than in the sixth form and at eighteen than at sixteen years of age. This can be seen clearly from the following table. This refers to the large sample of children born in 1940–41 in England and Wales that was investigated by the Robbins Committee on Higher Education.

Academic achievement of children at maintained grammar schools (percentages)

I.Q. at 11+	Father's Occupation	Degree Level Course	At least 2 'A' levels	At least 5 'O' levels
130 and over	A. Non-manual	37	43	73
	B. Manual	18	30	75
	A divided by B	2·06	1·43	0·97
115–129	A. Non-manual	17	23	56
	B. Manual	8	14	45
	A divided by B	2·12	1·64	1·24
100–114	A. Non-manual	6	9	37
	B. Manual	2	6	22
	A divided by B	3·00	1·50	1·68

(*Higher Education*, 1963, Appendix One, from Table 5, p. 43.)

If one considers the relative class chances as measured here by the line 'A divided by B', it is clear that the children of non-manual fathers have better chances than those of manual workers of gaining a given standard of education as successively lower IQ bands are taken, for example 3·00 times as against 2·06 in the case of university courses. Again, holding IQ constant the middle class, as measured here, have a greater chance of reaching each level of education than the working class, for example in the lowest IQ category 3·00 times as against 1·68. The exception to this last generalization is the expected one, namely that the class chances for the ablest category of gaining five 'O' levels are more or less equal.

In interpreting these figures it must be remembered that they only refer to those who have already entered a grammar school. Entrance to these schools is also linked to social class. Thus J. W. B. Douglas (1964) found that below the children who were in the top 2 per cent of measured intelligence, social background was an important factor in entrance to the grammar school. Thus for those with an IQ level of between 107·5 and 110·5 at eight years of age the rate of entry to grammar school at eleven that was achieved by the different social class divisions was as follows – the upper middle class 51 per cent, the lower middle class 34 per cent, the upper working class 21 per cent and the lower working class 22 per cent. It must be realized that the minimum IQ for entry to grammar school is in the region of 114, though great regional differences occur. The results quoted are in an IQ band well below the top 2 per cent of ability and hence much influenced by differences in social class learning.

E

After examining the way in which this inequality of educational opportunity is connected with social class learning, the second part of this chapter will be given over to the problems of the exact definition and measurement of equality of educational opportunity. Some of the problems that the existence of social classes raises for the analysis of educational opportunity will be considered, though a full discussion of the way in which the educational system selects children by social class and by ability will be left until Chapter 11.

A. Social Class Learning

1. *Infant Behaviour*

One of the pioneer investigations in the field of social class learning was that of the American Allison Davis (1948), carried out in the early 1940's. Conclusions from American evidence cannot be transferred directly to British situations, but they can be guides in examining our own similar problems. Davis showed that there were great differences between the social classes in the child's learning in such basic areas of behaviour as eating, aggression and sex. He traced these social class variations in behaviour and personality to very different patterns of mothering in infancy. More particularly he analysed the social class patterns of breast feeding and toilet training.

A survey (J. and E. Newson, 1963) has been made of 709 mothers of one-year-old children in the city of Nottingham. The object was to investigate contemporary ways of caring for infants, and the survey provides evidence that is comparable with that of Davis. It was found that although middle-class mothers were definitely more progressive in their attitude to child care, the influence of more enlightened methods was spreading down the social scale. But there were some major differences in approach. For example, the idea of what was meant by 'a spoilt child' varied. Basically the answer depended upon what each social class would indulge. The middle-class mother would put up with tantrums but would not feed an endless supply of sweets to her child; the working-class mother would not indulge her child's tantrums, but would give him sweets when he wanted them. The middle-class mother put up with more crying at night before going to comfort her child or giving him a feed. Further, how were the parents to ensure conformity? When a child offended, the working-class mother tended to use smacking immediately, though particularly in the case of mothers in unskilled workers, families, not very consistently, whilst the middle-class mother preferred to try 'to love her child out of it'. Feeding habits differed greatly. All the children had ample chance to suck, but in different ways according to their social class. The middle-class child was more often breast fed, but was weaned earlier; the working-class child was bottle fed for longer and was allowed a dummy. There was little thumb-sucking amongst the children (only 8 per cent), but, as may be expected, it was more pronounced amongst the earlier-weaned middle-class babies. The middle class began potty training earlier and were more successful at it; unskilled workers' wives were very much later than others. Genital play was stopped by working-class mothers, but permitted or diverted by the middle class.

2. *Personality Differences*

The overall impression of the Newsons' evidence, though not all the details, is much the same as that of Davis. The working-class mode of infant care was characterized by a pattern of indulgence that in Davis's view led to a lack of self-discipline in older working-class children and adults. These very different ways of socialization meant markedly different patterns of personality. Davis noted that the working class did not control their basic psychological drives in the same way as the middle class did. The working class tended to extremes. When money was available, they overate and overheated their rooms. They used aggressive action much more often, and this was particularly so with regard to sex. These ways of behaviour were approved as normal among the working class, whereas the middle class directed the identical drives into channels that were socially approved in their sub-culture. Working-class aggression became middle-class initiative; the same psychological drive could take the form in a working-class child of actually striking a teacher and in the middle-class child of hard work leading to good school marks that would earn him the name of 'teacher's pet'.

What evidence is there for similar personality differences in Britain? In the early 1950's B. M. Spinley (1953) investigated the development of personality in English children. She compared the upbringing and personalities of two contrasted groups of boys and girls, one from a London slum environment and the other from public schools. In the case of the slum group she collected evidence by interviews with mothers and social workers in the area and by participant observation in various roles in local clubs; for the public school group she collected life histories of her sample and interviewed nursery nurses in training on methods of infant care. She administered a personality test (Rorschach) to both groups. From this evidence Spinley was able to establish a different basic personality pattern for each sub-culture that she was considering. She attributed the differences to their particular patterns of socialization. It must be stressed again here that within the limits set by inherited temperamental differences personality is formed by the experiences that the child and later the adult undergoes. The personality of an individual is part of his mode of survival; it will within the genetic limits fit his environment or he will not easily be able to survive within his own particular culture.

Spinley found that the members of the slum group were basically insecure, since a newborn infant was made much of till the next came along or till it grew into a child and then almost put on one side. The children in this group rebelled against authority, since it had been weak and inconsistent in their own experience. They were sexually disturbed, as the male figure in their families was weak and often changed. They had an under-developed conscience and were unable to postpone immediate desires or tackle difficult problems, which they tended to brush to one side. To children with this personality type school poses many problems. The teacher is not liked as he is seen as a representative of authority who is trying to impose an alien code of moral behaviour and who sets difficult problems. Likewise the teacher has difficulties with these children beyond the obvious one of mere communication. It is hard to pass on a code of morals or impart religious instruction to rebellious children with weak consciences. These children have such totally different standards from their teachers that the instruction must unconsciously but almost inevitably become a criticism of the whole ethos from which the children come. Yet the personality which these children display by their behaviour is not a deviant one at home; it only becomes deviant at school where they spend a minority of their time. The children are exposed to living in two environments, each of which views the other as deviant. The clearest example of this is Spinley's discovery that the boys played football by the rules under the supervision of the teacher, but did not do so at home in the street, because no child observing the rules could survive in the free-for-all version of football played away from school.

The public school group provided almost a copybook contrast. The children were secure in their home lives. They had developed a satisfactory adjustment to their own and the other sex. They had strong consciences and had achieved a balance of respect for and criticism of authority which was to be invaluable to them in the move from school-child to prefect and from assistant manager to manager in their later careers. To these children the worlds of home and school were not in conflict; both were striving to form the same personality type. Hence there was a much greater chance of success at school for this group.

The Nottingham sample used by the Newsons was much more representative of the general population than that examined by Spinley which rather provided limiting cases at the extremes of the social spectrum. But the two opposing personality types that Spinley found are in a large measure what might be expected from the patterns of indulgence noted by the Newsons. The self-discipline that Spinley's public school group exhibited through possessing a conscience and in their more balanced attitude to authority can be traced back to the pattern of middle-class infant care found by the Newsons; its foundations lay partly in the early patterns imposed with regard to feeding habits and toilet training and in the way the mother tried to love her child out of wrong-doing. The opposite personality traits in Spinley's slum group have counter-parts in the opposite habits of infant care found in the working-class part of the Newson's sample. Therefore, although such extremes of personality-type cannot be attributed outright to the broad bands that make up the working and the middle classes, yet it seems likely that Spinley's two types are approximate descriptions of the basic personality found among many in the middle class and among certainly a large proportion of the lower working class. In between these social classes it seems likely that there is a continuum with the basic personality tending towards one or other of the extremes according to the social class being considered. The teacher, who is more often than not from the middle class, has to deal mainly with children from the working class and may well find that one of the main demands put upon him, if he is to achieve success, is the adjustment that he must make in order to teach children the majority of whom have a very different personality pattern from his own. Neither pattern is deviant in any moral sense; both were formed through the normal process of social class learning.

3. *Attitudes towards Education*
So far it has been shown that social class learning can result in children with a personality type that is not sympathetic towards school. Clearly

the attitudes that parents show towards their children's schooling can offset or reinforce this tendency. In an investigation carried out in south-west Hertfordshire and Middlesbrough during 1952–3 (J. E. Floud, A. H. Halsey and F. M. Martin, 1956) it was shown that the chances of a working-class child entering a grammar school were greater if he came from a home rated as having poor material conditions but where attitudes towards education were favourable than if he came from a good material environment but where the attitudes were unfavourable to education. Only 9 per cent in S.W. Herts. and 12 per cent in Middlesbrough of children from homes with poor attitudes but good material conditions gained grammar school places, whereas the figures were 23 per cent and 15 per cent respectively for those from homes with favourable attitudes but poor material conditions.[1]

It is true that not all middle-class parents have attitudes entirely favourable towards their children's education, but it seems that fewer parents of lower social class have attitudes favourable in this respect. F. M. Martin found that in 1952 in S.W. Herts. concern with secondary education varied directly with social class. Of fathers in professional occupations 82 per cent had thought a lot about their children's secondary education as against 38·3 per cent of fathers who were unskilled workers. Similarly 81·7 per cent of fathers in professional occupations preferred their children to go to grammar school compared with 43·4 per cent of fathers in unskilled work. Douglas found comparable results in his national sample. But in addition he found that the mother's interest in her child's school progress varied by social class and seemed to be of great 'importance' in deciding chances of entry to a grammar school. Thus, if measured intelligence is held constant, children with mothers who wish them to go to grammar school and stay there till seventeen gain 11 per cent more places than expected, whereas children of mothers who are undecided get 8 per cent fewer places than expected, whilst the children of mothers wanting them to go to a secondary modern school and leave at the minimum legal age have 60 per cent fewer grammar school places than expected.[2]

Once a child has gained entry to a grammar school his success there can be much influenced by his parents' attitudes towards education.

[1] J. E. Floud and others, op. cit., pp. 91–95. The position in Middlesbrough is complicated by differences for the Roman Catholic part of the population; see op. cit., p. 138.

[2] F. M. Martin, in D. V. Glass (ed.), op. cit., pp. 162–3 and J. W. B. Douglas, op. cit., pp. 21–22 and p. 45.

Himmelweit found in 1951 that working-class boys were less successful in certain London grammar schools than were middle-class boys, despite the fact that they realized that their present efforts at school were related to their probable future success in life. A major contributory cause seemed to be lack of parental support for working-class boys. Middle-class parents visited the school more often and came to watch school games or plays more frequently. The middle-class boys themselves thought that their parents were more interested in their progress at school. Their parents more often supervised homework.[1] Douglas reported that the possession of a separate room for homework varied directly with social class. This is partly, but not entirely, a matter of the type of house that can be afforded, and in this connection overcrowding is much more common under working-class than middle-class housing conditions. Homework in a crowded room with a television set turned on is very difficult.

A very thorough investigation of the effects of home environment on success at school was carried out by E. Fraser (1959) in Aberdeen in the early 1950's. The results were particularly interesting because the survey was planned so that the measured intelligence of the large sample of twelve- and thirteen-year-old children was held constant and the variation in academic attainments could be related directly to differences in the home environment. Of the four areas studied, namely cultural, material, emotional, and motivational, only the last is directly relevant here. Fraser found that consistent parental encouragement was most important in providing the incentive to effort that resulted in achievement at school. Such encouragement was born in attitudes favourable towards education.

There is a growing tendency for children to stay on at school after the present legal minimum leaving age of fifteen. This must to a large extent be due to parental encouragement. Douglas found that there was no real difference between older and younger parents in this respect and concluded that the change must be a general one that affected parents of all ages.[2] It is commonly held that this trend is due to the growing numbers of parents who have themselves undergone higher education and secondary education beyond the minimum legal leaving age. If such educational experience is 'infective' one would expect a growing number of the

---

[1] See H. T. Himmelweit, 'Social Status and Secondary Education since the 1944 Act: Some Data for London', in D. V. Glass (ed.), op. cit.

[2] J. W. B. Douglas, op. cit., pp. 50–51.

children of these parents to stay on longer in the educational system. This impression is reinforced by the following figures which cover the Robbins Committee sample of children born in 1940–41. If children of parents of whom one or both have had selective education are compared with those of parents of whom neither has had selective education, it is found that 5·9 times as many achieved entry to degree level courses, 5·2 times as many two 'A' levels, 3·5 times as many five 'O' levels and 2·4 times as many entered selective secondary schools.[1]

This last tendency is only indirectly related to social class in that in the past selective education has been more of a middle-class prerogative, and therefore the infective process did not spread far. It had more the nature of a feed-back system. However, it can be seen that attitudes towards education are an important determinant of chances of success in secondary education. Since favourable attitudes are found more often in the higher social classes, they reinforce the effects of social class learning on educational success that were discussed earlier in the present chapter.

4. *Thinking*

So far in this chapter we have been considering the effect of different social class patterns of learning on the personality of children and thereby on their chances of success in school. But as a result of recent work it now seems that social class learning has an important effect on the actual development of intelligence and perception. In recent years the generally accepted notion of intelligence has changed greatly. The work of two psychologists, namely the Swiss Jean Piaget and the American D. O. Hebb, has been of particular influence. Piaget has stressed the developmental aspects of intelligence, and Hebb has made the valuable distinction between inherited potential and present mental efficiency. The analysis here is based on the importance of the learning of language in the development of intelligence and of ways of thinking. Most thinking is done verbally. Bernstein (1958) has shown that sub-cultures transmit different modes of speech and hence different modes of thinking.

Bernstein has worked with middle- and working-class boys in London and found that in the working-class sub-culture there is on the whole a particular mode of speech that is characterized by its very restricted nature. Sentences are short, dependent clauses are few, vocabulary is small, adjectives few and not used with fine discrimination, abstract ideas are rarely used, and finally gesture is commonly used in addition to or in place of speech. This syntactically simple language may be called 'restricted code', and those who are brought up to speak this code will automatically be brought to think in the same uncomplicated way regardless of whether they are genetically capable of far more complex thought. To those who can use a more complex code of speech there will not be the same limit to mental development. In the middle-class sub-culture children hear the speech of their parents and imitate it. This tends to be a more elaborate mode of speech; sentences are long and contain a complicated structure of dependent clauses, many subtly chosen adjectives are used, the words 'it' and 'one' are common, abstract nouns are found, and gesture assumes a much less important place in communication. This is termed 'elaborated code' and gives its speakers the possibility of thinking of a much more complex and abstract quality than is open to those who speak in restricted code.[1] The middle-class child can understand both codes, but the working-class child is brought up to a restricted code and finds great difficulty in translating elaborated code into something that he can understand. It should perhaps again be added that the account given here for ease of exposition covers limiting cases. Between these limits there will exist combinations of the two extremes.

Evidence for this theory is provided by examining the results of members of the working and middle classes in intelligence tests. Bernstein gave a verbal and non-verbal intelligence test to two groups.[2] The first consisted of sixty-one Post Office messenger boys aged fifteen to eighteen, none of whom had been to a grammar school. This group could safely be considered as working class. The second group was made up of forty-five boys from a major public school who were matched for age with the first group. This was the middle-class group. For the working-class group the results on the verbal test clustered around an I Q of 100, whereas on the non-verbal test thirty-six out of sixty-one had an I Q greater than 110. For the middle-class group the results on both tests were all above an I Q of 100 and the distribution of results in the two tests were closely matched. If the mean scores were extrapolated for a mean age of sixteen, then the difference on the non-verbal test between

[1] For an American account of the same process see L. Schatzman and A. Strauss, 'Social Class and Modes of Communication', *American Journal of Sociology*, January 1955.

[2] B. Bernstein, 'Language and Social Class', *British Journal of Sociology*, September 1960.

the two groups was 8–10 points of IQ, but it was 23·24 points on the verbal test; that is, it was more than twice as great as for the non-verbal test.

To summarize, the language scores of the working-class group were depressed in relation to the scores at the higher ranges of the non-verbal test, but this was not the case for the public-school group. It would seem that the mental operations necessary to do non-verbal tests are available to both the working and the middle classes, but that the mental operations necessary for understanding the more complex parts of the verbal tests are only available to the middle class and have not become a part of the mental equipment of the working class.[1] Two things follow. Firstly, purely because of differences in social class learning the middle class have more facility in the mental operations necessary to pass the verbal intelligence tests mainly used for entrance to grammar schools, but, secondly, there must be many working-class children who have high innate mental ability, but who can not have this potential developed since the mode of speech they learn in their sub-culture is of too restricted a nature to furnish them with the mental equipment that is necessary and that they could have possessed. No firm answer can be given in the present state of psychological knowledge to the question of how late a child may delay the development of his innate potential mental capacity and not damage his chances of ultimately catching up.[2]

Therefore the working-class child may well come to school with a twofold handicap. His innate intelligence is under-developed in certain aspects that are important for success in our educational system as it is now organized, and his personality is so structured that he is unlikely to do well in school. It is to a fuller examination of the effect of this personality structure on the child's perception of the school situation that we must now turn.[3] The working-class child has not had his spare time carefully organized for him, as is often the case with middle-class children. He has a very general notion of the future and is incapable of pursuing long-term goals. This reinforces the already mentioned difficulty of postponing his present whims. To such children arbitrary luck rather than rigorously planned work appears to be the reason for success.

[1] J. W. B. Douglas, op. cit., p. 46 found a slight tendency for the middle class to do better in verbal and the working class in non-verbal tests. The difference was not statistically significant, but certainly confirms other studies.

[2] See J. McV. Hunt, op. cit., for an account of this problem.

[3] B. Bernstein, 'Some Sociological Determinants of Perception', *British Journal of Sociology*, June 1958.

On the other hand the middle-class child comes to school with his intelligence developed in the direction required for success. In addition his personality has been moulded in a very different social setting so that he sees the importance of long-term goals and perceives that he himself, rather than good fortune, is the main influence on his chances of achieving such goals. These two ways of perceiving the school situation that are due to personality differences may explain the paradoxical finding of Himmelweit in her survey of London grammar schools where working-class boys did not do as well as middle-class boys despite the fact that they knew that their success at school could influence their long-term chances in life.[1]

Social class learning results in the school learning situation appearing very different to each social class. Clearly communication will be difficult between those who tend to speak and to think in different codes. It has been pointed out that the stress on the transmission of an elaborated code and on the moral code associated with the middle class may be perceived by a working-class child as an implicit criticism and devaluation of his own background. Yet the working-class child may come to feel unease at his failure at school, the responsibility for which may well not be his own. If we consider actual school subjects, it will probably be in his English lessons that the working-class child will most feel that his teacher is trying to change his code of speech, his method of thought and even his mode of perception. His whole system of communication seems to be under attack. Difficulties will occur in mathematics; mechanical operations, such as addition and multiplication, will be within his grasp, but the transfer of these operations to symbols that is involved in algebra could cause trouble.

The description of social class learning that has been given here has stressed limiting cases. It can be appreciated that such cases are useful tools of sociological analysis, yielding results from which it is possible to work. But in the world of the school all is not so clear cut. The situation is blurred by the existence of 'illiterate' middle-class parents who care little for their children and do not provide an environment favourable to their full development and also of working-class parents who perhaps through extensive further education have come to value education and who can speak in both codes. It can, however, be appreciated that a knowledge of the extreme effects of differential social class learning on

[1] See H. T. Himmelweit, op. cit. See also E. Bene, 'Boys' Attitudes Towards Education', *British Journal of Sociology*, June 1959.

the personality and intellect of children will be of great assistance to all who work in schools.

B. Equality of Educational Opportunity

1. *Definition*

A modern political ideal that is widely held in Britain is that of equality of educational opportunity. Like many of the catch-phrases of politics this is not an easy ideal to define. A politician has said that equality of educational opportunity exists when all have equal chances to become unequal. This is a stimulating thought, but is not a close definition. A philosopher might develop his definition along lines somewhat as follows. Equality in this context exists when all children have the same chances to develop their abilities and aptitudes to the fullest possible extent. This is a more exact definition, but raises difficulties of measurements. How are we to know when all children have equal chances? Or how are we to measure the 'mature' individual? A sociologist who wants to know just what is happening in a given educational system will demand a definition that enables him to measure how much equality there is by the chosen criteria. This tendency to want to quantify problems is strengthened because sociologists usually tackle social problems with the hope of influencing administrators by their findings. Such an aim encourages the use of exact measurement.

In the present British educational situation a practical definition of equal opportunity that is capable of making discoveries that may influence policy can be worded in the following way. Equality exists when all children of the same measured intelligence have the same chance of going to a grammar school. Here the criteria used are I Q and entry to the grammar school. I Q tests are suspect on technical psychological grounds and also raise awkward questions with regard to those whose I Q develops after the crucial test to a level high enough for entry to a grammar school. But in contemporary Britain where there is a shortage of grammar school places and a need to fill them in as objective a way as is possible I Q tests are the most efficient way of rationing these places out amongst the children with the capability at that moment of undertaking a grammar school course. The second criterion of entry to a grammar school can also be attacked on the grounds that this school is the basis of an inegalitarian system aimed at educating an *élite*. This may be true, but the grammar school is what many parents want for their children and in addition is the main educational source for many of the higher grades of labour necessary for the country's economic survival. This definition also totally ignores the whole question of social class learning; the extent of this problem is very difficult as yet to measure, though an indication can be gained from the measurements of wastage of talent to which reference will be made in Chapter 11.

This definition is a working one that can be applied to the existing educational system to give us some guide to what is actually happening. It also provides a model for other similar definitions which could be used in somewhat different circumstances. Thus if there were no entry examination to grammar schools, a completely comprehensive system of secondary education, and no private system, it would be possible to find out if there was equality by measuring whether all adolescents of the same I Q had the same chances of entering the sixth form or the university, or perhaps even of gaining a degree.

2. Social Class and I Q

When considering equality of educational opportunity it is necessary to know how measured intelligence is distributed by social class. A naïve approach to this question would assume that, since there are more working than middle-class children, there should be a higher proportion of working than middle-class children in the grammar school. Though this can be true, it totally ignores the fact that above a certain level of measured intelligence there is a higher proportion of middle- than working-class children who have this level of intelligence. In other words there is a higher proportion of middle- than working-class children with high I Qs.

The causes of this bias in the distribution of I Qs must be sought in two main areas of knowledge, in genetics and in psychology. Firstly, though there is a spread of the I Qs found in any one occupation, those employed in occupations of lower status tend to have lower mean I Qs. As has already been indicated there is a positive correlation between the I Q of parent and child. Therefore the children of the lower social classes will tend to have lower I Qs than those of the higher classes. Secondly, however, there is the effect of differential social class learning. Even if the working-class child is born with high innate mental potential, this may not be developed because of the quality of experience to which he is exposed in his home environment. The low I Qs of such children will then contribute to the class bias in the distribution of measured intelligence. It must be stressed that this latter argument should in this context be treated as a matter of fact and not as a cause for moral indignation.

Furthermore, the exact psychological mechanism by which intelligence is developed may well not be the same for bright as for dull children. A survey was carried out in Manchester in 1951 (S. Wiseman, 1964) as a result of which the intelligence, arithmetic and reading tests of 5,374 children between fourteen and fifteen years old were analysed. By using the statistical technique of factor analysis four factors emerged, two of which were particularly important in accounting for the variations in the test results. Backwardness was defined as shown by those scoring in the lowest sixth of the results and was almost entirely accounted for by a factor named 'social disorganization', which was in the main genetic, but which was also closely connected with such purely social circumstances as a high illegitimate birth rate or a high rate of neglected children. Brightness was defined as shown by the top sixth of the results and was a far more complex phenomenon. Especially in the reading results, but also in intelligence, brightness had a strong connection with a factor named 'maternal care', but the 'social disorganization' factor was nearly as important. It would seem that social class learning does not operate in a homogeneous way but rather works in different ways at the two poles of intelligence.[1]

The exact nature of the distribution of IQ scores can be seen from two surveys. In the Scottish Mental Survey occupations other than agricultural were coded into seven categories. The mean test scores of measured intelligence and the proportions of the sample obtaining them were as shown on page 79.

In Douglas's investigation the average test scores of children at eleven measured in IQ points were as follows for each social class: Upper Middle = 115, Lower Middle = 106, Upper Manual Working = 100, Lower Manual Working = 96.[2]

High scores are distributed throughout the social classes, but low scores are bunched in the lower classes, so that the proportion of high IQs is lower in the lower than in the higher classes, but below a certain level of IQ the actual number of those with high IQs is greater in the lower than in the higher classes. It is among this latter group, the intelligent working-class children, that the chance of gaining entry to a

[1] S. Wiseman, op. cit., pp. 93–96.
[2] From Table VI(d), J. W. B. Douglas, op. cit., p. 151.

Occupational Class	Description	Mean Score (Max = 76)	% of Sample	Number Scoring 50 and over	% of those in that Class	Number Scoring under 20	% of those in that Class
1.	Professional and large employers	51·8	3·7	141	63·8	2	1·1
2.	Small employers	42·7	5·3	125	37·4	29	8·7
3.	Salaried employers	47·7	3·9	119	50·5	9	0·4
4.	Non-manual wage earners	43·6	9·1	202	36·2	26	4·7
5.	Skilled wage earners	37·2	39·3	549	23·8	368	15·3
6.	Semi-skilled wage earners	33·2	19·8	184	15·3	252	21·0
7.	Unskilled wage earners	31·1	18·9	134	11·7	296	25·9
All	(including those in Agriculture)	37·786	100·0				

(From Table XXIII, p. 47 and Table XXXVIII, p. 113, *Social Implications of the 1947 Scottish Mental Survey*, London, 1953)

grammar school is low. Amongst a representative sample of National Service recruits who joined the Army in 1956–7 it was found that in the top ability group (the top 11 per cent of the sample) only 1 per cent of the sons of fathers in professional and managerial occupations had left school by fifteen, whereas 28 per cent of the sons of unskilled manual workers had done so; in the second ability group (the next 30 per cent of the sample) 27 per cent of the sons of the highest social group had left school by fifteen compared with 86 per cent of boys whose fathers were unskilled workers.[1]

Some of the determinants of this process of selection will be examined in Chapter 11, but it is quite clear from these figures that by the very conservative definition used here equality of educational opportunity has not yet been achieved. This conclusion takes no account of the even greater inequality that social class learning must introduce.

[1] From Table Ib, *15 to 18*, Vol. I, 1959, p. 119, and op. cit., Vol. II, 1960, p. 113.

3. A Model

In order to apply this definition of equality to any given geographical area it is possible to devise a model (J. E. Floud, A. H. Halsey and F. M. Martin, 1956). First, the distribution of the IQs of the children to be considered must be known for each of the relevant social classes; it will be realized that all the difficulties of defining social classes are raised here. These figures may be totalled cumulatively in a table like the following:

I.Q.	Middle Class	Lower Middle Class	Working Class	Total
130 and above	8	9	8	25
125 „ „	11	15	13	39
120 „ „	15	32	28	75
115 „ „	20	50	65	135
110 „ „	26	73	136	235

This table shows the way that the lower down the scale of IQ one goes the more possibility there is that the total numbers of the working class with a given IQ will be greater than the total for the middle class. Let us next assume that in the school catchment area under consideration there are 135 places in grammar schools available for this year's entry. It is clear that an IQ of 115 is the 'cut off' point; children below 115 will not achieve entry to grammar school. The 'perfect' entry that will provide equal chances to each social class will then be twenty middle-class, fifty lower middle-class and sixty-five working-class children.

This model provides the perfect entry in any one year, but the conditions that govern the competition for places may change from year to year. The fact noted earlier that the different social classes have different birth rates can alter the distribution of IQs. There may be a differential rate of immigration or emigration at work in the area; for example, the building of a council estate will raise the proportion of working-class children in an area, whereas an increase in speculative building can have the opposite effect since these new houses will be bought in the main by members of the middle class. The rate of use of private boarding-schools or the presence of a direct grant day school in the area will be another fact that must be taken into account. All these considerations will vary from year to year and from region to region. In practice, therefore, the problem of an exact calculation of class chances of entry to grammar school becomes very complex, although in theory it may be simple.

4. *Conclusion*

Social classes are sub-cultures within which there are different patterns of learning. Social class learning affects three psychological concepts -- personality, perception and thinking. Because of this children from each social class have varying chances of doing well at school. In an egalitarian age this tendency raises the problem of whether it is possible to diminish these social class differences. If the re-interpretation of the thesis of embourgeoisement that Goldthorpe and Lockwood have suggested is true, the tendency towards one new class under the impact of common contemporary social and economic changes could produce a common class culture. However, this is a long way off and raises problems of culture transmission through the schools that must be dealt with in the second part of this book. Another policy that might alleviate the problem of social class learning has been suggested. The structure of the British educational system could be changed to a comprehensive one at secondary level as it is now at primary level, so that the children from all classes went through a similar pattern of schooling. Again we shall be in a better position to analyse the problems of our present structure of secondary education when we have examined the way these schools act to select the children within them by class and ability. But even at this early stage the reader must be warned that this is a problem bedevilled by political considerations and rarely treated in the impartial way that a sociologist of education hopes to examine it.

As the political ideal of egalitarianism has come to exercise more power so more stress has come to be laid in the administration of education upon ensuring equal chances for children of all social classes in the schools. In the inter-war years the IQ test was seen as the means of achieving this equality with the criterion of entry to the grammar school. Though for measurement purposes such a definition of equality can still be useful, since the war a more subtle analysis based upon the idea of differences in social class learning reinforced by parental attitudes towards education has uncovered deeper reasons for inequality. The measurement of the scale of this problem, to which reference will be made in the next part, forms one of the present growing points of the sociology of education.

F

BIBLIOGRAPHY

B. Bernstein, 'Social Class and Linguistic Development: A Theory of Social Learning' in *The Reader*.★

A. Davis, *Social Class Influences on Learning*, Cambridge (USA), 1948.

J. W. B. Douglas, *The Home and The School*, London, 1964.

J. E. Floud, A. H. Halsey and F. M. Martin, *Social Class and Educational Opportunity*, London, 1956.

E. Fraser, *Home Environment and the School*, London, 1959.

J. & E. Newson, *Infant Care in an Urban Community*, London, 1963 (Pelican)

Social Implications of the 1947 Scottish, Mental Survey, London, 1953.

B. M. Spinley, *The Deprived and the Privileged*, London, 1953.

S. Wiseman, *Education and Environment*, Manchester, 1964.

★ *Education, Economy and Society*, by A. H. Halsey, J. E. Floud and C. A. Anderson, New York, 1961 will be referred to as *The Reader*.

6

The Economy

Economics is probably the most developed of the social sciences, partly because it has a longer history as a discipline recognized in its own right than the other social sciences. It now covers a great number of special fields. For example, two topics which have little direct relevance to education but which have been of great importance traditionally in economics are the study of international trade and the examination of how the individual firm operates under varying degrees of competition and monopoly. In this book we can only deal with a limited number of these specialized subjects. The aim will be to cover topics that are of immediate relevance to education, and at the same time to give as balanced a picture as possible in the space available of the way that the British economy works today. Therefore this chapter will contain three sections. In each a brief analysis of an important economic concept will be given. This will be followed by an account of contemporary developments in this particular field. The three concepts to be covered are capitalism, the division of labour, and full employment.

A. Capitalism

1. *Analysis*

The fundamental problem of all economic systems is the allocation of the scarce resources amongst the many possible uses. There is no problem in deciding who should have fresh air since plenty is available. Difficulty arises in the case of commodities such as coal or skilled labour. What system can we evolve to allocate these scarce resources? Economists use the term 'capitalism' to refer to one particular type of economic system. The principal characteristic of the system is that the instruments of production, such as the factories, tools and raw materials, are owned by private individuals. In classical economic theory these individuals are known as 'entrepreneurs', a word significantly translated in many American textbooks as 'enterprisers'. The entrepreneur is assumed to follow a policy of self-interest. He will buy his raw materials as cheaply as he can and sell his products as dearly as possible, thereby maximizing his profit. Under strict *laissez-faire* this policy is held to result in the most efficient allocation of productive resources and therefore in the greatest material benefit to all. The pure doctrine of the early nineteenth-century Manchester school of *laissez-faire* prohibited all State interference as inimical to the best distribution of resources. Twentieth-century neo-Liberals allow sufficient State intervention to offset any undue exploitation of those with little power. It would be a fair summary of their views to say that the State should set the rules within which the *laissez-faire* system must operate.

There are further implications of this system. One of the economic commodities that is bought by the entrepreneur and sold by those who have it is labour. Its price is the wages or salaries paid to attract it. These rates will vary according to the quality of labour considered; one of the more important determinants in Britain today will be the education required in the grade of labour to be hired. The highly qualified technologist will command a higher reward than the less-well-qualified technician, who in turn can expect more than a craftsman. The markets in which labour and other products are exchanged are assumed to be free of restriction so that all commodities, including labour, will move to their highest reward. Further, no dealer must command so large a proportion of the market in any commodity that he can control its price; obviously a market controlled by one buyer or seller is at the mercy of this sole operator. This point raises the problem of the contemporary size of economic unit. Under the conditions of classical capitalism an entrepreneur could easily enter an industry to start his own small firm.

A final assumption vital to classical capitalism is that all who took economic action behaved rationally. A man who wants to sell his labour, whether manual or intellectual, goes for the highest reward. This implies that upward social mobility was easy for the able worker. A person who wishes to buy an article for consumption or a raw material for use in production always pays the lowest possible price. This assumes that all consumers have the knowledge and the desire to distinguish between rival goods. Disbelief of these last two implications should cause the reader to doubt whether the classical picture of the way that capitalism works serves as anything more than a starting-point for an analysis of the contemporary British economic system.

2. Developments

(i) *Size of Unit*. The impression given in the classical theoretical analysis is that the size of economic unit, whether for production or distribution of goods, is small. An individual who wanted to start up a new business enterprise could enter the industry easily since the amount of capital required would be relatively small. An examination of the size of units in manufacturing industry will show the contemporary trend. The usual criterion for measuring size of unit is the number of employees, though this is not equally applicable to all types of economic activity.

Size and Number of Manufacturing Establishments in Great Britain, 1935 &1961

Size of Unit	Number of Establishments				% of Total Employees	
	1935	%	1961	%	1935	1961
11–99	37,614	76·9	40,049	72·6	25·6	20·5
100–499	9,750	19·9	12,213	22·1	39·1	32·2
500–999	1,047	2·1	1,693	3·1	13·9	13·7
1,000 and over	533	1·1	1,206	2·2	21·4	33·6
	48,944	100·0	55,161	100·0	100·0	100·0

The move towards larger establishments as measured by the criterion used here can be seen. In 1935 76·9 per cent of all manufacturing establishments were in the smallest group; by 1961 this percentage had fallen to 72·6. In the largest category in 1935 only 1·1 per cent of all establishments employed 1,000 or more, but by 1961 the proportion had doubled and the actual number much more than doubled. Furthermore, this very small proportion of the total number of manufacturing units employed just over a third (33·6 per cent) of all factory employees, as compared with about a fifth (21·4 per cent) in 1935. When the percentages of those employed in each size group in 1961 are compared with those for 1935, the tendency is clear; there is a move towards fewer employees in the smaller and more in the larger factories.

To complete the picture, however, there were even in 1961 a large, but unknown number of factories employing less than eleven employees.

The total of these small units was believed to be around 140,000. These are the small units of the modern economic system. They still exist, but there is a definite tendency for the amount of capital needed to enter most industries today to be so high that the private individual cannot start a manufacturing business on his own out of his personal resources. As the size of manufacturing unit has grown so that the economies of large-scale production can be gained, rising costs of entry have prevented the small man from becoming an entrepreneur. This must modify the traditional analysis of capitalism and poses the question of who today owns and controls these large enterprises.

(ii) *Ownership*. In 1855 and 1862 laws were passed in Britain that enabled joint stock companies to have the privilege of limited liability under fairly stringent legal conditions. Thereby, if a company became bankrupt, it was only liable for debts up to the limit of its legally registered capital and no longer, as had been the case previously, could the shareholders be called upon to stand all the debts of the company. These laws enabled British industry and commerce to tap the growing wealth of the country for additional capital. Eventually ownership of shares became more widespread, and there was a much greater chance than beforehand that the actual day-to-day control of an enterprise might be in different hands from its ownership. In theory the owners of a company are the ordinary shareholders who have the maximum voting rights within the company. In most limited companies there are a large number of shareholders and they appoint managers to look after the business on their behalf. As long as profits are satisfactory, the shareholders will not worry and in all likelihood will never attend the company's annual general meetiings. Thus ownership and control can come to be in the hands of two totally different sets of people. Those in control may have no financial stake in the company that they run.

An example of the present situation is provided by the British iron and steel industry. In 1956 the typical shareholding in a steel company was small, namely 150 shares. Yet an analysis of eleven large companies producing 70 per cent of the privately produced output of steel showed that the 5 per cent of largest shareholders then owned 56 per cent of the total capital. Since anyone who can control more than 50 per cent of the voting power in a company can outvote the remaining shareholders, it is clear that a small number of individuals can control a large company. In practice ownership is often so divided that any individual or group who control even 20 per cent of a company's ordinary shares can usually dictate its policy. It therefore becomes important to know who owns industrial shares. The owners of the steel shares mentioned above were very largely insurance companies, nominees of banks and institutions specializing in investment (J. H. Dunning and C. J. Thomas, 1961). Who do these owners appoint as their managers? One survey made in 1951 of 1,173 directors of large public companies showed that between 50 and 60 per cent started their careers with the advantage of a business connection in the family. Nineteen per cent were directors of firms of which their fathers were directors before them, though only 8 per cent were leaders of firms that had been in the same family for more than three generations.[1] Even allowing for this 50 or 60 per cent, many of whom may not have had a large financial stake in the companies that they were controlling, there still remains a large number of directors who can be regarded as professional managers. Particularly at a slightly lower level there are a large number of managers who have made their careers in such companies, who have much power and a relatively high income, but own no shares in the companies for which they work.

It was this increase in the number of men who were managers but not owners that led the American, J. H. Burnham, in 1943 to publish his well-known book, *The Managerial Revolution*. Burnham developed an argument put forward by an earlier American, the economist Thorstein Veblen, that the split between ownership and management had gone so far that industry had come to be controlled by a more or less self-perpetuating *élite* of managers. These men were the directors of companies. Since they were efficient, profits satisfied the owners and, therefore, there was so little intervention by the owners that the director-managers could follow their own policies, particularly as they were more knowledgeable about the business than the owners. These professional managers could perpetuate the situation by electing whom they wished to fill any vacancy caused by a director resigning or retiring.

The joint stock company presents a very different picture from the entrepreneur of classical economic analysis. The question may be asked as to who in our present system exercises the function of the entrepreneur of entering new fields and starting new enterprises. It would seem that in the major section of industry which is organized on the joint stock principle the boards of the companies act as entrepreneurs in a corporate fashion. Though it can be shown from the point of view of social class

[1] G. H. Copeman, *Leaders of British Industry*, 1954, London, pp. 95–96 and p. 98.

that the managers and the owners often come from the same class, yet from the economic standpoint it remains crucial that control and ownership are now often split, particularly in the large manufacturing companies that have been seen to be growing more common. This raises important questions that must be considered in the next chapter as to how these managers are recruited from the educational system.

(iii) *Nationalization.* During the period of office of the Labour Government between 1945 and 1950 a substantial sector of British industry was taken into public ownership. Nationalization now covers a large part of the transport industry including the railways and most of the airways, the electricity and gas industries, and coal mining. Some measure of the important share that these industries now have in the economy as a whole can be judged from the following facts. In 1962–3 the nationalized industries employed about two million workers or about 8 per cent of Britain's labour force. These industries produced 15·2 per cent of the gross output of this country and undertook 19·5 per cent of the fixed investment.[1] Thus they employed nearly a tenth of the workers and accounted for almost a fifth of investment.

The policy of nationalization affected the trends already considered in this chapter. The actual size of manufacturing unit did not necessarily increase, though this did happen, but the size of economic unit controlled from one source did grow. The worker in a coal mine that was owned by a joint stock company often knew who his boss was, whereas under the National Coal Board the ultimate source of authority and control is many steps away up the hierarchy of management. Furthermore, ownership is now in the hands of the State, a very abstract concept for a man at the coal face to grasp. Ownership and control have seemed to be even more divorced than before nationalization.

There are many similarities between these large-scale industries owned by the State and run by professional managers who are responsible to a Minister of the Crown and ultimately to Parliament and such giants of private enterprise as Unilever, Shell, or the Imperial Chemical Industries. These companies are also run by professional managers, the great majority of whom will have no financial stake in the company for which they work. Such men, particularly at the middle level of management, lead a bureaucratic life not dissimilar from many Civil Servants. In this situation the drive to work is of a very different quality from that assumed to operate in the classical entrepreneur or even in his employees.

[1] *Treasury Bulletin for Industry,* November, 1963.

(iv) *Equality*. The tendency towards a more egalitarian society has already been mentioned in the context of social class, but it can also be viewed as an economic phenomenon. Wealth has been slowly redistributed under the impact of heavy death duties. An estate of £1 million will attract estate duties at a rate of about 80 per cent. At lower levels the rate is less and it is therefore still possible, despite taxation, to pass on substantial fortunes at death. In addition there are legal means of avoiding the maximum impact of estate duties, such as making gifts prior to death. Thus the policy of redistributing wealth has been slow to take effect.

The attempt to create a less widely spread income structure has had more success than that of lessening inegality in ownership of wealth. Between the start of the century and 1939 it seems that about 10 per cent of the population received nearly half of the national income, whilst the other 90 per cent got the remaining half (J. R. Hicks, 1960). During the Second World War a big redistribution took place so that about 10 per cent of the national income was transferred from property owners to wage earners. The trend has probably moved slightly in the other direction since 1945, particularly in the late 1950's and early 1960's. The shift towards a somewhat more equal income distribution has been effected partly by fiscal policy through a steeply graduated taxation system, but one of the most powerful influences has been of a purely economic nature. A larger proportion of the working population now works in the more productive industries which pay higher wages. The greater the proportion of wage earners in these high paying industries, the greater will the proportion of national income tend to be that goes to wage earners as a whole.[1]

The calculation of how egalitarian the British income structure is has become a complex statistical problem. One of the main complications is that many welfare payments and services must be taken into account before a true picture can be given. All social classes are entitled to payments such as children's allowances and maternity benefits, and to services such as free education and medical treatment. Whether these services are of more benefit to the middle or the working class is at the moment a matter for economic controversy. All that can be said with certainty is that our income structure is somewhat less widely spread than in 1939 and that the raising of the whole level of real incomes (i.e. after allowing for the inflation in prices) due to the increasing produc-

[1] D. Seers, op. cit., and 'Salaries', *The Economist*, 23 and 30 May 1964.

tivity of industry since 1945 has taken some of the sting out of the still existing inequality for many of those in the lower income groups. However, here, as in the three preceding sections dealing with contemporary developments in capitalism, we find that a measure of intervention has replaced complete *laissez-faire*.

3. *Capitalism Today*

Marx viewed capitalism as one type of economic system and as one economic stage through which a society had to pass along a predetermined pattern of development. He recognized that this system had achieved much in improving methods of production and thereby increasing wealth, but he thought that capitalism would fail because of the faults inherent in the system itself. Marx was proved wrong for a variety of reasons, some of which were discussed when considering his theory of social class. In this chapter the more egalitarian income structure has again been mentioned, but with stress on the economic viewpoint, and in the next part of this chapter the rise of the new middle class will also be examined for a second time, but here for its economic implications.

The failure of Marx to foretell the future course of capitalism has not discouraged the attempts of others. In 1942 Professor Schumpeter of Harvard University published a very influential book, *Capitalism, Socialism and Democracy* in which he also foretold the eventual end of capitalism not because of its failures as did Marx, but because of its successes. He noticed the tendency towards large-scale manufacturing units which raised productivity and increased efficiency. He saw that in some industries one company already produced the output sufficient to satisfy almost the whole national market for its products. In this situation nationalization seemed to him a logical consequence of capitalist growth. The problem to Schumpeter was to ensure political freedom under such conditions.

Schumpeter's thesis is not yet proved. What can we conclude is the state of capitalism today? The work of Professor Sargent Florence (1953) can help us to find an answer. Sargent Florence examined the economies of the USA and the UK and found common forces at work in both. The same industries tended to be large in both economies, though scale in the USA was larger than in the UK. The same enterprises on the whole were concentrated in one or a few geographical regions and the same were distributed throughout the whole area of each country, for example in both economies the motor industry was concentrated and hairdressing was widely spread. He found the same patterns of ownership and control in the two economies. From such evidence he concluded that there was a fundamental logic of economic development that operated in all situations. The same logic is presumably also at work in other industrialized nations such as the USSR.

The USA and the UK are called capitalist economies, but in addition to the interference necessary to follow the policy of greater egalitarianism there is in both economies much central planning; this affects all the industry of both countries. There is also a considerable sector of State-owned industry in both countries, though this is more the case in the UK than the USA. In the USSR industry is basically nationalized, but there is a small free sector and, as the economy grows richer, the consumer is being given somewhat more say in what shall be produced. None of these economies is, therefore, a pure type, but all three economies are developing under the same logic. In the case of an economic as opposed to a political analysis, we may often stress what is common in each case and not what is different and, using Freidmann's (1953) term, speak of 'industrial society'.

B. The Division of Labour

1. *Analysis*

In 1776 Adam Smith wrote what is often regarded as the first modern book on economic theory, *The Wealth of Nations*. He began this work with a chapter on what he called 'the division of labour' and he chose the manufacture of pins as one example of this process. One man carrying out the whole process 'could scarcely, perhaps, with his utmost industry, make one pin in a day, and certainly could not make twenty'. But he noted that the job was now divided up into a number of branches, each of which was done by a specialist. In one factory that Adam Smith had visited ten persons in this way 'could make among them upwards of forty-eight thousand pins in a day' or four thousand eight hundred each as against twenty made by the one relatively unspecialized man. Thus the division of the job amongst many labourers who each specialized on a small part of it brought a great rise in productivity.

This is the principle upon which most industry is now organized. Craftsmen do not operate in this way, but a modern economy is characterized by mass production rather than by craft industry. There are therefore today a very large number of semi-skilled occupations in our labour force. It is possible to enumerate these occupations under main headings that are usually chosen on an industrial rather than an occupational basis. This gives an indication of how the labour force is employed in any country and provides a rough picture of the occupational structure. It is not exact because workers in any one occupation (e.g. lorry driving) may be employed in several industries.

In the UK in 1962 out of a population of approximately 52 millions there were 24·6 millions in civil employment of whom 8·5 millions were women. The broad outline of the occupational structure was as below (figures in 'ooo's):

I		II		III	
Agriculture ⎰ 1,709 Mining ⎱		Manufacturing		Transport,	
		Industry	9,029	Communication	1,717
		Construction	1,697	Distributive Trades	3,439
		Gas, Electricity,		Professional, Com-	
		Water	394	mercial, Services	5,327
				National and Local	
				Government	1,326
				Registered Unemployed	432
Totals	1,709		11,120		12,241

(Annual Abstract of Statistics)

On the basis of these figures a broad comparison can be made with an under-developed country, and this will indicate a way of analysing the occupational structure. The labour force of an under-developed country will contain a far larger proportion than in the UK in the economic sector that develops first, namely the agricultural group of occupations. This category has been called the primary sector. As a country begins the process of economic development, it will shift part of its labour force out of the primary sector into the manufacturing or the secondary sector. At this stage only a small proportion of its workers will be employed in the service industries, such as banking, insurance or distributive trading. As a country moves towards economic maturity the proportion employed in this final or tertiary sector grows. It can be seen that in the UK the tertiary employment by any count is large. On a very rough grouping 12·2 millions are employed in this sector against 11·1 millions in the secondary and 1·7 millions in the primary sectors, but, though the principle is clear, it is possible to dispute the exact boundaries to the statistical categories used in such a division.

2. Contemporary Developments in the Division of Labour

(i) *Specialization*. The Classification of Occupations that was used for the 1961 Census of Britain showed approximately 35,500 different occupations. The sub-division of labour is now very great. One Midlands manufacturer of men's clothing has broken down the making of a waist-coat into sixty-five separate units of work. The farther this process goes, the more specialized, but the less skilled, does the work become. The production line becomes the standard method of large scale manufacture; a line of highly specialized workers is stationed before a slowly moving carrier-belt along which the product passes, gradually assuming recognizable shape as each worker adds the piece for which he or she is responsible. Little knowledge of the materials used is necessary. Speed, precision and dexterity are the qualities demanded.

From this it may be imagined that the ratio between the skilled part of the labour force and the unskilled is falling. However, there are two forces at work in the opposite direction. Firstly, there is the great growth in the tertiary sector of the labour force. Many of those employed in these occupations are in work of an administrative or clerical nature. This is true within manufacturing industry itself. Large production lines working on a mass-production basis require careful control and present complex problems of management. Nothing must be allowed to stop production, since idle machinery makes no profit. The importance of this force can be appreciated if one realizes that the number and proportion of the workers in British factory trades employed as administrative, technical and clerical staff grew from 512,000 (11·8 per cent) in 1924 to 1,093,000 (20·0 per cent) in 1948. Even between 1959 and 1962 the proportion of those employed in this category in all manufacturing industry grew from 21·1 to 22·6 per cent. Different industries employed higher or lower percentages, but the general trend was clear. For instance, between 1959 and 1962 the percentage employed in chemicals and allied industries rose from 32·3 to 34·8 per cent, in vehicles from 24·1 to 25·1 per cent and in clothing and footwear from 11·0 to 11·6 per cent.[1]

There is a second force working to preserve the ratio of skill. Production lines are complicated trains of machinery. Some very skilled

[1] P. Sargent Florence, op. cit., p. 139 and *Annual Abstract of Statistics*.

men are necessary to maintain the machines essential to modern industry. Thus the percentage of maintenance men is rising. Many of these men are craftsmen who not only need the skills to repair complex machines, but also must be able to diagnose just what has caused the breakdown. In a typical steel company the number of craftsmen as a percentage of the total labour force rose from 7 to 11 per cent between 1925 and 1953.[1] An exact balance of the forces operating on the need for skilled workers is difficult to assess, and it must be left until we have considered the move towards automation.

(ii) *The Changing Nature of Industry.* So far in this chapter we have considered the changing pattern of employment, the development in the size and ownership of industrial units, and the increase in the direct intervention of the State in the economy. There are three additional changes which affect the very nature of British industry. Firstly, the industries based on science are growing more predominant. This encourages a second and logically separate trend, the move towards a greater use of research and science throughout industry. Lastly, connected with this, but again partly autonomous, is the application of new techniques to industry, exemplified particularly by automation (J. H. Dunning and C. J. Thomas, 1961).

(a) *Science-based Industries.* The old staple industries upon which Britain's prosperity in the nineteenth century was founded were not renowned for the application of science to their processes. It may have been that at that time their nature and the state of scientific knowledge was such that it was not possible to apply science to the textile, coal and heavy engineering industries, though this is doubtful. But by the mid-twentieth century other industries are basic to our survival as an industrial power with a high standard of life. The chemical industry has become important both in itself and as a supplier of raw materials to other industries. Many of the industries using and producing the new synthetics, such as plastics, clothing fibres and detergents, are based on raw materials provided by the chemical industry. The survival of old as well as the welfare of new industries has come to depend on an industry of a highly scientific nature. In 1963 it employed 6 per cent of those working in manufacturing industry.

The character of the engineering industry has changed greatly. Within this heterogeneous statistical category there has been a switch to lighter products and, more particularly, the electrical engineering industry has

[1] *Men, Steel and Technical Change*, DSIR, London, 1957, p. 8.

become important. In 1953 the engineering, shipbuilding and electrical goods industries together employed 30·0 per cent of the workers in manufacturing industry; by 1963 the proportion had grown to 33·6 per cent. But during the same ten years the proportion of workers employed in electrical engineering rose from 23·9 per cent to 28·6 per cent of the whole engineering group. Since 1900 two new industries have risen, namely the aircraft and vehicle industries (vehicles 8·6 per cent and aircraft 3·1 per cent of all workers in manufacturing industry in 1963), both of which rely heavily on science and high standards of precision.[1]

The needs of two world wars have played a big part in this move towards a structure of industry that must be more firmly based on the application of science. Since 1945 these changes in the nature of British industry have been powerfully affected by the struggle for export markets. The pressure of international competition has been felt more strongly than in the depressed 1930's. In the 1950's our share of total world trade dropped from over 20 per cent in the immediate post-war period to about 15 per cent by the early 1960's. British industry has to change from its traditional empirical methods to a greater application of science in order that its products should stand international comparison.

(b) *Research and Science.* In 1867 Marx pointed out in *Das Kapital* that capitalism, unlike earlier systems of production, does not regard existing technical methods as definitive. Competition forces the search for new products and methods. This process has been accelerated by the coming of full employment. Change is more worth while in surer markets where sales seem more likely. At the high British standard of life many consumers have to be persuaded by advertising that they need a new product or that it is essentially different from what it replaces and so must be bought. Rapid obsolescence and replacement by the new but slightly different article become an integral part of a fully employed advanced economy. Change is now built into our economic system.

Behind this search for new and 'better' products is the science-based activity of research. The decision to commit manpower and resources to research is an economic one largely dependent upon the search for profits, though whether industry's attitude towards science is favourable or not will also be important. Recently there has been a rise in expenditure on research and development; from 1955–6 to 1961–2 the proportion of the gross national product spent in this way rose from 1·7 per cent to 2·7 per cent. Though only about a third (33·6 per cent) of the

[1] Figures for 1953 and 1963 from *Manpower Studies No. 1*, 1964.

funds were supplied by private industry as opposed to the Government, almost three-fifths (58·0 per cent) of the actual work was carried out by private industry. The amount spent varied considerably from industry to industry, but those referred to above as the science based industries were the ones with the highest expenditure per employee. Thus in 1961–2 the totals spent on research and development per employee were as follows, the aircraft industry £506, mineral oil refining £207, electronics £182, chemicals and allied industries £116, electrical engineering £88, mechanical engineering and shipbuilding £35, and textiles and leather £9, with an average for private industry of £54.[1]

(c) *Methods.* The stress on science in industry has extended beyond an increasing application of the results of pure scientific research to industry. There has been a growing application of scientific methods of management. This had begun early in the century in the USA when F. W. Taylor had introduced what came to be known as the Scientific Management Movement (G. Friedmann, 1953). The aim was a realistic assessment of economic efficiency at every level of industry. The application of Taylor's ideas were often inhumane. Since 1945 much of British industry has begun to use more scientific but humane techniques of management. The rational layout of the management structure, particularly in large companies, is now given more attention. It is more common to find stress put on accurate methods of cost accountancy and on the application of systems of wage rates to individual jobs, so that the worker is given maximum incentive. These new techniques of management require complex calculations, as do the increasingly difficult problems posed by stock control in large organizations, and the use of computers may become necessary.

(d) *Automation.* Almost a symbol of all these changes is automation, the product of a new and scientific industry that implies up-to-date management techniques. The word 'Automation' is much used and little understood. It is therefore proposed to define it. The term is usually applied to an industrial plant that has a very high ratio of capital equipment to labour employed and is in addition characterized by one or both of two particular types of mechanism. Firstly, the plant is a chain of machines that were formerly separate, but are now linked by transfer mechanisms that pass the semi-finished product from one process to the next without the use of any manpower. Secondly, throughout the train of machines there is a succession of feed-back mechanisms that auto-

[1] *Treasury Bulletin for Industry,* February, 1963.

matically send information to other stages of the process, if the product is not meeting the specifications required at that particular stage; a correction is made automatically so that the final product is to specification. For example, the exact thickness of a rolled steel plate can be ensured to narrow predetermined limits. Automation, it can be appreciated, may lessen the manpower needed, certainly reduces the decision taking and skill of the traditional type required by the operative, and probably improves the quality of the product (DSIR, 1956).

Though very often an installation is tailored to an individual company, there seem to be some general effects of automation as, for instance, changes in the composition of the labour force of the type associated with mass production, more particularly a larger maintenance staff. This trend would seem to reinforce the continuing requirement for skill already mentioned above. There will also be an increase in the need for men trained in the new technologies, such as electronics. The new demands on the men employed in automated plants are only beginning to be understood. It seems that both the operatives and managers require a broad grasp of the whole process, if they are to control it satisfactorily. At all levels except the highest different sensori-motor skills are needed; there is much more need to act quickly by, say, pressing a button as a result of reading information on a dial. New types of job are being created which have new requirements and which in turn have new implications for education.

Automation seems to be the most advanced of the technical changes now affecting the British economy, but change is at work in every sphere, in the office as well as on the shop floor and in commerce as well as in industry. Nor is it sufficient to adjust to one change, because change is now a part of our way of life. We must keep up with a succession of changes. As producers there are new jobs and new techniques that must be mastered, but as consumers also we have to cope with change and understand the nature of the new products that a modern science-based industry offers us.

C. Full Employment

1. *Analysis*

Since the beginning of industrial capitalism in Britain in the mid-eighteenth century there has been an alternation of active and depressed business conditions that economists have named the trade cycle. The

G

whole cycle of boom and slump varied in length but averaged seven to eight years. The proportion of the working population still unemployed at the top and bottom of the cycle also varied. Conditions were very bad in the inter-war years when the rate of unemployment averaged 12 per cent of the insured labour force, rising to 23 per cent in 1932 and never falling much below 10 per cent even in the best year of the late 1920's. The incidence varied and the old staple industries, particularly ship-building, suffered most. Since these industries tended to be concentrated in particular regions, some areas, such as Clydeside, the North-west and North-east, were more hardly hit than areas, such as the South-east, where the newer type of industry was already growing important.

During the inter-war years economists gave much thought to the causes of the trade cycle. They noted that its course was disturbed by wars, and that it never occurred in wholly planned economies. In 1936 J. M. (later Lord) Keynes, the Cambridge economist, published his book *The General Theory of Employment, Interest and Money*, which provided the key to the understanding of the trade cycle. Out of Keynes's work came the idea of a full employment policy. If there are unemployed resources in an economy at any time, this is due to a lack of demand backed by the money to buy goods. The Government can create the deficient demand in two ways. It may make conditions favourable so that business men will undertake more activity, thereby employing unused resources including labour. Secondly, the Government itself can expand its own activities by, for example, undertaking public investment. Both policies will create wages which will be spent so that the demand for other goods and services is increased. This in its turn will help to bring still unused resources back into work so that unemployment is reduced.

In 1944 the three political parties forming the wartime Coalition Government issued a White Paper on Full Employment Policy in which they all pledged themselves to use Keynesian-type policies to maintain full employment in Britain after the war. Since 1945 there has never been more than just over 3 per cent or less than just under 1 per cent unemployment, though regional variations still exist; the North, Scotland and N. Ireland have continuously had higher rates than London, the South-east and the Midlands. Yet the situation has changed dramatically for the better since 1945.

Full employment was defined in 1944 by Lord Beveridge in his book *Full Employment in a Free Society* as '3 per cent unemployment'. There will always be some workers in the process of moving from one job to another in a modern economy. Now that cyclical unemployment has been reduced to a mere trace of its pre-war severity, the object of policy is to lessen the impact on the individual worker of such 'technological' unemployment as is inevitable when changes in industrial techniques cause redundancy. With the aid of unemployment benefit and retraining facilities the period out of work accompanied by a lower income can be shortened, so that the individual worker suffers the minimum of the indignity of unemployment. A brief mention must be made of the 'unemployables'. The National Assistance Board estimated in 1951 that out of the 60,000 unemployed who were receiving assistance from them, there were 'not more than 7,000 (5,500 men and 1,500 women)' who 'could be working if they really wanted to work'. This seems a very small percentage of a total labour force at that time numbering 23·5 millions.

Keynes pointed to a fundamental fault in the working of the capitalist system that prevented it from running smoothly. The logic of his theories indicated some Government intervention to ensure full employment. In Britain the benefits of a so called 'free economy' were considered great enough to keep intervention to a minimum, and the rate of unemployment that can be tolerated politically seems to have settled at Beveridge's figure of 3 per cent, though the tolerable rate in the USA is double and in Australia less than half the British rate.

2. Developments

One of the main results of the state of full employment that has existed in Britain since the war has already been discussed. This is the acceleration given to the rate of technological change. There was always present in the capitalist system a force towards change, but it is now very pronounced. As a result there is a need for the labour force to be adaptable so that workers can easily turn to making similar, but slightly different, products or even move to totally different occupations. This adaptability will have to be shown not only by younger, but also by the older workers, since technical change affects all age groups alike. Traditionally the old are viewed as less adaptable than the young. This is important in view of the present demographic trend towards an ageing labour force. The proportion of those of sixty years and over will rise in the following way between 1962 and 1972 – for men from 10·7 to 12·1 per cent of all men in the working population, for single women from 8 to 8·7 per cent and for married women from 5·4 to 6·4 per cent.[1]

[1] Treasury Bulletin for Industry, January 1963.

The most noticeable consequence of full employment to the man in the street has been the constant slow inflation of prices since the war. The economists seem to have conquered mass unemployment only at the price of inflation. There has been a constant attempt to invest too much which has led to the bidding up of the prices of resources in all sections of the economy. One of the clearest results has been the almost continuous shortage of labour in many industries, which has led either to the raising of wages and salaries or at least to little opposition by employers to demands for higher remuneration.

The high demand for labour has been very pronounced in the rapidly expanding industries to which reference was made above. Therefore this demand has often translated itself into a need for youths capable of training as technicians and craftsmen in science-based industries. This has important implications for the schools. Such youths often want to stay at school beyond the legal minimum age to reach the necessary standards in the subjects required. However, during this same period there has been a relative shortage of youths on the labour market partly due to the low birth rate up to 1945 and partly because of the growing tendency to stay longer at school. Thus the wages of youths have risen more than those of adults, and this in its turn has acted to attract youths into work before they have had the education of which they are capable and which would ensure them a better job both from their own and the nation's point of view.

D. Conclusion

The reality of the twentieth-century British economy is very different from the picture conjured up by the phrase 'laissez-faire' or the word 'capitalism'. Very often we do better in considering the economy to think of an 'industrial society' that has many similarities with other advanced industrial nations regardless of their political system. When analysing an economic problem in this way comparative evidence from other countries may become more suggestive in the British context.

The fundamental logic of economic development seems to ensure that industrial society is characterized by large-sized units of production, by professional managers and by Government intervention. This intervention may be political in aim as in the case of the British egalitarian policy on wealth and incomes, but it has economic effects seen very clearly in the case of full employment. Though less space has been given above to full employment than the other two economic concepts, two results of the high level of employment now found in Britain were considered, namely the accelerated rate of technical change and the chronic tendency towards a shortage of labour that is either formally qualified or capable of qualification, and both are of vital relevance to contemporary education.

There is a constant inter-play between these tendencies and the move to an economy that is more dependent on science and gives a high regard to the application to industry of the findings of research in the field of pure science. Both the acceptance of science and the new stress on technical innovation in our economy demand favourable attitudes in the population, young and old, towards science and change. These attitudes can be inculcated in the educational system. The new recruits to the contemporary British economy need knowledge as well as favourable attitudes. The proportion of the labour force employed in the tertiary sector and in similar occupations in the secondary sector is growing, and this raises the question of the link between the school curriculum and future occupation, especially if the nature of this occupation will change rapidly. Despite the forces working for a large, if not increasing, proportion of skilled workers in the labour force, the specialized and trivial nature of many repetitive jobs poses very difficult problems of how best to educate children whose future work is not going to be of much interest to them after the first day or two, the brief period needed to learn their responsibilities. It is to these and similar questions linking education with the economy that we must give our attention in the next chapter.

BIBLIOGRAPHY

T. Caplow, *The Sociology of Work*, New York, 1954.
Department of Scientific and Industrial Research, *Automation*, London, 1956.
J. H. Dunning and C. J. Thomas, *British Industry*, London, 1961.
P. Sargent Florence, *The Logic of British and American Industry*, London, 1953.
G. Friedmann, *Industrial Society*, New York, 1955.
J. R. Hicks, *The Social Framework*, London (3rd Edition), 1960.

7

The Economy and Education

In this chapter the connections between the economy and the process of education will be examined under the same three headings as in the last chapter, though the same sub-divisions will not be followed. Many of the ideas and facts that were given in the last chapter will not be used directly, but will form an essential background to what is said or will be used later in this book. In some ways this chapter is an introduction to Chapter 12, which deals with the economic functions of the educational system. In the present chapter we shall concentrate on showing the connections between education and the economy, whilst in the later chapter the focus will be on the way in which the British system deals with these connections.

A. Capitalism

In this section we shall consider three important points raised by the equivalent section in the last chapter. Firstly, the connection between education and the spirit of capitalism will be examined. Next, some of the consequences for education of the managerial revolution will be analysed. Lastly, the effect that the growth of the size of productive unit has had on educational organization will be assessed.

1. *Education and Capitalism*
The question of why the capitalist system replaced the feudal system that preceded it has raised much controversy. The German sociologist, Max Weber, influenced the answer given by the majority of scholars when he wrote a series of essays in 1904–05. These were later published as his famous book, *The Protestant Ethic and the Spirit of Capitalism*. Weber believed that the Reformation, fundamentally a theological movement, indirectly influenced the values that govern economic action. The new

faith, especially in its more strictly Puritan forms, laid great stress on regular and hard work, on thrift and abstinence.

Recent American work has concentrated on the 'need to achieve' as a major source of economic effort in the higher levels of the labour force and has connected this need with the level of aspirations set by parents. A crucial determinant of parents' values in this respect seems to be the extent that the family religion stresses individual, as against the ritual, contact with God. The Protestant ethic with its stress on the individual approach to God can be seen as a special case of the general law here, since certain pre-literate societies that were studied were found to fit the same pattern. Self-reliance appears as an essential trait.[1] This and the other Protestant economic virtues are all character traits that can be stressed in school as well as in church. Particularly since the time of Thomas Arnold, the headmaster of Rugby from 1828 to 1842, teachers in Britain have given much attention to the formation of character in their pupils. It is therefore possible that the schools may educate for capitalism by stressing the particular traits of character that are necessary if the capitalist system is to work smoothly.

British psychologists have shown in experimental work that the way in which the teacher organizes a classroom can determine the type of personality found in the children concerned.[2] It is certainly true that British schools lay great stress from an early age on competition in school work. This is usually done through lists of marks and of positions in class. Many parents have had the experience of the five-year-old who comes home from school and reports that he 'got three out of four in a spelling test'. Education for competition may be assumed to be of more importance than education for co-operation in a capitalist economy. In this connection it is of interest that the US business monthly *Fortune* once complained that the diet of great American literature fed to undergraduates at colleges put the business hero in a bad light.[3] It has to be admitted that the critical study of novels such as Sinclair Lewis's *Babbitt* does not seem to have cut off the supply of those with a high 'need to achieve' in the American economy.

This last example does show how complex the connection is between the educational system and the formation of those character traits that the capitalist system requires. It is true that Protestantism stressed what

[1] See D. C. McClelland, *The Achieving Society*, Princeton, N.J., 1961.
[2] K. M. Evans, *Sociometry and Education*, London, 1961, pp. 77–78.
[3] Quoted by R. Lewis and R. Stewart, *The Boss*, London, 1958, p. 188.

Weber called 'worldly asceticism', whereas the more ritualistic Roman Catholicism seems not to have emphasized qualities such as thrift. Individual accumulation of capital had occurred before the Reformation and the coming of capitalism, though it had tended to be less open. A recent critique[1] of Weber's theory has pointed out that the Protestant countries on the whole developed capitalist economic systems before and faster than Catholic countries, but the latter countries are now growing at the more rapid rate. It may be that the Protestant ethic provided the right qualities for early capitalism, whereas a different set of qualities is needed in an advanced industrial society where much of the thrift and abstinence that leads to accumulation of new capital is provided not directly by individuals, but indirectly by large-scale companies or by the State. Yet the schools may still form character traits that are valued by industry. Many business men when choosing a recruit to management will put more weight on the dependability that a public school is assumed to guarantee than on any proof of intellectual power. The only conclusion to be drawn is that there can be a definite connection between the type of character aimed at by the educational system and that which the economy requires.

So far we have been considering how education can help the production side of the economic system. It is also possible to speak of education for consumption. The modern consumer in a capitalist economy lives in an environment marked by many advertisements pressing him to buy a multitude of new products. How is he to learn to discriminate between the choices presented to him? The schools can help in two ways. They may try to form the qualities and to teach the knowledge that future consumers will need. The main quality necessary to face the pressure of commercial advertising is rationality so that the consumer may choose with logic. The clearest example of the teaching of knowledge in schools in this connection has been the recent campaign against smoking. Because of the possible economic effect on the industry concerned there were objections to this direct education for consumption. If less specific education for consumption is given, it can have indirect economic results. In the terms of the classical theory of *laissez-faire* more perfect knowledge and greater rationality in the decisions that affect consumption will bring about a more efficient use of scarce resources amongst the possible uses.

[1] S. Andreski, 'Method and Theory in Max Weber', *British Journal of Sociology* March 1964.

Adolescents can see a direct relevance for education for consumption. To use one's wage to the best advantage has a definite appeal. Much of what might be called education for production is only indirectly relevant, but, what is probably more important, it is seen to clash with what happens outside the school. Teachers may urge self-denial in the tradition of the Protestant ethic; teenagers do not practise this virtue out of school nor do advertisements urge them to do so. If the educational system aims to teach the traits that meet the needs of the capitalist system, both types of education must be considered.

2. The Managerial Revolution

One consequence of the growth in the number of professional managers should more logically have been considered in the last section. Most managers today lead a bureaucratic type of business life. The administrative type of work done by most professional managers does not need the qualities of personality that the entrepreneur must show, but rather those usually associated with the stereotype of a good Civil Servant. These would seem to be conscientiousness rather than energy, a co-operative rather than an individualistic spirit, and a fine balance of judgement rather than single-minded drive to follow a hunch. These problems of personality formation have been little studied and hence once again we can only note the connection.[1]

When we consider the formal educational qualifications demanded in managers, the position is clearer (G. L. Payne, 1960). The increasingly technical nature of industry has raised the level of education required in managers of all types, whether scientific, financial, or administrative. The rise in 'the educational threshold'[2] to management has caused a much greater demand for formal educational qualifications, and this trend is growing more pronounced because the proportion of the labour force that is employed in managerial and administrative capacities is rising. To some extent part of this new demand for qualifications is due to fashion. 'Good firms employ graduates and so must we.'[3] However, basically it is a necessary change and one to which we shall often return.

Education has therefore come to be associated with positions of high social status and is seen as the main agent of social stratification. This point has already been made, but must be taken up again in an economic

[1] See, however, R. Bendix, *Work and Authority in Industry*, New York, 1956.
[2] Burton R. Clark, *Educating the Expert Society*, Los Angeles, 1962, p. 48.
[3] A. Collins and others, *The Arts Graduate in Industry*, London, 1962, p. 9.

context. During the period that formal qualifications have grown important this country has followed the policy of moving towards a more equal distribution of wealth. Largely due to the joint pressure of these two forces education has to some extent taken the place of property as something that can be inherited. Fathers see a need for education to ensure their children's future; more especially is this so in the case of boys. Many middle-class parents spend capital on the private education of their children in preference to leaving wealth at death that is liable to a high estate duty. By this means they hope that they will pass their own social status to the next generation. Much of the enduring prosperity of the British public school can be seen as a side effect of the managerial revolution.

3. *Size*

As the size of productive units grows the problems of management become increasingly complex, and therefore the tertiary sector of industry employs more workers. This raises the demands for technical, administrative and clerical workers. It is usual for the larger companies to specify the formal qualifications that they require for entry to each grade of their managerial and administrative staff. Smaller companies who have to compete for labour find that they must imitate the larger companies if they wish to recruit labour. A general level of qualifications is established that matches the hierarchy of the labour force. Some indication of the present level can be gained by a quick glance at newspaper advertisements for vacant jobs. It is this tendency that Michael Young (1958) satirized in *The Rise of the Meritocracy*. This book is a social history from 1870 to 2033 of an England where merit alone guarantees success in life. It is important to stress that in Britain today formal qualifications only admit the recruit to a certain level of industry. A youth with five 'O' levels can become a trainee laboratory technician, but his progress after entry depends upon his own efforts and character. Personality still matters. Michael Young defined 'merit' as 'intelligence plus effort'.[1]

In the large public companies that are coming to be typical of British industry today nepotism would seem to be less important than it was, though it must be common in smaller firms. Some industries, such as the wool textile industry, are still characterized by family firms. In a survey of the managers of twenty-eight firms, made in the Manchester area in 1954–5, R. V. Clements (1958) found only twenty-eight (or 4 per cent)

[1] M. Young, op. cit., p. 89. (Pelican edition).

out of a total of 646 managers who were what he called 'crown princes'. These were men whose start in a firm could be ascribed to close family links with the ownership or management of the firm. It must be noted that this was not nepotism in its widest sense since these men appeared to deserve their successful careers. They may have had an advantageous start to their lives in industry, but very often they had been educated and trained almost from childhood so that they would want and be able to run the family firm with success.[1] The proportion of these instances seems small and on balance does not destroy the force of the previous argument.

Greater size makes possible the supply of facilities for education and training by industry itself. The nationalized industries and many large public companies now run schools that provide education in the widest sense as well as more narrowly vocational training. This is an anomalous position from the point of view of the finance and the structure of education. It raises the questions of who should provide education after the minimum legal leaving age and of what the curriculum should consist. The British educational system more than ever comes to resemble a patchwork quilt made up of institutions of different quality and type. The educational structure of a country can be altered to meet new economic and social conditions, or these changes can be accommodated in an empirical way by new growths which may not be a part of the existing structure. It seems that the recent developments in industrial education have been in the last category; they were not planned to fit into the overall structure.

The provision of these new facilities within industry has brought some new life to one of our oldest continuous educational institutions, namely the apprenticeship system. With the coming of industrial capitalism in the eighteenth century the nature of apprenticeship changed greatly from the traditional residential form that existed in medieval times. In several European countries the apprenticeship system is still viewed as a part of education and therefore has close links with the educational system. In Britain by the early twentieth century the way of learning a trade was aptly summarized in the phrase common in industry, 'sitting by Nelly'. There were no sanctions upon employers to give definite instruction to apprentices. Typically an apprentice today must start his training at a definite age and serve a fixed number of years after which he becomes a craftsman without undergoing any test of competency. This

[1] R. V. Clements, op. cit., especially Chapter III.

is a rigid system that makes no allowance for variations in ability of individual apprentices or in the needs of different trades (K. Liepmann, 1960).

B. The Division of Labour

1. *The Quantity of Labour*

As the structure of the labour force changes under the impact of the various forces described in the last chapter the emphasis put on the various subjects in schools and universities will alter. Particular instances are easy to quote, for example, the new need for physicists. In addition there are more general effects. The gradual growth of the tertiary sector means that more youths are required capable of administrative and clerical work. In terms of the school curriculum this may be interpreted as a need for the skills cultivated in English and mathematics. At the very simplest level a girl who does not know her alphabet cannot file letters efficiently. In the secondary sector of the labour force industrial occupations are more scientific in their needs. Here we can see at its clearest the growing stress on science as a school subject. The qualifications sought in both new recruits and in older workers who are moving from one job to another reflect these developments. In turn the demands upon secondary and further education are influenced.

The education that a future worker receives must not only fit him for present economic conditions, but he must be able to meet future changes. These are usually unpredictable. This makes the forecasting of future manpower needs a difficult exercise. When the quantities of the particular types of education cannot be specified in advance, the quality is of the utmost importance. Many physicists are needed. It is hard to say how many. Therefore it is vital to ensure that the physicists who come forward from the educational system at each level have the combination of knowledge in their field that will serve them best under contemporary economic conditions. The same conclusion holds for all ranks of the labour force and all occupations. British educationists have always distrusted talk of quantity and preferred to stress quality. The next few pages will show that sociological analysis reinforces a preference based on educational grounds, since the way to meet problems of quantity seems to be to concentrate on the quality of the education given. However, the recent publicity given to the numbers of those with particular educational qualifications could have one important consequence. In the USA the great demand for those with formal education has raised the status of those who do possess such qualifications. They now have a more honoured place than was given to them by the practical men of nine-teenth-century capitalism.[1] The need for quantity could have a similarly beneficial effect in Britain. Where men give a high priority to formal education, a greater number of young men and women will have the chance to gain the qualifications that the economy demands.

2. *The Quality of Labour*

The changing character of the division of labour as described in the last chapter has two other important consequences for education. These are due, firstly, to the increasingly trivial nature of many of the routine manual and clerical jobs that must now be done and, secondly, to the need to ensure that the whole population, those at work and their de-pendents, have the attitudes towards science and change that are favour-able to contemporary economic conditions.

(i) *The Triviality of Work.* The sheer factual knowledge needed to do most of the highly specialized jobs that many workers do is very small (H. Schelsky, 1957). If the worker can read instructions, carry out easy calculations so that he will only produce the required number of articles and fill in a simple report form or work ticket, this will be sufficient. The '3 R's' at a relatively low level are enough. To master such jobs may take only a day or two, and after this brief training period is over little thought is required to do one's daily work. In pre-industrial days the life of a peasant or craftsman, though far from idyllic, was in some measure an education in itself. Life today is not built round work as was then the case. Nor do jobs today allow the exercise of the faculties of judgement and initiative that most humans need for psychological health. Work no longer provides either satisfaction or the feeling of being someone that matters. The worker must look elsewhere, perhaps to his family or friends for the fulfilment of these needs. A few companies are experiment-ing with the aim of overcoming the triviality and lack of satisfaction inherent in much contemporary work. They have re-organized some production lines so that workers move from one specialized task to another, taking turns to do all the jobs involved on that production line. Such 'job rotation' is, however, very rare (G. Friedmann, 1961).

The tendency for life away from work to grow in importance com-pared with time spent at work has become more pronounced as a result

[1] R. Hofstadter, *Anti-Intellectualism in American Life*, London, 1964, p. 396.

of another consequence of the division of labour. Specialization has raised productivity greatly so that most workers now have considerably more leisure than fifty years ago. The five-day week is now common to most industrial workers. Can the schools help the future workers both to use their increasing leisure and to find satisfaction in a life marked by an uninteresting job?

Educational theorists have suggested that the schools can help the worker to adjust to modern conditions of work in two ways. In the first place the school can teach children how to make the best use of their spare time. Life away from work will be full enough to compensate for the dullness of the time spent at work. Secondly, the schools can teach in such a way that children want to continue to learn. Then men and women will have the desire and the intellectual equipment with which to seek a worthwhile life away from their jobs. The way recommended to achieve this aim is that schools should teach children how to find out rather than the knowledge itself. A curriculum based on this aim tends to ignore facts and to stress discovery. In fact the same curriculum will also impart the qualities that are equally important in those who do have satisfying jobs. There is, however, a danger. Although this approach is valuable, workers must have some sheer factual knowledge if they are to do their jobs efficiently. The comparison between an Indian peasant and a British farm worker demonstrates this. In Germany most craft occupations have been analysed; technical school curricula have been drawn up and are regularly revised to meet changes in the needs of each occupation. In Britain little is known as to what knowledge is necessary to undertake individual occupations at any level in the labour force.

On the grounds of common sense it would seem that the curriculum to match the needs of today's labour force would stress general intelligence rather than particular faculties, would give a background of contemporary economic and industrial knowledge, would impart a minimum level of literacy and numeracy, and would emphasise a willingness to co-operate with others on the same job. We are only considering economic needs, and therefore we have ignored many other important parts of the curriculum. But here once again we are only starting to ask the questions; exact psychological and sociological data upon which to formulate the answers is not available.

(ii) *Attitudes*. The need for men and women at all levels of the labour force who have some knowledge and training in science must by now be very clear. The nature of the most rapidly expanding industries and their dependence on research has been described. Full employment has intensified the scientific basis of industry since change based mainly on scientific research is now normal. The labour force must therefore not only have scientific knowledge but must exhibit attitudes that are favourable towards science and change.

(a) *Science.* The conversion of British schools and universities to the teaching of science in the nineteenth century was a slow and difficult process (Sir Eric Ashby, 1958). Mainly because of this a negative approach to science has much hindered many British industries.[1] The way in which science is taught in schools and other educational institutions can powerfully affect the rate of response of the economy to scientific change. Managing directors who are lawyers or accountants by training, as well as operatives, can hold attitudes hostile to or unappreciative of science because of faulty teaching and thereby stand in the way of the development of the modern economy. Modern industry is based on science and development depends upon research in the field of pure science to lay bare the theoretical principles relevant to its working. The research is usually undertaken in a university, namely in an institution that is within the educational, and not the economic, system. Upon the principles that are discovered can be built a technology round which will grow the whole structure of technical education backed by curricula, textbooks and examinations. Therefore the work of pure scientists is the source upon which applied science is built, but a fair proportion of intellectually bright young men and women ready and able to use the results of contemporary research must go into industry. The important point is that of balance. If we examine the way that the UK and the USA employed their stock of qualified scientists in 1956, we find the percentages were as follows: in industry USA 60, UK 38; in Government USA 20, UK 12; in education USA 20, UK 50. Allowing for the difficulties of international statistical comparisons we may say that Britain employed twice as many as the USA of her pure scientists in schools, colleges and universities, whilst the USA employed half as many more of her scientists in industry as the UK did.[2]

The world of science in Britain is very inbred and attitudes are easily passed from one generation to the next, but few of the scientists are in the community outside education to spread a knowledge and understanding of modern science throughout industry and commerce. Those

[1] C. F. Carter and B. R. Williams, *Science in Industry*, London, 1959.
[2] G. L. Payne, op. cit., pp. 41–43.

who are not science specialists at school must not lack the knowledge that they need as producers and consumers. In addition all must have attitudes favourable to the application of science to industry and commerce.

(b) *Change*. Innovation in any field whether artistic or scientific depends on existing knowledge. The wider this is spread, the more easily can additions to knowledge be made and the easier will be applications of new knowledge. The scientific knowledge necessary for the invention of the Bessemer Converter, which ushered in the age of cheap steel in 1856, was known at the start of the nineteenth century, but it was not known widely or in the right places, so that application was not easy. When the invention was eventually made, there was enough understanding of the process for the invention to be taken up by the industry quite quickly, though lack of scientific knowledge was one reason that prevented the new product from being accepted in some quarters as rapidly is should have been the case. For both consumption and production a high level of literacy and numeracy is even more essential in the mid-twentieth century, when change is more rapid than was the case in the mid-nineteenth century.

Since the educational requirements of most occupations are constantly altering, there is difficulty in specifying the content of a curriculum to meet change. The most serviceable education would appear to be a general one out of which specialization can grow. The deeper the specialization, the further the general education must be carried. The specialist requirements of a metallurgist need a longer general education, especially in general science, than is necessary for a first-hand melter on a steel furnace. A broad general education will assist adaptability since a worker will be more able to understand future changes in his field and to relate them to his own particular job. If the job is changed, the worker can return to the basis provided by his general education to start out afresh. If the steel industry switches to a new process, the metallurgist with a broad education can more easily cope with this change, as can the operative on the furnace at his own level of education.

Attitudes will govern the application of this knowledge. Four are of especial importance, namely the attitudes towards education, science, industry and that towards change itself. Unless education is given a high priority, the proportion of the national income spent on education will not be large enough to create an adequate educational system. If science is not thought to be important, neither sufficient time nor money will be given to it in schools and universities. The schools themselves influence the attitudes towards education and science. A teacher may transmit an attitude towards a subject without having a full awareness that he is teaching the children anything. A good example of this process was the low status of science in schools in the nineteenth century which had grave repercussions on the technical adequacy of our industry as compared, for example, with German industry. The schools did not educate enough men at any level, but particularly at managerial level, who understood the scientific advances of the time. During this same period the schools and universities gave their pupils an attitude towards industry such that able young men of the upper middle class were very unwilling to enter industry.

But the most vital attitude is perhaps that towards change. Very little is known about how this is learnt or taught in schools. Adaptability is a factor of personality whose source has not been deeply explored. The willingness to accept change is a necessity for young workers who are just entering industry and for older workers who may have to move to new jobs because of technical innovation. In Western European countries since 1945 younger workers have tended to receive higher pay than older men. The benefits of technical change seem to go to the younger men with the formal qualifications.[1] We must therefore consider how to teach the present generation in school to meet change, but in addition we must give older workers every chance of re-training themselves to meet new techniques. The revolution demanded in the views of operatives and managers is great if a worker or a manager aged forty-plus is to go back to school to re-learn his job or to learn a totally new one. The educational techniques involved in teaching such pupils would seem to be very different from those at present used in technical education.[2]

The educational system and the economy are two social institutions that are closely linked in any society, though many do not realize the nature of their mutual relationship. Industry in Britain has tended to put its faith in the practical man and in effect to say to the schools, 'You teach the three R's and we'll do the rest.' In the schools there has been little knowledge of or sympathy with the industrial and commercial life of the nation. Any social institution can oppose the general direction of the development of the society that contains it. There may be a conscious aim to reform the society. But if there is a general consensus of the aims

[1] OEEC, *Steel Workers and Technical Progress*, Paris, 1959, p. 27.
[2] See C. E. Belbin, *Training the Adult Worker*, DSIR, London, 1964.

H

of the society, the place of the educational system is clear. The schools must teach and shape personality in a way that recognizes economic developments. If children, particularly, though not entirely, of a low socio-economic status, are to cope with greater leisure, an increasing triviality of work, and rapid technical change, then there is scope for research and thought of a more sociological nature in the schools on the topics discussed in this section.

C. Full Employment

The standard of education required for entry to all levels of the labour force has been rising since 1945 for all occupations except the unskilled. Full employment has contributed to the higher educational threshold. As already indicated the growth of company training schemes is in part a result of the shortage of trained or trainable labour and in part of the accelerated rate of change, both of which have owed much to the state of full employment. We shall discuss two other topics here that have connections with full employment, namely labour discipline and the views of the trade unions on education.

1. *Labour Discipline*

The smooth running of any organization, economic or otherwise, demands that the orders of those in authority should be obeyed. Authority may be enforced or accepted willingly. Before the last war a manager could dismiss a man at the least provocation and find a replacement with ease because of the existence of a large pool of unemployed labour. The fear of unemployment acted to enforce labour discipline. Those who gave the orders in industry, the managers, foremen and charge-hands, did not need to persuade men to accept authority, as is very often the case today when full employment makes the replacement particularly of skilled or trained men very difficult.

The traditional source of future leaders in Britain has been the public schools. Since the inter-war years a growing proportion of industrial managers have come from this source. One of the ways by which the responsibilities of leadership is supposedly taught is the prefect system. The grammar schools and more recently the secondary modern schools have widely imitated this institution. During the last thirty years there has been a major change in the way that the prefect system has operated. Due to the influence of the more progressive educational theories on

THE ECONOMY AND EDUCATION 115

corporal punishment prefects are now encouraged to stress the responsibility rather than the disciplinary aspect of their functions. Prefects should lead rather than force younger boys into doing things. During the same period the fagging system, where it still exists, has grown more humane. A similar change in secondary modern schools was observed by the Newsom Report, which found that some heads were in favour of a less authoritarian form of discipline.[1]

These changes occurred because of change in the prevailing philosophy of education, but they match well the contemporary needs of the labour force. Those destined for positions of authority in industry or commerce at whatever level will have learnt through experience at school that discipline must be accepted willingly rather than forced on those for whom they have responsibility. From the point of view of those who do not give the orders the result may well be an increased questioning of authority that is inconvenient to management. This new attitude towards authority is, however, a fact with which industry must reckon. The 'bloody mindedness' of the British worker may now be strengthened by developments within a hallowed educational institution, the prefect system.

2. The Trade Unions and Education

Up to 1939 the trade unions showed little real interest in education. Either the educational policy of the unions was purely political in that they demanded secondary education for all on grounds of social justice, or it was economic. This latter part of their policy must now be examined. The first trade unions that were stable and powerful were those organized on a craft basis in the mid-nineteenth century. Because of the nature of their membership they came to have an interest in recruitment to craft trades and hence in the apprenticeship system. It has already been noted that apprenticeship can be an educational institution, but the trade unions did not see it in this way. They did not wish to control the curricula and methods by which apprentices were taught in factories or technical schools. The unions gave their attention to controls of an economic nature. If they could limit the number of craftsmen in any trade, they might keep their members in employment when many others were unemployed, and they might also keep their wages relatively high.

[1] A. C. D. Peterson, *Educating Our Leaders*, London, 1957, p. 58; J. C. Dancy, *The Public Schools and the Future*, London, 1963, p. 96; *Half our Future* (Newsom Report), 1963, p. 67.

Unions established a system of apprenticeship ratios by which they limited the number of apprentices in a trade or in an area; for example, one apprentice might be permitted to every six trained carpenters (K. Liepmann, 1960).

Full employment means that such controls are on the whole unnecessary. Unions will still want to guard against redundancy, due to technical change. But apprenticeship ratios militate against the quick expansion of skilled occupations that is often now necessary. The agreements between unions that limit the work that individual crafts can do also introduce rigidity, because new jobs, such as those connected with electronics or with instruments controlling automatic machinery, cannot easily become recognized crafts. It is no use a technical college running courses if the relevant unions will not permit industry to recruit the apprentices who will take these courses. There are signs that apprentice ratios are becoming more flexible, and that the unions are coming to take a greater interest in technical education as such rather than as an adjunct to a method of controlling the entry to skilled trades.

D. Conclusion: The Economics of Education

Education of all types is now central in an analysis of the economy. The rate of flow of educated manpower to the economy has a vital influence on the rate of economic development. Much academic education has come to be viewed as vocational. This is not a new situation. The classical education that up to the sixteenth century was almost the only one available in separate educational institutions, apart from the apprenticeship system, aimed for the most part to provide a vocational education for priests. Today passes in 'O' level mathematics or degrees in modern languages are gained through academic education, but are demanded by industry as vocational qualifications. Education is the avenue to worthwhile employment. This has been discussed here in its economic context but was also relevant to the study of social stratification. In examining the complex connections between education and the economy we have seen that the triviality of much work today and the chance of greater leisure as productivity rises is forcing many to look for the satisfaction formerly found in their work in their families. All three of the social institutions studied in the first part of this book are closely related and influence each other. To analyse them apart is necessary for clarity, but nevertheless the result is an artificial and partial picture. But in each case, whether considering the family, social class, or the economy we have seen that the educational system is of great and of growing importance.

A possible criterion of the importance of any social institution is the purely economic one of how great a proportion of a country's gross national produce (GNP) is spent on it. The rapid growth in the importance of education to Britain over the last few years can be judged from the following figures. In 1952 3·2 per cent of GNP was spent on education; by 1957 the proportion had risen to 3·8 per cent and by 1962 to 4·8 per cent.[1] The proportion has grown in recent years at an accelerating rate. The quality of any educational system must always depend largely upon the economic wealth of the country concerned. Yet paradoxically as a country grows into an advanced industrial society the educational system ceases to be determined by the state of the economy and becomes a determinant of the rate of economic development of the country concerned. Education is no longer a neutral, but a causative agent.

It is because economists have realized the new position of education in industrial societies that they have tried to work out an 'economics of education' (J. Vaizey, 1962). Education now employs a large and growing labour force. Between 1959 and 1962 the total employed in educational services rose from 876,000 to 997,000, of whom 321,274 were teachers in grant-aided schools and establishments.[2] This growth may be considered as part of the general move to a larger proportion in the tertiary sector of the labour force. The educational system now employs more workers than the iron and steel industry. In many ways education can be considered an industry. Is it an efficient industry? How can its productivity be measured?[3]

Economists have attempted to answer these questions along two main lines. Firstly, there have been investigations into the direct returns to educational expenditure. For example, in Britain in 1963 Dr Abrams took a random sample of 6,500 men who were aged over twenty and were heads of households.[4] He found that amongst the 85 per cent who were

---

[1] *Treasury Bulletin for Industry*, October 1963.

[2] *Annual Abstract of Statistics* and *Ministry of Education Statistics*, Vol. I, 1962.

[3] For a survey on recent work in this field see *Higher Education* (Robbins Report), 1963, Appendix 4.

[4] Mark Abrams, 'Rewards of Education', *New Society*, 9 July 1964. For the USA see H. P. Miller, 'Annual and Lifetime Income in Relation to Education: 1939–59', *American Economic Review*, December 1960.

willing to divulge their earnings annual income varied with the age at which schooling ended in the following way; for those who left school at fifteen the median income was £636, between sixteen and eighteen £1,034, and for those who left at nineteen or over £1,583. Thus the private benefit of an extra two or three years at school beyond the minimum leaving age was £400 per year or about £20,000 over a working life. These figures make very clear the connection already noted between education and socio-economic status. But here we are considering their purely economic relevance. The longer anyone stays at school, the greater is the total expenditure involved. A calculation of the extra return received for every extra year of schooling gives one measure of the direct return to the individual as a result of additional educational expenditure. From an economic point of view if the return from investing in education expressed as a percentage is lower than the percentage return that could be gained from investing in some other way, then there has been a waste of economic resources. The first difficulty in such comparisons is that the return to education cannot be judged by purely economic criteria. In addition there are economic problems in such calculations. Thus over a definite period of time the earnings of one group of labour, for example of scientists or builders' labourers, may be determined by the scarcity of those workers rather than by any educational consideration. Again, the return to a particularly talented individual may be goverened by his psychological or physical make-up rather than by his education; Yehudi Menuhin or Charlie Chaplin are examples.

The other main line of attack has been to try to measure the indirect benefits of education. Here economists have followed the tradition of welfare economics, a branch of their subject that measures the benefit accruing from any particular expenditure to society as a whole rather than to individuals. There are immense problems of a statistical nature involved in disentangling education from the many other factors that influence a society's economic gains. Many assumptions of dubious validity are needed to quantify the evidence. One calculation reckoned that for the USA the average annual growth in the real national product (i.e. measured in goods and services, not in money) was 2·93 per cent over the period 1929 to 1957. Of this increase 0·67 per cent, or about a quarter of the annual rate of growth, could be attributed to expenditure on education.[1] What is not yet known is how much greater this rate of growth could be if more were invested in education. Since the British economy is fully employed, this would entail a transfer of resources from some other use. Decisions of a political nature would have to be made as to which expenditure had the highest priority. Nor is it known up to what point investment in education can go without reaping diminishing returns to successive increments of expenditure. The optimum rate of investment will probably differ with economic and social conditions; an underdeveloped country will not be in the same position as an advanced industrial society.

Since the Government, either at national or local level, finances the majority of educational expenditure, it is more than ever important to see that this major growing industry is efficient. In 1862 the Chancellor of the Exchequer, Robert Lowe, speaking of the Revised Code, a new means of controlling educational expenditure, said to Parliament, 'If the new system will not be cheap, it will be efficient, and if it will not be efficient, it will be cheap.' Undoubtedly we can control educational expenditure in a more humane spirit than this. At the least the educational system should use the economic resources that are handed to it out of the fruits of taxation on the functions expected of it by society. There is the possibility of autonomous growth within the educational system. Institutions established for one purpose can come to serve another. A clear example of this was the case of the Department of Science and Art. This was set up in the early 1850's to teach science and commercial art to industrial workers with the specific intention of avoiding any interference in secondary education. By 1899, when the department was merged into the new Board of Education, it was mainly involved in providing scientific education to secondary schools.[2] At a humbler and more mundane level most managers of industrial enterprises can be held responsible for an exact sum when waste occurs. This is rare in the case of teachers. Few attempts have yet been made to cost the work of the teacher or to compare different ways of teaching so that a scarce resource, the trained teacher, can be used in the most efficient manner.[3]

In any study of the economics of education it is apparent that the

[1] E. F. Dennison, *The Source of Economic Growth in the US and the Alternatives Before Us*, Committee for Economic Development, Washington, January 1962.

[2] M. Argles, *South Kensington to Robbins*, London, 1964, pp. 20–21.

[3] See, however, H. Kay, J. Annett, and M. E. Sime, *Teaching Machines and Their Use in Industry*, DSIR, London, 1963, pp. 29–30.

functions of the educational system becomes an issue. It is important to ask upon what we should spend money. So far in the first part of this book we have considered the connections between three of the major social institutions and education. We have now reached the point where we must pass on to an examination of what the functions are that an educational system fulfils in a modern industrial society.

BIBLIOGRAPHY

Sir Eric Ashby, *Technology and the Academics*, London, 1958.
R. V. Clements, *Managers: A Study of Their Careers in Industry*, London, 1958.
G. Friedman, *The Anatomy of Work*, London, 1961 (especially Chapters III and IV).
K. Liepmannn, *Apprenticeship*, London, 1960.
G. L. Payne, *Britain's Scientific and Technological Manpower*, London, 1960.
H. Schelsky, 'Technical Change and Educational Consequences', 1957, in *The Reader*.
J. Vaizey, *The Economics of Education*, London, 1962.
M. Young, *The Rise of the Meritocracy*, London, 1958 (Pelican).

PART II

The Social Functions of Education

8

Introduction

In an earlier chapter we considered the family and its place in the social structure. It was found that the family, as an institution, served certain functions. It is possible to analyse most social institutions in this way and to discover in what ways they help to maintain the society in which they exist. These are their social functions. Therefore we may ask the question, what are the social functions of the educational system? Just as we look at a car engine and say what each part of this machine is doing, so we may examine the educational system as a whole or one part of it, for example, one individual school, and decide what functions it is performing. Furthermore, in the same way that machines do not always run smoothly, so it may be that social institutions do not fulfil their functions in an efficient manner.

In this analysis it is not the aim or purpose of the schools or any one school that is being considered, although this will be implicit in the way that the educational system is organized. To revert to the analogy of the car, we are not considering where the car is going or that it is carrying passengers, but the question is rather whether the car is going well and carrying its passengers in an efficient manner. Such an analysis can be free of value judgements. The social scientist should be willing to bow to the philosopher and learn from him the skills of classifying the aims of education. But once this is done he can undertake a neutral analysis of how the educational system is functioning. From this he can help in the understanding and right working of the country's educational provision.

This analysis will not only be of the internal working of the various parts of the educational system from primary school to university, but also of the relations between these parts and between the educational system and other social institutions, such as the family or the economy. It may be found that the way in which education is organized is bringing disharmony to the social framework. The sociological term used to describe this state is 'dysfunction' and comes by analogy from the field of medicine. Just as illness brings dysfunction to the body, so there may be dysfunction in the social system. Furthermore, this element of dysfunction may be either 'latent' or 'manifest'.

When we look for the functions of any social institution, we tend to focus on the way in which that institution helps the rest of the social system at one moment. The picture is static, but we know that society is in flux. Institutions once established begin to have lives and to create values of their own. In consequence we must remember that we are examining a system prone to change. Equilibrium is rare; tensions are common. Often there is a balance between the consequences of contemporary social organization. In some ways it is functional and in others dysfunctional. A political decision may be necessary to re-arrange the institution so as to meet the nation's present aims.

It is convenient to consider the social functions of education under five headings:

(i) The transmission of the culture of the society; here the need is basically the conservative one of passing on the main patterns of society through the schools.

(ii) The provision of innovators; someone must initiate the social change that is necessary for a society to survive under modern conditions. Such change may be technical, political or even artistic.

(iii) The political function; this may be looked at in two ways. There is firstly the need to provide political leaders at all levels of a democratic society and, secondly, there is the demand that education should help to preserve the present system of government by ensuring loyalty to it.

(iv) The function of social selection; the educational system is central to the process by which the more able are sorted out of the population as a whole.

(v) The economic function; here the need is that all levels of the labour force should be provided with the quantity and quality of educated manpower required under the current technical conditions.

These five functions should be considered as the tools of analysis that will be used in the next four chapters in an endeavour to see what the educational system is really doing. It is suggested that to apply these same tools to some of our contemporary educational disputes might clarify the issues considerably. More especially it would show where there were no facts upon which to base a decision and therefore direct attention to those places where research was needed.

9

Stability and Change

There is a very delicate balance in any community between stability and change. Though new techniques are constantly altering the material conditions in which we live, many of the values by which we govern our lives are based on Christianity, a religion which is nearly two thousand years old. New types of car come to make more difficult the struggle to maintain the old courtesy on the roads. Both the techniques and the values are part of the culture which a society transmits to its next generation. In a primitive society changes in the culture were rare. Today, for reasons, which are often economic or political, few societies can maintain such stability. If, however, change were to grow very rapid, any continuity of culture might prove difficult to achieve. This is the type of problem some African societies face today as they industrialize.

The tension between stability and change is well illustrated by what happens when a country decides to industrialize and to switch from being a 'conventional society' to a society where much that is traditional must go. It can be seen that here the problems of culture transmission become acute. How much of the old social structure should be preserved and handed on to the next generation ? How much will the new generation accept and pass on to its children ?

In primitive societies the coming generation learn the ways of their culture within the extended family system. We saw this in our study of the family. Today in Britain much of this function of the family has been passed over to a special institution, namely the school. A very clear example of this process can be taken from English educational history; during the nineteenth century the public schools grew as upper and upper middle-class families came to rely on these, mainly boarding, schools to form the character of their children. The important position that all schools play in Britain today in passing on culture can be appreciated.

Another aspect of the equilibrium between stability and change is the consideration of who pushes a society on to the road of change. These men are the innovators. In the British industrial revolution the innovator was often self-taught, but under modern conditions much specialized knowledge is needed to achieve change in almost any field. It can be seen that for this reason alone the provision of innovators has to be considered as one of the functions of education.

Any consideration of stability tends to raise the problem of change and vice versa. Certainly the educational system of a modern community has a function in respect of both. It is because they are so closely connected, though opposites, that the function of providing stability through transmission of culture and the function of assisting change through a supply of innovators have been placed together in this chapter.

A. Culture Transmission

1. *Conserving the Culture*

When looking at primitive cultures which are very different from our own, as, for example, those described by Margaret Mead, it is relatively simple to appreciate their particular customs and to see how their children learn these patterns of behaviour. It is more difficult to examine our own culture and discover which parts are passed on by the family and which by the school. The extent and nature of culture transmission through the school can perhaps best be shown by a series of examples. Some of these will be extreme cases, since these throw a very clear light on just what is happening.

Let us take the case of a five-year-old British child who comes from an Agnostic home. When he goes to his primary school, this child will spend much of the latter part of each autumn term preparing the classroom for Christmas. It is almost impossible that the child shall not learn something of the Christmas story from a Christian viewpoint and this learning will be reinforced yearly till the child leaves school. It is difficult to imagine this process not taking place. By law State-aided schools must give religious instruction, and the religion taught is almost always Christianity. A child may be withdrawn from religious instruction if his parents demand it. But even in such a case this aspect of our culture would almost inevitably be transmitted to the child. The classroom walls will be covered with pictures or decorations, many of which his classmates have made; his friends will eagerly talk of what they have done and this may include the making of a nativity scene in the corner of the classroom; the new songs learnt will be carols. The theme of Christmas will recur throughout all his work and play. How can he escape learning about it?

A second example of the same extreme type is the case of the British school in a foreign land, such as the Argentine, or even in a Commonwealth country, such as India. In this school a British child will not only learn the English language which, as will be seen later, is an important vehicle for transmitting the culture and which he will be accustomed to using in his own family circle, but he will learn much that will make him a Briton and which his family's restricted pattern of experience cannot provide. Perhaps the most obvious example is seen in the games that he will play; cricket overseas is a well-worn joke. Less obvious is the particular way in which the British of the social class to which the child belongs mix with others of their own age and sex. The triumph of the British school abroad is that the British at home shall say of its old scholars, 'You would never have thought that he was brought up abroad.'

As a child grows older he is constantly learning new patterns of behaviour and at the same time expanding his vocabulary. These two processes bear a unique relation to each other in any single culture. Under modern conditions much of both types of learning occurs at school or under its influence. In this way what is considered polite, whether in actions or in words, is often 'picked up' at school and may well be considered wrong in the family. Much of the work that is done in the classroom under the heading of 'English' is of the nature of moral education and therefore attempts to transmit cultural values.

Our language is full of metaphors and, particularly in poetry, of images that are peculiar to us as a nation. Children undertake many comprehension exercises during which these cultural images are attached to words and analogies are explained. One has only to try to read contemporary American or Australian poetry to children to realize that what is ostensibly the same language carries very different meanings, references and values, all of which are part of an alien culture. Or again one should note the difficulty of using American children's books, even when illustrated, in English schools. The young child is of an age at which he is unable to appreciate that culture transmission is taking place during an English lesson, whilst the parents are either unaware or in some respect wish the process to occur.

From the examples given it is clear that on the whole culture transmission is conservative. The teachers in the schools tend to pass on what they have been given. Conformity to what went before is stressed. The schools help the family, which plays a more predominant part in infancy, to pass on the national culture, which may be taken to include the national character.

This last point is best exemplified from American educational history. The task of the typical American city school, especially on the eastern seaboard, has always tended to be the creation of good American citizens from the children of the most recent immigrants (M. Mead, 1951). They had to learn not only a language, but a national character. The symbol of this task is still the Stars and Stripes on the teacher's desk. In passing it is worth commenting that this task has become more common since 1945. For example, immigrants into Australia, the so-called 'New Australians', have had to be made into Australians, and Jews from all over the world into Israelis; also in Britain the assimilation of white and coloured immigrants has brought problems of an educational nature.

In all these instances the schools seem to be assisting in the creation of personality. From the point of view of the individual this is true, but, if one examines what is happening from the point of view of the community as a whole the schools are acting in a neutral way in passing on the existing culture to new members who may or may not have been born in that community. The schools have been given a task and administrative means may exist to ensure that they carry it out. Schools may be inspected with this end in view; syllabuses and textbooks may have to be approved officially, as they are in many countries outside Britain.

2. Changing the Culture

The educational system may, however, be given a more positive role in transmitting culture. A political decision may be taken that the existing way of life ought not to continue, and the Government may want to use a social institution which is as central to this purpose as the educational system in an attempt to change the culture. The Russian schools were in this position in the 1920s, though by today an existing culture is being transmitted. One of the clearest examples of an attempt to alter the culture of a country was that made in Germany by the Nazis after they came to power in 1933. In this case the full extent of the term 'education' can be seen. The Nazis used every type of school for every age range and all the facilities for further education including universities and technical colleges. They used the existing institutions for adult education and created new ones. Finally, they used the apprenticeship and training system in industry, always considered a part of the educational system in Germany. Though this attempt failed, it is a reminder of how many and varied are the institutions which we lump together under the heading 'the educational system'.

In Britain we may think that what the Russians succeeded in doing and what the Germans attempted to do was morally wrong, but we should remember that a similar role is sometimes suggested for our schools today. The argument runs somewhat as follows: the modern adolescent is not of the type that, according to some, is good for Britain today, or, according to others, of whom they approve. He must be changed, and the schools must play a big part in this policy. To put it bluntly, the child must be saved from society. There is a long history, especially in nineteenth-century England, of the teacher as a social worker, as a missionary to better the way of life of his pupils. It is a worth-while exercise for any teacher to examine his role and see whether he is neutral or positive in the way in which he passes on his country's culture. And can he justify either his neutral or his positive position?

The child stands between two powerful influences, the school and the family. Every teacher needs to remind himself constantly that the family is often the stronger of the two influences, especially when the child is young. Yet paradoxically teachers of children in primary schools probably have more direct influence on their pupils than teachers at any later stage, more particularly because of the greater influence of children of their own age group amongst children of the secondary age. But at all stages the influence of the school and later the university or college is great, especially in the introduction of ideas to older pupils. An inspiring teacher can create what the Crowther report has called 'intellectual discipleship'. The great French sociologist, Durkheim (1956), spoke of the teacher as 'the interpreter of the great moral ideas of his time and his country'.[1] It is clear that these ideas may be Marxist or Christian, but the teacher in his role as teacher will pass them on to the next generation.

3. Sub-cultures

(i) *Regional Differences*. So far we have spoken as if it was one culture that was being passed on by the schools. We must now face the question of whether the educational system does or can transmit only one culture. Let us take a concrete example. In several parts of rural Britain there are secondary schools in villages that are close to RAF aerodromes. These

[1] E. Durkheim, op. cit., p. 89.

I

schools must cater for two types of pupils, the children of the local people and the children of the RAF personnel. Children of the former type are country born and bred, whilst the majority of the latter type come from the great industrial conurbations. In fact, both of these divisions represents a sub-culture, the rural and the urban. They are both within the overall British culture, but each has distinctive differences of its own. Can the school give the same way of life to both types of child? In one case of which details are known this proved to be impossible.[1] Despite their period under the influence of a country school the city children still showed in their work, more especially their English compositions, the marks of their strong attachment to their own sub-culture. Deep differences in the ways of thought of the two types of children were seen. The city children had a greater factual knowledge of the technical world of today and on the surface were more sophisticated; the village children showed a deeper understanding of the ways of the country and because of this had a subtler feeling for life and death, growth and decay. Whilst the city child appeared the more mature, in reality the country child was so in his appreciation of the feelings and emotions around which life revolves. The school could not here change what had been begun, nor could it combat the influence of the aerodrome to which the city child returned after school each day.

Sub-cultures exist within our society. T. S. Eliot (1948) has argued that the tensions produced by their existence bring gain and that therefore the resulting whole is greater than its parts. R. Hoggart (1957) has traced the way in which the traditional rural English culture was taken by migrants during the nineteenth century to the great northern industrial cities and how by today the traces of this traditional way of life have in some respects disappeared, though in others remain. A school set in the midst of any sub-culture will find it hard to pass on the culture in any form other than that in which it is interpreted by that sub-culture. This is particularly true when the differentiation is mainly along material lines, as is perhaps so in the case quoted of the rural and urban sub-cultures. It would be hard to teach a rural way of life against a background of tall chimneys.

(ii) *Educational Sub-cultures.* There is another aspect of the passing on of one culture which must be considered. This is the problem known today as 'the two cultures controversy'. In its modern form, which is relevant

---

[1] B. Jackson, 'Report from a Country School, *Universities and Left Review*, Autumn 1958.

to all levels of education, including higher education, it was sparked off by C. P. Snow (1957). In brief the argument runs that specialization in education is nowadays so intense that even in the final years at school, but certainly by the time higher education has been reached, it has become impossible for those following arts courses to understand and communicate at any depth with those following science courses and vice versa. The effect created by specialization goes further than difficulty in understanding the material with which the other side is dealing, but extends to the fact that the two sides are learning totally different modes of thought.[1]

The validity of this argument in such an extreme form can be questioned, but there is an element of truth in it. For perhaps the greater part of the last hundred years the claims of science to a place in the school curriculum have been overlooked despite the fact that the contemporary culture was growing more scientific throughout the period. The influence of this neglect is still with us. It is therefore true to say that in organizing a curriculum which fits children and older students for the modern world the whole of the present culture must be considered. To use the word coined by the Crowther Report 'numeracy' as well as literacy is important if the schools are to come near passing on the culture in this respect.

(iii) *Social Class Differences.* There is another difficulty, similar in some ways to that of the rural and urban sub-cultures. This problem lies in the fact that social classes may be considered as sub-cultures. This affects the schools in various ways, but one important aspect is found in the relation between teacher and taught. Very often the teacher is middle class and hence has middle-class values. Even if he has come from a working-class background, the teacher will in all probability aspire to the middle class and hence hold the values of that class more strongly. Since the majority of pupils in schools come from the working class and in the case of many secondary modern schools it would be nearer the truth to say not the majority, but all the pupils, the teaching situation is normally one where a member of one sub-culture tries to communicate with members of another sub-culture. Very often, as we saw when considering social class learning, the teacher is trying to teach his pupils a way of life and set of values that is alien to them.

---

[1] C. P. Snow treats the same problem in his novel *The New Men*, London, 1950 (Penguin), though here he introduces an intermediate sub-culture, that of the engineers.

It is useful here to consider a special case, that of 'the scholarship boy'. This is the child from the working-class home who achieves social mobility through the educational system. This has been the way of social advancement of many teachers and therefore has an especial interest in this context. Does the scholarship boy stay loyal to his class of origin or transfer his allegiance to his achieved social class? B. Jackson and D. Marsden (1962) made a pioneer study of this problem in a large industrial community in the North of England. They concluded that on the whole such children transferred their loyalty, sometimes in an exaggerated fashion, to their new and higher class. This did not happen without soul searching and often was accompanied by emotional difficulties. But it is clear that the grammar school education which is so necessary for achieving upward social mobility not only gives the child the factual knowledge that he must have, but has as well a stereotyping effect on many children. It tends to turn out young adults who have middle-class values, whatever the social class from which they originally come.[1]

As we already know, the majority of the children in the grammar schools come from the middle class, as do their teachers for the most part. Even to a child of eleven it is apparent that to succeed in this environment he must adopt certain new values and modes of behaviour. Support for him in this course often comes from home, especially from his mother. This takes the form of encouragement to succeed without a full realization of what this will entail for the child in a change of values, leading perhaps to difficulty of communication between parents and child. In extreme cases the cost of success is not just inability to communicate, but that the child does not wish any longer to see his parents. Thus it is a relatively easy task for the grammar school to assimilate a minority of working-class children and initiate them into a new sub-culture. In comparison the attempt to introduce an overwhelming majority of working-class children to the values and way of life peculiar to the English middle class seem an almost impossible task, if in fact it is what the teacher wants to achieve. Once again it would repay many teachers to examine their aims in education in the light of this analysis.

(iv) *Differences by Types of School.* Up to this point little attempt has been made to define the part played by the various types of British school on the process of culture transmission. Is the problem made more

---

[1] For a novelist's picture of the life of a scholarship boy to manhood see Raymond Williams, *Border Country*, London, 1960 (Penguin).

difficult because of the way secondary education is organized? Children at first attend a primary school that is common to the majority including, for at least a year or two, some of those who are going to enter the private school system. From about eleven secondary education is given in several types of school. A brief examination of the main types of school will show that dysfunction is caused by this method of organization, at least in respect of the particular function of the educational system here under consideration. Each type of school chooses from what is available in the culture as a whole and passes on only what it wishes.

The public school exists to train an *élite*. This has always been so and is so today. In medieval times Winchester and Eton were founded to train a priestly *élite*, during the great expansion of these schools in the nineteenth century the *élite* was a political one, whilst today it has become largely a managerial *élite* with perhaps a bias more towards commerce than industry. The clients of these schools pay so that their children shall be taught the qualities of character thought necessary for leadership. Certainly many of the products of these schools seem to assume that they will be leaders.

The maintained grammar school has imitated the public school in many respects. It has taken over what are often considered the virtues of the public school; a sense of duty is stressed and training for taking responsibility is given. But the majority of the pupils of these schools have not been able to assume that their path onwards after school was assured. Therefore, if it was one's duty to use one's abilities well, but one had to make one's way, success in school and more particularly in examinations became important. The ethos of the new grammar school came to be marked by duty and competition.

The secondary modern school was a product of the 1944 Act and the attempt to give a secondary education to all. It is here that clash of two sub-cultures can be seen most clearly. The teachers, products of the grammar schools, who believe in the values that they learnt there, have tried to teach a way of life based on these values to mainly working-class pupils. Over the last century the hard experience of unemployment and industrial strife has taught the working class to trust in a way of life based on solidarity and co-operation, not duty and competition. The coming of full employment may alter the ethos of working-class life, but as yet it is difficult to assess how much the secondary modern school has achieved. Many teachers might question whether in some cases it is not the middle-class values that should give way to those of the working class.

It is apparent that the three types of school considered in so brief and generalized a way are passing on very different versions of the British culture. The secondary technical school may provide a fourth version, but even less evidence exists about it than for the other schools mentioned. It has been suggested that this dysfunction can be corrected if the secondary system were organized on the basis of the comprehensive school, the argument being that a single type of secondary school would transmit one basic common culture. This claim must, of course, be tempered by the qualifications described so far in this chapter. Though a greater measure of 'social cohesion' might be achieved the elimination of, for example, regional sub-cultures would probably be impossible. There is as yet little factual evidence of what does happen in this respect inside comprehensive schools. One criterion would be whether the different social classes mixed in school, at play and continued to do so out of school. There is evidence to show that in American high schools mixing out of school between children of different social classes does not occur. There is, however, some slight evidence comparing one London comprehensive school with a nearby grammar school which indicates that such mixing may be more common in the comprehensive school.[1] In other words the case for social cohesion through this type of school is not as yet proved. Nor is it easy to see how the comprehensive school could ever overcome the problem of social class learning, since the fundamental differences in thought processes caused in this way occur long before the child reaches the secondary stage. Further, as long as parents can contract out of the State system and buy their children a different culture in the private system, the transmission of one single culture cannot be achieved. Nor, perhaps, should this be our aim for several reasons, one of the most cogent of which is the need to provide religious education of different types.

(v) *Sub-cultures within the School.* There is one final difficulty which must be examined. Within schools themselves it is possible to identify sub-cultures. Often there exists a group whose main aim in school is to play games well, whilst at the other extreme there is a group whose whole aim is academic work. Again in some schools, particularly in the poorer urban areas, there is a small group whose interests seem centred in

[1] W. L. Warner, *Who Shall be Educated?*, New York, 1946, and G. V. Pape, 'Mixing in the Comprehensive School', *Forum*, Spring 1961, pp. 71–74.

activities best described as delinquent. The only analysis of schools that
has so far been undertaken along these lines was made by J. S. Coleman
(1961) of the American High School. Coleman identified three main sub-
cultures which he named the fun, the academic and the delinquent sub-
cultures.

The children who formed the fun sub-culture put a low value on
academic success and intellectual matters, but gave much importance to
social success; to the boys athletic prowess and to the girls good looks
were what really mattered. It was on the whole not the aim of the
teachers to perpetuate this set of values, which seem to have been im-
ported from life outside the school. Yet this system of values now exists
within these schools and is therefore willy-nilly passed on to many
children. An academic sub-culture also exists in the American high
school. Here we find a very different set of values marked by a stress on
things of the mind, though it was the case that neither sub-culture was
mutually exclusive. There are signs that the academic sub-culture is
growing stronger today in America.

The fun culture in the shape of organized games has for some time
been consciously used in British schools with definite objects in view. It
has been assumed that games trained character. In the present state of
psychological knowledge there is more justification for two other of the
aims sometimes given, namely that by organized games loyalty to the
school can be increased and that healthy exercise lets off much emotional
steam, thereby easing the problems of keeping discipline. However, this
aspect of the fun culture, games, has often come to have such importance
in many British schools as to encroach seriously on the academic sub-
culture. Games mattered and work did not. Intellectual pursuits such as
poetry and art have not a very high standing in our culture. How much of
this is due to the games cult in our secondary schools? Certainly it is true
that teachers must be careful what values they attach to the various
school activities, since they hope to transfer these values to their pupils.

Sanctions that are external to the schools may well be strengthening
the academic sub-culture. Industry and trade are coming to put more
stress on proof of academic success; children have to pass examinations
to find a good job. Examinations are now more common in the secondary
modern schools. It may well be that the academic sub-culture is being
sought, as has happened often in the past, not for itself, but for vocational
reasons.

Coleman found that the delinquent sub-culture was marked by

avoidance of and rebellion against the school. This was not mere adolescent negativism, but a conscious total rejection of the school. It was found in Britain that, when the school leaving age was raised from fourteen to fifteen, the peak age for juvenile delinquency also rose, so that it still occurred in the final year at school. There seems to be a conscious revolt against a system where the adolescent is treated as a child. This rejection is symbolized by the boy who had just left school and 'was asked by his former headmaster what he thought of the new buildings. "It could be marble, sir," he replied, "but it would still be a bloody school."'[1] If the delinquent sub-culture is strong in a school, the transmission of the present culture becomes very difficult. The children who become friendly with the members of the delinquent group will learn to reject much or even all that the school stands for, and thereby most of what the majority of adults would think worth while. An extreme example of this process occurs in the Approved Schools, where the only pupils are those classed by the courts as deviants from the generally accepted culture of this country. The aim of these schools is to establish the values of the majority in the minority. But these institutions fail in as much as a large proportion of their pupils who are first offenders leave these schools only to be re-committed. The teachers in such schools try to pass on a set of values from which the majority of their pupils dissent. As has been indicated earlier in many cases their values and resulting behaviour are not deviant in their own home environment. In the schools the delinquent sub-culture is so strong that in many cases it, rather than the school culture, wins the adherence of those whose crime might have been their only one, but who become regular criminals.[2]

It must be added that Coleman found few traces in the American high school of the vocational sub-culture which is to be found in many institutions of higher education such as the university with its medical or law schools, the college of education with the stress on teaching, and the technical college. It may well be that this sub-culture with its stress on values relevant to success in one's chosen career is to be found in Britain in the secondary technical school. These values may provide a substitute for those of the fun or delinquent sub-cultures.

The function of transmitting culture is a complex one. Much of this process is now carried out in the educational system, but the creation of

---

[1] *Half our Future* (Newsom Report), 1963, p. 2.

[2] An interesting novel relevant to this paragraph is Alan Sillitoe, *The Loneliness of the Long Distance Runner*, London (Penguin), 1959.

institutions has in some cases built in dysfunctions which are often not recognized. Sub-cultures can provide a healthy tension, but this is not always the case. We have to consider whether our educational aims are such that when we recognize dysfunction we should reform the institutional framework which our analysis reveals to have caused it.

B. Innovation

The function of providing innovators clashes with that of transmitting culture. Innovation brings either new ways or new ideas and therefore challenges what was formerly considered to be usual. The educational system has here two parts to play. It must provide the innovators and also ensure that the necessary changes take place with the minimum of friction. Opposition to change is common where traditional ways have ruled for a long time; this is the case in many societies now meeting industrialization for the first time. But change is not welcomed in some complex industrial societies either because it will hurt vested interests or, as in Britain, because the traditional is held in high regard.

1. The Schools and Change

This twofold role of the educational system is particularly important in modern Western economies. Even before 1939 research of a scientific nature was being applied to industry; this had raised the rate of introduction of new industrial products. But we have seen that since 1945 full employment has further increased the rate of industrial innovation. The American economist, J. K. Galbraith, has suggested that in a modern high consumption economy change is essential to provide employment for all; new cars with slight differences from the previous model must be sold in order to keep the industry in full employment. In brief this is Galbraith's 'Dependence Effect'.[1] The place of advertising in this process is clear. What part can the schools play if change is to occur as easily as possible?

There has been a move towards more general education at many levels of the educational system, and this matches the needs of workers who meet changes in methods of production. As more children are staying at school beyond the minimum leaving age, they pursue their general education for longer. This in itself is an advantage, but it also means that adolescents may possibly choose their first occupation more wisely since

[1] J. K. Galbraith, *The Affluent Society*, London (Pelican), 1958.

they are somewhat more mature. The new universities have tried to introduce broader degree courses in many fields of study, and in the sixth forms of secondary schools many headmasters are trying to reduce the tendency to early specialization that marks British education.

Much more direct help in adjusting to change is given by that part of the educational system that gives technical education. Since the 1956 White Paper on Technical Education the Government has spent far more in this field.[1] The links between education and industry must be good so that teachers in technical colleges can know the changing needs of the economy. Though unofficial links between industry and education exist on some examining bodies, on the whole there are not strong channels of communication. In Germany the situation is very different. Communication is assured because representatives of management, the unions, the Government and education sit together on official committees that are responsible for laying down and revising the syllabuses for the examinations taken by all German craftsmen before qualification as a skilled worker.[2] In Britain the Industrial Training Act of 1964 lays down that boards responsible for vocational education shall be set up in each industry. The Government has appointed the first boards and therefore has made a start in establishing the machinery needed to keep technical education in line with the needs of the economy. This system is geared to teaching younger workers, but recently more attention has been given to the creation of facilities to help older workers to meet change by training them for new jobs.

We do not know much about the education of recent innovators. During the industrial revolution many were self-taught, but this is no longer common in industry, if only because of the extensive knowledge needed to understand present-day techniques. Recent research in the field of psychology has, however, revealed a disturbing possibility. Our teaching methods, certainly up to the age of sixteen, tend to demand the one right answer and throughout are marked by examinations which encourage standard answers. It may be that we turn children who are potentially creative into adults whose only wish is to succeed through conformity. Psychologists now believe that some people have an innate mode of thinking such that they tend to give the expected answer or follow the usual line of thought, whilst others have a mode that enables

[1] See M. Argles, op. cit., especially Chapter 8.
[2] See Lady Gertrude Williams, *Apprenticeship in Europe*, Chapter II on Western Germany, London, 1963.

them to diverge easily from the conventional. It is suspected that the emphasis in our schools may teach the 'diverger' to think in a more conformist manner and thereby crush potential creativity.[1]

We may not know the educational background of our innovators, but recent work in the U S A has revealed two facts that we may suspect to be true in Britain. Despite the growth of research in large teams about half of industrial innovations still seem to be made by individuals.[2] This emphasizes that, if the schools do stunt the creative potential of individuals, they are acting in a dysfunctional way in that they are stopping the flow of innovators. Secondly, there seems to be no difference in the quality of the output of American scientists from schools or colleges in which the expenditure per pupil is high and those where it is low.[3] Anyone with experience of British education might go as far as saying that the correlation in Britain was inverse!

The educational system has itself changed so as to ease adaptation to continuous technical innovation. The institutional framework that links the economy with education is growing stronger. The movement towards staying longer at school and towards less specialized courses at all levels of education is helping to meet change on the side of production. But what little we know of the education of our present innovators leads us to believe that here the educational system is acting in a dysfunctional way in that it may well be checking the supply of innovators. This would seem a serious fault in a country traditionally as conservative as Britain.

2. Autonomous Change

The educational system is a social institution which can develop autonomously. The dysfunctional attitudes towards science cited above developed within the educational system itself. Often schools, which were started at least in some measure to assist social change, have become sources of ideas that have hindered change. A recent example, which will be discussed fully in Chapter 12, is the way in which the supply of scientists from the schools has risen greatly since 1945, but many of the children have learnt unconsciously to see their future careers as spent in research rather than in industry where the need for scientifically trained

[1] For an account of work in this field see J. W. Getzels and P. W. Jackson, *Creativity and Intelligence*, New York, 1962.

[2] J. Jewkes and others, *The Sources of Invention*, London, 1958.

[3] For schools see an unpublished survey in Connecticut in J. S. Coleman, op. cit., p. 235, and for colleges see R. H. Knapp and H. B. Goodrich, *Origins of American Scientists*, Chicago, 1952, pp. 45–46.

young workers is perhaps greater. The task of checking the autonomous growth of attitudes dysfunctional to the smooth acceptance of change is difficult, but a first step is analysis to find where such attitudes exist.

It must be realized that, whereas industry makes some attempt to plan the direction in which it is going to change, the educational system itself causes much unplanned cultural change. This can be seen in three ways. There is one obvious example. Universities are a source of new knowledge and ideas, which are usually the result of research pursued for its own sake rather than because of any possible commercial application. Nor is it only in the field of pure science where discoveries are made that bring cultural change. It might be argued that one of the most beneficial of inventions in this century has come from a social scientist, namely Keynes's discovery of the mechanism of the trade cycle. Important new ideas are also generated in the arts faculties. A very good example is the influence of the school of literary criticism that grew up in Cambridge under Dr F. R. Leavis in the 1930's. We have seen that this has influenced not only the way we look at literature and teach it in schools, but has changed the sense of values inherent in this teaching, and hence influenced the way we look at newspapers and advertisements.

Another source of unplanned change is the sheer spread of education. More children are staying longer at school and this must affect their values and tastes. This could have an impact on the publishing industry; the growth of the paperback has proceeded simultaneously with the spread of education both in Britain and the United States. Perhaps more important is the effect of longer education upon attitudes held. In both the United States and Germany it has been found that the longer the education that people have had, the more tolerant their attitudes seem to be.[1] The cause of this is uncertain, but it may be due to deeper knowledge or to a greater breadth of social contacts. When we encourage or legislate for longer education, we are never sure what the eventual effect will be.

The final example of unplanned cultural change also stems from the greater length of educational experience. When the majority of the population attended the elementary school up to fourteen, they underwent an educational experience that was fairly common to all. It was pointed out in the last section that secondary education in Britain today provides a variety of experience and thereby instils different sets of values. If a larger proportion of the population go beyond the secondary

[1] S. M. Lipset. *Political Man*, London, 1960, pp. 109–11.

stage, many more people will not only experience the various types of secondary schools, but also the differing sub-cultures of the university, the college of education or the technical college. This could be of more importance relatively to women than men, since women are seriously under-represented in many of our institutions of higher learning. Longer education is itself a powerful instrument for further differentiating culture. It could therefore make the problem of culture transmission a more complex one.

3. *Conclusion*

Once again a consideration of social change and innovation has led us back to the problem of providing stability. As was observed at the beginning of this chapter the two are closely linked. The very decision to hand part of the task of socializing the young to an institution other than the family builds in the chance of change. As more educational institutions are set up, so sub-cultures can be born within them. This can result in healthy tension, but it can also lead to dysfunction which may be latent until a careful analysis is made. The results of such an examination may drive us to justify a particular sub-culture; this will force us out of the realm of a neutral sociological analysis into the field of politics or philosophy, since we must then consider our aims in education. Our knowledge of the effects and sources of change is very limited, particularly in the field of education. The very least that we can do is to be aware all the time that in the modern world this is an important problem and has a relevance to what and how we teach.

BIBLIOGRAPHY

(i) *Culture Transmission*

J. S. Coleman, *The Adolescent Society*, New York, 1961.

Emile Durkheim, *Education and Sociology*, Glencoe, Illinois, 1956.

R. Hoggart, *The Uses of Literacy*, London, 1956 (Pelican).

B. Jackson and D. Marsden, *Education and the Working Class*, London, 1962.

M. Mead, *The School in American Culture*, Cambridge, Mass., 1951.

C. P. Snow, *The Two Cultures and the Scientific Revolution*, Cambridge, 1958.

Books on types of schools

J. C. Dancy, *The Public Schools and the Future*, London, 1963.

R. Edwards, *The Secondary Technical School*, London, 1960.

R. Pedley, *The Comprehensive School*, London, 1963 (Pelican).

F. Stevens, *The Living Tradition*, London, 1960 (for the Grammar school).

W. Taylor, *The Secondary Modern School*, London, 1963.

(ii) *Innovation*

B. R. Clark, *Educating the Expert Society*, San Francisco, 1962 (Chapter I).

Sir F. Clark, *Education and Social Change*, London, 1940.

10

The Political Function

In its political function the educational system has two tasks. Within any political unit there is a need that all its members, especially the new generation coming to the age when it can exercise political power, shall be loyal to the assumptions underlying the present system of government. This consensus is often taken for granted, but one of its main sources, whether consciously pursued or not, lies within the educational system. Secondly, there is the necessity that the country shall be led. Whatever is the type of government that exists in the country, its leaders must come from within it if it is to remain independent; the schools can play a major part in both the selection and the training of leaders.

1. *Consensus*

Whatever the régime that rules a country, its leaders will hope to gain the acceptance of that country. This should help to ensure the continuance of the régime. This will be so whether the country is democratic or not. Since Britain is a democratic society, it is natural to give more attention here to this type of political system. The assumptions that underlie a democratic system demand a high level of political sophistication. Most important are the tolerance of minorities by the majority who for the time have power, and the acceptance by the minorities that the majority has legitimate power. It has been said that one of Britain's greatest political inventions is the office of Leader of the Opposition, a politician paid by the State to ensure that an opposition exists able to take office if voted into power. Certainly the Leader of the Opposition symbolizes many of the basic assumptions of a democracy.

The decision that the schools should have a definite part in promoting political consensus can be a conscious decision. The part the school plays in Russia is a good example. In our view much of the history taught in Russian schools is given a bias with the intention of making the children loyal to the Communist régime so that they will see the world in the way that the rulers of Russia wish them to do. However, it is possible that most countries do much the same thing unconsciously in their own schools. History textbooks provide many examples. For instance in describing the War of the Spanish Succession, British books tend to mention only British victories and omit French ones. French books tend to minimize or omit the part played by Marlborough. Both sides claim to have won the war. In the case of the Hundred Years War British texts make much of Crecy, Poitiers and Agincourt, so that British pupils are left wondering how we came to lose so many of our French possessions by 1453. Spanish textbooks have omitted any mention of the Armada.[1]

It may be thought that it is easiest to build up loyalty to the country in such school subjects as history, geography and the teaching of the mother tongue, and that this process will be more powerful when the child is at the secondary stage. But this is not so. The textbooks of many countries could be quoted. A careful study of anthologies of verse for young children with their stress on national folk heroes would be relevant at this point. But here examples from German textbooks will be given.[2] An elementary reading book dated 1906 will show how the ideal of militarism, then considered a political necessity by the rulers of Germany was inculcated into the young child.

'We want to play soldiers,' said Albert. 'Yes, soldiers,' cried the others. He divided them into two armies, four boys in each. Charles led his army to a large sand heap. Albert had to storm this with his soldiers. Shouting, 'Hurrah! Hurrah!' they ran up the sand heap, came to grips with the enemy and took them prisoner. Thus Albert won the war with his soldiers.

Or, again, under the Nazi elementary arithmetic was used to teach the young child the political aims of the new régime. The child became familiar with large numbers by reading how 13·25 millions were called up by Germany in the First World War and 11·25 millions by Germany's allies. These men carried on the 'heroic' fight, against the 47·5 millions of the league of Germany's enemies. Language can be used in an emotional way even in elementary arithmetic textbooks. Again, the child learnt how

[1] E. H. Dance, 'History Textbooks and International Revision', *History Today*, April 1956. For further examples see J. W. Hunt, *English History Through Foreign Eyes*, London, 1954.

[2] These and many other examples will be found in R. H. Thomas and R. H. Samuel, *Education and Society in Modern Germany*, London, 1947, *passim*.

to multiply and divide using money from tables comparing the sums spent yearly on education and on lunatics; the intention was to show at the same time what an expensive liability the mentally handicapped were to the State. Similar problems were given using the number of Jews in Germany.

These examples are very obvious and were part of a conscious policy; the same process occurs in Britain unconsciously. If one makes historical examination of the relevant journals and official reports, there are only rare references to be found to the conscious use of education to create political consensus. They can be found in the official reports issued in 1917–18 at a time when there was considerable political unrest of an extreme left-wing nature. They can occasionally be found in the speeches of moderate trade union leaders reminiscing about the slump of the early '30's; loyalty to the democratic way of life was preserved for these men in some cases through attendance at classes of the Workers' Educational Association. However, consensus is maintained in many ways. Partly it is a matter of culture transmission; the great stories of the nation that are told from the earliest years in school are important here – the Armada and Trafalgar. Partly it is determined by the questions teachers ask and omit to ask; are there no disadvantages to our *laissez-faire* system? Is 'the West' always right and Russia always wrong?

The connections between education and democracy are well documented in certain particular instances. Thus it has been shown that in the case of various countries those with a longer education tend to vote more regularly than those with less education (S. M. Lipset, 1960). This raises the difficult question of whether a basic minimum of education is essential for a stable democracy. In the case of Britain it is true to say that one of the main influences that brought about the establishment of a State-aided system of elementary education in 1870 was the extension three years earlier of the vote to the male urban working class. It may well be that the experiment in India of running a democracy in a country still marked by mass illiteracy may, if successful, disprove this connection. However, Lipset has shown that degrees of democracy correlate positively with several indices of education. He compared firstly stable democracies with unstable democracies and dictatorships in Europe and secondly, democracies and unstable dictatorships with stable dictatorships in Latin America; the division into these categories had necessarily to be somewhat arbitrary. Lipset found that in both comparisons the more democratic group had a higher index on four educational criteria.

K

These were the percentage literate and the percentages in primary, post-primary and higher education. Though the statistics were by their very nature not strictly comparable, the differences between the two groups, both on average and when considering the ranges, were in each case so great as to leave the general conclusion in little doubt; the more educated countries were the more democratic. Certain exceptions at once come to mind, more particularly France and Germany. These exceptions raise the problem of national aims in education. As has been shown above, for much of the last century the German educational system has been used to further undemocratic ends.

One of the most influential of modern philosophers of education has built his entire philosophy around the need for a full education in a true democracy. John Dewey, particularly in his *Democracy and Education* (1916) argued that, if a democracy was to survive, the educational system must teach certain knowledge about the society and its traditions, and inculcate certain qualities so that citizens will both wish and be able to participate in the ruling of their country. It is hoped that such an education would lead to a greater tolerance of views of others and provide a basis for more rational political choice. There is a suspicion amongst political scientists that less sophisticated people have a simpler view of politics and are therefore more likely to fall under the power of extremist political leaders. It has already been pointed out that there is a connection between length of education and the degree of tolerance of opposing views. But more particularly the fear is that it is the working class because of their shorter education who will surrender to extreme political views. Hoggart (1957) pointed out that the education of the working class probably gives 'little idea of a continuing tradition'. This class will not have the same wide general perspective as the more educated middle class, nor will they have the same sense of a past, a present and a future, which is an important element in political continuity. Evidence on the latter point comes from Spinley's (1954) work; it will be recalled that she found that her sample of working-class children tended to live for the present and were unable to forgo present pleasures for future benefits. Psychologists have found that this kind of limited or fixed frame of reference is one condition for easy suggestibility, which is in itself a major explanation for political extremism. Spinley also found that because of their upbringing these children were more prone to use violence and to rebel against authority.

To sum up the argument, many working-class children come from a poor home background, have an education of a poor standard and leave school as soon as they can. This start in life is followed for many by a job in which they mix with adults from a very similar background. Limited educational experience is followed by low mental stimulation. This situation could well be a breeding ground for extremism. The Communist Party has always seen the leadership of the slumbering masses as one of its historic roles. This rather pessimistic picture is perhaps truer of some of the emerging countries in Africa or Asia than of Britain today, but nevertheless it allows us to draw a general conclusion that is relevant to this country and that is often forgotten. Education may not be a sufficient condition for democracy, but it certainly is a necessary condition for its survival.

2. Leaders

When we talk about 'leaders' in a democracy, to whom are we referring? We certainly include political leaders such as members of the Cabinet. We should include Members of Parliament and the more active members of the mainly hereditary House of Lords. The higher grades of the Civil Service must be added, since they are a part of the governing machinery of the country and have considerable powers of their own. Mention must be made of the counterparts of these national leaders at local government level, namely councillors and aldermen, and the full-time officers, such as the Director of Education, who carry out the policy determined by our democratically elected representatives on the local council. It will be noticed that economic leaders are omitted; they will be considered, when we examine the economic functions of education.

(i) *National Leaders*. Where are our political leaders educated? There is a description of their education which is almost a caricature. It runs as follows: a private preparatory school leads to a public school followed by Oxford or Cambridge University. The distinctive point of this education is that it is an education apart from those who are to be led. Further it is not only the pattern supposed for Conservative Party leaders, but also for a considerable number of Labour leaders, more particularly for the intellectuals of the party. The trade unionist section of the Labour Party must be excepted, since by the present convention British trade union leaders must rise from the ranks of the unions that they lead. How true is this stereotype of leaders educated in the main apart?

Recent work by W. L. Guttsman (1963) has shown the changing social background of our political leaders over the last century. The Cabinet has become less predominantly aristocratic in its recruitment and is now recruited more from the upper middle and middle classes. Yet there still persists a strong aristocratic connection. There also remain traces of the great 'political families', the younger members of whom have an earlier start in politics, often because of greater financial independence. By our present constitution a certain number of Cabinet members must sit in the House of Lords, though the possibility now exists that the Labour Party could appoint life peers, rather than hereditary aristocrats, to fulfil this need. There was a lag of a generation between the changes in the constitution that broadened the social composition of the House of Commons and the subsequent changes in the social composition of the Cabinet. The lag was not just a question of political connections, but the new political generation had to serve its apprenticeship before reaching high office and positions of leadership. The old political *élite* had been marked by an aristocratic connection with the more exclusive public schools. The new *élite* seems to have been drawn principally from the professional classes and more especially from lawyers. Business men are under-represented, perhaps because of the greater difficulty in their case of combining the earning of a living with Parliamentary duties. The intellectual level of the new *élite* is high. Some have been to the old public schools, but a fair proportion come from the new public schools that grew up in the nineteenth century in answer to the demand of the new middle class. Oxford and Cambridge are well represented amongst these new men whose careers at university indicate more interest in things academic than the old aristocratic *élite* had shown at these same universities in the nineteenth century.

(a) *The Cabinet*. When Baldwin formed his first Government in 1923 he said that one of his first thoughts was that 'it should be a Government of which Harrow should not be ashamed'. Similar sentiments were attributed to Macmillan in the 1950's except that in his case it was Eton and not Harrow that was important. In 1951 82 per cent of ministers in the new Conservative Government had attended public schools; ten years later the proportion was 76 per cent. The public schools still seem to be the educational source of an important section of our political leadership; they are still considered to give the worth-while lessons in loyalty, obedience and leadership that are thought necessary for public life. Later in this section consideration will be given to the validity of the claims that these characteristics can be taught.

(b) *Members of Parliament*. Cabinets are drawn from Parliament and largely from the House of Commons. What types of school have Members of Parliament attended in recent years ? In the case of the Conservative Party the position was almost the same in 1955 as between the wars. In 1955 75 per cent had gone to public schools and 16·5 per cent to other secondary schools, whereas the inter-war averages were 78·5 per cent from public schools and 19 per cent from other secondary schools. For the Labour Party the proportion who had been to public schools rose from 9 per cent in between the wars to 19 per cent in 1955, and from 15·5 per cent to 29 per cent for those attending other secondary schools; these increases were at the expense of those who had attended elementary school only. In 1955 the percentage of Members of Parliament of all parties who had been to public school was exactly 50 per cent.[1]

(c) *The Civil Service*. Before considering the consequences of this recruitment the third component of political leadership must be examined. There are two main avenues of entry to the senior, or administrative, grades of the Civil Service; entry may be by open competition through an examination or by promotion from the executive or clerical grades. Entry by examination would be thought to supply a genuine career open to the talented. However, during the inter-war years more than 80 per cent of the entrants to the senior grades by this method of entry and about 50 per cent of the entrants by other means came from the independent public schools. During the years 1944–52 56 per cent of entrants by open competition attended independent public schools, 17 per cent direct-grant schools, many of which are in fact Headmasters' Conference schools, and 28 per cent maintained grammar schools.[2] The picture here is similar to that of Parliament. There is a fall in the public school representation and a rise in that of maintained grammar schools, but a substantial proportion, about half in both cases, came from the public schools, using a wide definition of the term.

It must be realized that there is one possible justification for this situation to continue or, at least, not to undergo rapid change. Those who are our leaders can possibly mix more easily with those who have the same upbringing as themselves. In this way proper communication will ensure efficient government. However, two powerful arguments exist on the other side. The first is purely on the functional level. There is no

[1] J. C. Dancey, op. cit., p. 112. A public school is here defined as one of the approximately 200 Headmasters' Conference schools.
[2] R. K. Kelsall, *Higher Civil Servants in Britain*, London, 1955 gives full details of the education of this group (percentages rounded off).

guarantee that men or women educated apart in special schools for a small proportion of the country and drawn predominantly from one class will have any understanding of those whom they will govern and from whom they have been segregated almost completely since birth. Secondly, a general contemporary political aim is equality of opportunity in all spheres, and it would seem that those who attend the public schools still have a greater chance of success in national politics.

(ii) *Local Leaders*

The rise of the Labour party in local politics has made a considerable change in the educational sources of local leaders. From the few relevant surveys[1] in this field the expected stereotype seems to be true. Most local Conservative leaders, whether on the council or the committee of the local party are drawn from local managers, small business men or shopkeepers, many of whom have been to grammar school and a few of whom have gone to public schools. This seems to be the case in both urban and rural areas. Most local Labour Party leaders come from lower managers, and from clerical and skilled manual workers, few of whom have been to grammar schools, but a greater proportion of whom in the near future will go to grammar schools because of the greater stress on formal educational qualifications at this level. One of the social problems of the near future will be to provide a replacement for the old type of local Labour leader, particularly of the type connected with the trade union. In the past these men have been mainly recruited from the able men whose social background in childhood prevented their having the education for which their ability fitted them. Today such men are diverted at eleven-plus to the grammar school and often then rise up the social scale. In the USA the trade unions feed such men back from the universities into the higher levels of the union and local politics, but in Britain on the whole convention as yet will not allow this.

The equivalent at local level to the national Civil Servant is the local government officer. The senior grades, for instance the Director of Education or Town Clerk, must by the nature of their occupations have had a long formal education. In one large Midland city F. Musgrove (1963) found that 76·9 per cent of the senior local government officers had been to grammar or public schools. At the middle levels of the local

---

[1] See A. H. Birch, *Small Town Politics*, London, 1959; T. W. Brennan, E. W. Cooney, H. Pollins, *Social Change in West Wales*, London, 1954; M. Stacey, *Tradition and Change*, London, 1960.

government service it would seem that many make a career who have left grammar school at sixteen. The grammar and public schools were also found to provide the education of many local leaders, both men and women, in voluntary organizations such as the scouts and guides, and the Red Cross.[1]

(iii) *Education for Leadership*

It has been made very clear that at national level a majority of our political *élite* is educated at public schools and at local level at maintained grammar schools. The influence of the public schools on the aims and organizations of the grammar schools is well known; some aspects of this will be discussed in Chapter 14. One of the most important claims of the public schools has been that they can train boys to become leaders. They aim to give our future leaders the sense of duty and responsibility to their country which will ensure that their former pupils will use their talents as leaders, and these schools further believe that they can inculcate the social skills needed by leaders. In other countries, such as the USSR and to a large extent the USA, political leaders are not educated apart. Can the British system be justified?

The early attempts of psychologists to study the nature of leadership concentrated upon the character traits displayed by those considered to be leaders. The results were inconclusive. In a critique of twenty studies made up to 1936 seventy-nine different traits were reported.[2] Only one trait was common to as many as ten of the studies and that was intelligence. Similarly in Britain intelligence was found to be the most efficient predictor for choosing officers in the armed services during the 1939–45 war (E. James, 1951). Many of the twenty studies reported traits that were obviously contradictory.

As a result of the failure of this type of investigation psychologists have turned their attention away from the concept that the leader is a person with special qualities to the concept that the leader is a person who fulfils a special role in a group of people with a shared set of values (T. H. Newcomb, 1952 and G. Homans, 1951). The only factor common to all leadership situations is that the other roles in the group are dependent upon the leader's role to fulfil the aim of that particular group. But in different situations a different set of qualities is required to

[1] See Rosalind C. Chambers, 'A Study of Three Voluntary Organizations', in D. V. Glass (ed.), op. cit. for a contrary conclusion in the case of voluntary organizations consisting mainly of women.

[2] C. Bird, reported in T. H. Newcomb, *Social Psychology*, London, 1952, pp. 6 2–3.

fill the role of leader. For example, the role of the army captain in action demands different traits from that needed by the scientist leading a research team. To a school teacher it is clear that the headmaster of a public school must have different qualities from the headmaster of a secondary modern school. The conclusions to be drawn here are that the character traits demanded in leaders vary from situation to situation, but that the position of the leader is marked by the structural dependence of the roles in the group on his role. Possibly the only personality trait that may be demanded in a leader is that of intelligence.

There are groups that need leaders at all levels of society. We should not be surprised to read that adolescent boys in Liverpool organized a football league with matches every Saturday morning, each team in charge of a boy captain; they did this without any help or encouragement from adults.[1] Again, a recent investigation compared leadership amongst two school classes of thirteen-year-old boys in Glasgow. One group was from one of the best fee-paying schools, whilst the other was in one of the toughest non-selective secondary schools in the city. It was found that the general trait of leadership was distributed in each group according to the curve of normal error.[2] At all socio-economic levels men and women fill the role of leader.

The claim of the public schools to train leaders has usually been based upon the fact that they could bring out the qualities essential for leadership in boys. We can now see that this is impossible, since different qualities are required in different situations. It is even difficult to argue the case put by the public schools in their own terms since no one has been able to agree what are the traits that are vital in leaders. What then can the educational system do to educate the potential leaders that exist at all socio-economic levels ? It would seem that any policy of educating for leadership must be based on the foregoing analysis.

In the first place at every level of leadership intelligence seems necessary. Any educational system that selects by intelligence will influence the supply of leaders. Entry to the grammar school is largely determined by measured intelligence, and therefore these schools are bound to be the main source of leaders for many of the higher positions of leadership in Government, industry and other spheres. As long as we have a selective system of secondary schools, it must be arranged to find the

[1] J. B. Mays, *Growing Up in the City*, Liverpool, 1954, Appendix A, pp. 169–73.
[2] J. Kelly, 'A Study of Leadership in Two Contrasting Groups', *Sociological Review*, November 1963.

maximum number of intelligent children who may become leaders. But leaders are also required in the lower ranks of society. Therefore attention to the education of leaders is needed in all, not merely in selective, schools.

A second lesson to be drawn from the analysis of leadership is that no one will take the role of leader unless he feels impelled to do so. The motive is essential. The public schools did give many young men a deep sense of service, particularly of a political nature, and this, rather than any special training in the necessary character traits, led such men to grasp the role of leader that was offered to them in many different situations. Under the social conditions found in Britain up to 1939 few others had the education, the time and the will to take these roles, and traditionally leadership went to the class who patronized the public schools. Under modern conditions it is therefore necessary that at all levels of intelligence there should be people who want to be leaders in the many spheres of action open to them. It is here that the secondary modern school has a place in educating for leadership. Many of its pupils must leave school with the desire to lead and the interest that will supply a motive to leadership in some activity that is open to them.

Finally, the prefect system was supposedly an agent in training leaders. Originally, as we have seen, it rested on domination by force, but in its present less authoritarian form it can have a place in educating leaders. Children who are prefects have the chance to lead others in all the activities in a school. If the many activities in any school could be systematically divided and children given the chance to lead in each sphere, far more children than under the present unitary prefect system would have the chance of acting as leaders.[1] This experience would be valuable only if the lessons learnt in the particular situation at school could be transferred to other situations on leaving school. Transfer depends upon conscious thought. Therefore the vital lesson in all school leadership situations must be pointed out to the children, namely that the dependence of the led is common to the role of all leaders.

There is another problem of a theoretical nature. Some sociologists have considered the nature of leadership in society (T. B. Bottomore, 1964). For example, Karl Mannheim believed that leadership could be exercised within the framework of a classless society. At the head of each sphere in a society there would be an *élite* consisting of the out-

[1] For further consideration of this topic see K. G. Collier, *The Social Purposes of Education*, London, 1959, Chapters XI and XII.

standing men in that sphere. Entry to this group would depend upon ability and experience, not upon the influence of class, family or other connections. This theory of *élites* has been opposed, especially by T. S. Eliot (1948), on the grounds that the family cannot avoid passing on the culture of that level of society to which the parents belong or which they have achieved. This sub-culture must contain some elements of the leadership implicit in the parents' position. Such an argument is reinforced by the known positive correlation between measured intelligence in parents and their children, since, as has already been explained, a minimum level of intelligence is needed for leadership. It therefore seems clear that, though there may not be a system of *élites* to which entry is completely open, there will be an *élite* from which many leaders are bound to come.

3. *Conclusion*

Obviously the educational system has two important parts to play from a political point of view. As was shown in the first part of this chapter it must ensure that the political leaders at each level are followed even by those in loyal opposition. Democracy is a system of government that demands a fair standard of education to ensure its continuance. Secondly, the educational system must be organized so that those with the intelligence necessary to lead can have the chance to do so. At present this is basically part of the selective function of education to which we now turn.

BIBLIOGRAPHY

T. B. Bottomore, *Élites and Society*, London, 1964.
G. D. H. Cole, *Studies in Class Structure*, London, 1956 (especially Chapter V).
T. S. Eliot, op. cit. (especially Chapter II).
W. L. Guttsman, *British Political Élites*, London, 1963.
G. Homans, *The Human Group*, London, 1951 (especially Chapter 8).
Sir E. James, *Educating for Leadership*, London, 1951.
S. M. Lipset, *Political Man*, London, 1960.
F. Musgrove, *The Migratory Élite*, London, 1963 (Chapter 5).
T. H. Newcomb, *Social Psychology*, London, 1952 (especially Chapter 17).

11

The Selection Function

A political aim common to many countries is that of ensuring equality of opportunity. This aim is often held especially strongly in the case of education. Certainly no political party in modern Britain could afford to forgo the provision of equality of educational opportunity as one of its main policies. Politically the educational system is seen as a possible way of selecting some children and giving them a better start to their adult life than others. However, we are trying to view the working of the educational system in a neutral way. Here we must attempt to answer two questions, namely what is the selection function and how is it being fulfilled in Britain today?

At any time the population of a country contains children who have different abilities and personalities. It is essential that by the time they are adults these children shall be able to use their talents to the utmost. This may be justified in several ways. One may argue on moral grounds that each child ought to be given the chance to develop fully or on psychological grounds that only by a full use of his talents will the child grow to be a mentally healthy adult. Again, there is the economic case that in the modern world no country can afford to neglect the greatest of its resources, the native talents of its population.

In this context we can consider the educational system to be acting in a way akin to a sorting mechanism. Children with many individual differences are helped to the starting places for their adult lives which are most suited to their own particular qualities. If the educational system is undertaking the selection function well, then the country will make full use of the personal and intellectual qualities of its people. It is the sum of these qualities that is sometimes called 'the pool of talent' or 'the pool of ability'. For reasons which will become clear 'the pool of capability' is perhaps a more apt term.

A. The Pool of Capability

In recent years some thought has been given to the more exact analysis of the pool of capability. Interest has been stimulated in two ways. There has been a political interest based on the desire that able children of all social classes should be given the fullest education of which they are capable. There has also been competition on an international scale to achieve higher economic productivity; this has directed attention to the comparative output of technicians and technologists from the institutes of higher education in various countries including the USA, Russia and Britain. This interest in the pool of capability has led to attempts to measure the size and distribution of the reserves of ability. Statistical exercises endeavouring to answer this problem for Britain have been made, for example, by the Crowther (Vol. II, 1960) and Robbins (Appendix I, 1963) Committees. Similar work has been done in Sweden and Holland (P. de Wolff and K. Härnqvist in A. H. Halsey (ed.), 1961).

The initial attempts to measure reserves of ability were based on the use of tests, usually of IQ, which were considered to have a value for predicting future academic success. A typical method was to calculate the proportion of the population of a given IQ that was thought to be the minimum requisite for a given level of education, for example, to achieve success in a grammar school course as measured by passing five 'O' levels or for university entry. This proportion was then compared with the proportion that was in fact undergoing that level of education at that particular time. Any shortfall would indicate the order of the reserves of ability. This calculation has been called an assessment of 'reserves in the narrow sense'. Usually the sole criterion is IQ, whereas it is well known that many other considerations are important for the progress of children at school or of undergraduates at university. Apart from the influence of the home and the rest of the environment there is the whole complex of personality factors. Many teachers know that relatively dull children succeed at school because of perseverance or the support of their parents, whilst more intelligent children can do less well than expected due to some defect in personality or a lack of parental interest. It is for such reasons that Vernon wishes to talk of 'the pool of capability' rather than 'the pool of talent'.[1] The statistical measurement of reserves of capability must obviously be a much more complex task.

Although no adequate allowance has yet been made for personality

[1] P. E. Vernon, letter in *British Journal of Educational Studies*, November 1958.

factors, measurements of 'reserves in the broad sense' have been made. The population has been divided into strata, usually by social class, and the distribution in these strata of measured intelligence or some such measure of school success as passing a given examination has been calculated. If it is assumed that the highest strata covers the optimum conditions for all the possible variables, then the shortfall in the lowest strata can be calculated. Some calculations have attempted to allow for the effect of removing the economic hindrances to success at school. It is hoped that such methods can be extended to the measurement of the reserves of special ability such as is needed by mathematicians and scientists. This is partly dependent on further improvements in the psychological tests used to measure such special aptitudes. When thinking about these methods it is worth while reminding ourselves constantly that it is ability usually and not capability that is being used as the criterion. In this connection we should remember that 'merit' has been defined as 'IQ plus Effort'.[1]

Some indications can be given of the quantity of capability that must be wasted in Britain. The very framework of the analysis used will show some of the causes of this waste, since it will make clear the way in which this country fails to allow many individuals to develop and use their capabilities to the full. It is possible in this context to make comparisons between countries, the sexes, geographical regions within the same country, social classes and between types of school.

1. *International Comparisons*
There is immense difficulty in international comparisons of educational statistics, mainly because of differences in standards. Yet the fact that in 1957–8 in the USA 16·65 per cent of the relevant age group gained first degrees compared with 2·92 per cent in Britain cannot be attributed entirely to the somewhat lower standards of some American universities. Again it is known that in the early 1960's 13 per cent of the relevant age group in Sweden passed the university entrance qualification compared with the 6·9 per cent of boys and girls who gained two 'A' levels in England and Wales in 1961.[2] This difference can hardly be attributed to a higher level of innate intelligence among the Swedes than among the British. Some measure of the possibility of university expansion is

[1] M. Young, *The Rise of the Meritocracy*, London, 1958, p. 94 (Pelican ed.).
[2] A. H. Halsey (ed.), *Ability and Educational Opportunity*, OEEC, 1961, pp. 192–3 and *Higher Education* (Robbins), Appendix I, p. 7.

indicated by this comparison, but calculations by Professor Härnqvist (A. H. Halsey (ed.), 1961) suggest that even in Sweden there are reserves of capability, since he believes from his figures that at least 28 per cent of boys and girls could attain university entrance standard.

2. Inter-sex Comparisons

It is generally held that there are no significant differences in the innate intellectual potential of men and women. Differences in kind may exist, but not of level. Yet in 1961 whereas 8·7 per cent of boys in the relevant age group left school with two 'A' levels, only 5·1 per cent of girls achieved this standard.[1] The same type of inter-sex difference can be found at 'O' level though of a smaller order of magnitude. Yet it is also known that once women are at university they do on average as well as men.

Any attempts to calculate reserves of capability are complicated when comparing the sexes by the fact that girls often study a different curriculum from boys even in co-educational schools. This can be seen clearly in the table below which shows the proportions of different types of sixth forms in maintained schools in England in 1959.

	Science	Arts	General
Boys' Schools	59%	39%	2%
Co-educational Schools – Boys	72%	21%	7%
Girls	23%	64%	13%
Girls' Schools	23%	56%	21%

15 to 18, Vol. I, 1959, p. 253)

This tendency is as pronounced in the universities where the proportions of young men comes near matching the occupational structure, whereas a much higher proportion of women are in arts rather than science or technology faculties. Though there is no doubt that this matches the structure in women's occupations, the swing to the arts appears to have gone further than economic needs would demand. There is, therefore, a tendency built into the school system to divert young women into one particular educational avenue which may be dysfunctional, if one is considering the optimum use of available capability. Marriage and consequent withdrawal from the labour force also compli-

[1] Robbins, Appendix I, p. 7.

cate the issue and make calculations, for instance, of the reserves of women teachers a very difficult task. However, these complications should in no way be allowed to obscure the fact that in Britain, and indeed in many other countries, women do not receive an equal chance compared with men to be educated beyond the minimum school leaving age. It is, therefore, amongst women that one of the untapped pools of capability lies.

3. *Geographical Comparison*

In view of the very different social characteristics of the areas for which the local education authorities in Britain are responsible it is not surprising that the proportion continuing school beyond the minimum school leaving age of fifteen varies throughout the country. Explanations for this might be sought in the fact that there is difficulty in matching the rate of population change in any area to such a 'lumpy' piece of capital investment as a new school. Each local authority has reached its present pattern of provision by a different historical route. The problems of educational provision are not the same in rural and urban areas. Social class differences in measured intelligence exist and often characterize a local authority's catchment area; thus different patterns of the distribution of measured intelligence will be found in Southport and in Salford. Yet after allowing for all such considerations the recorded variations between areas in Britain in 1960 seems unduly high. Amongst counties Cardiganshire had the highest proportion of seventeen-year-olds at school with 27·9 per cent, Lincolnshire (Holland) the lowest with 5·5 per cent; the highest county borough was Merthyr Tydfil with 15·2 per cent and the lowest Bury with 2·5 per cent.[1] Such large regional variations, which on the whole mirrored the provision of grammar school places, can in no way match differences in the distribution of capability or even of measured intelligence, nor for that matter do they bear any relation to the availability of fee-paying schools.

These differences are often founded on local attitudes towards education. Thus an analysis of similar regional inequalities in France has shown that the southern third has on average higher attendance rates in secondary education than the rest of France (J. Ferez in A. H. Halsey (ed.) 1961). This was attributed partly to the strong cultural tradition left by the Roman civilization in this area and partly to the fact that the small-scale vineyard owners of this area see in education an escape from

[1] Robbins, Appendix I, p. 65.

their own economic uncertainty, whilst the industrial areas of northern France have provided a more certain demand for labour amongst those who could leave school at the minimum age. A further comparison was made between the dispersed rural areas and the concentrated urban and suburban areas. In the latter the provision of secondary schooling does not demand boarding facilities or long journeys, both of which are needed in rural areas and demand exceptionally favourable attitudes towards education.

In the USA place of residence has been found to influence the desire for university education.[1] Thus in Wisconsin the intelligent sons of prosperous farmers were less liable to want to go to university than were equally intelligent urban boys, since higher education was regarded by the farmer's son as irrelevant to their chosen career of farming. Their sisters, however, could not easily find an occupation at home and chose a career, such as teaching or social work, for which higher education was necessary.

Little is known of this nature with regard to Britain. Yet similar forces must be at work. It is in an analysis of this kind that we must seek the answer to the question why it is that both the five counties with the highest proportion of children staying at school until seventeen and the five counties with the highest proportion entering higher education are Welsh. When the proportions vary between local education authorities as much as those given above, it can be clearly seen that here is another source of inequality and of unused capability.

4. *Social Class Comparisons*

The argument about the reserves of ability is often stated in terms of social class. Sometimes crude comparisons are made between the proportions from various social classes at different stages of the educational system, for example, the percentage of the children of manual workers at university. Apart from the by now familiar warning against confusing ability with capability, there are two other considerations to be taken into account. Comparisons between the measured intelligence of the various social classes may for many purposes need to be corrected to allow for the skewed distribution of IQ by social class. But perhaps of more importance is the influence of social class learning as described in Chapter 5, which works so that many able children from working-class

---

[1] W. H. Sewell, and others, 'Social Status and Educational and Occupational Aspiration', *American Sociological Review*, February 1957.

homes cannot gain the experience necessary for the full development of their intelligence.

It is possible to quote statistics that show clearly the differences between measured intelligence and academic attainments in each social class. For example, during the course of its inquiry the Crowther Committee examined a representative sample of 5,940 National Service recruits to the Army. It found that in the top 11 per cent of measured intelligence the proportion who gained the entry qualifications necessary for higher education, namely two or more 'A' levels or an Ordinary National Certificate, was 68 per cent in the case of children of fathers in professional or managerial jobs compared with 52 per cent for those whose fathers were in clerical employment, 45 per cent for the children of skilled manual workers and 31 per cent in the case of children of semi-skilled and unskilled workers. It is not so much amongst the very able that these differences are so apparent. Thus in the second level of ability 69·1 per cent of the children of fathers in professional and managerial occupations are in independent, grammar or technical secondary schools, whilst only 26·3 per cent of the children of fathers in unskilled manual work are; at the first level of ability the respective percentages are 96·2 and 77·2.[1]

Using this type of statistic it is possible to calculate the reserves of ability 'in the broad sense', but such a figure would be very artificial, since the academic achievements of children in the upper social classes has improved greatly in recent years, but there has been only a small reduction in the differential rate of achievement between the social classes. All classes have been affected more or less equally by the recent expansion in education. Therefore any calculation of the reserves of ability made in the future may well result in a higher estimate than at present, if this differential rate of achievement were to diminish. It is clear, however, that there is a dysfunction in the British educational system so that it is not playing its proper part in sorting out the capability available in all the social classes of the population. After the next brief section it is to this problem that the rest of this chapter will be given.

5. Type of School

The four comparisons made so far have all relied on factors external to the educational system. It is possible to tackle the problem in a different way. This examines the educational achievements of children who have

[1] Crowther, Vol II, pp. 120 and 122.

the same apparent capacity as measured by intelligence tests or by some form of teacher's report, but who have taken different routes through the secondary school system or have left before taking certain examinations. The difficulty inherent in this type of estimate can be seen from the fact that in the report on *Early Leaving* (1954) heads of a sample of grammar schools in England and Wales thought that 33 per cent of their entry were capable of a course leading to two or more 'A' levels, but by 1962 well over 40 per cent of their pupils had begun such a course. In fact, in 1960–61 26 per cent of all grammar school leavers had obtained two or more 'A' levels. Rapid change can confound most calculations in this field.

At the moment little is known of the effect of different types of secondary education on children of equal measured intelligence at the time of entry. In a recent national sample of 5,362 children it was shown that there is a considerable overlap in the IQ scores of children in different types of secondary school. The ranges within which 90 per cent of the children's IQ scores fell were: grammar schools 106–127, technical schools 100–122·5, independent schools 85–124, secondary modern schools 76–107·5.[1] It is known that in some independent schools children attain much higher academic results than might be expected from their IQ scores. It is also known that children can lose points of IQ through the experience of being placed in the lower streams of a primary school (J. W. B. Douglas, 1964). It therefore seems possible that the very act of putting a child in a certain type of school may provide him with the experience that can help to develop or hinder the growth of his intelligence.

6. *Conclusion*

The problem of the pool of capability viewed from an educational standpoint is whether the schools and other educational institutions are so organized that they help to bring about the full development of the capability potentially available to the country. Perhaps the best way to epitomize what has been said is to take an imaginary, but not untypical case. What is lost to the country when the daughter of an unskilled labourer just fails the selection test for the grammar school at the age of eleven and becomes a member of the top stream of a single-sex secondary

[1] J. W. B. Douglas, *The Home and The School*, London, 1964, p. 21 (T. Scores converted to IQ points as on p. 7). S. Wiseman, op. cit., pp. 21–24 and p. 132 found a similar overlap in his work in the Manchester area.

modern school in an urban area with a ready demand for unskilled young women in the local labour force? Mention of selection at eleven leads straight to the other main problem of this chapter, namely how does the educational system carry out the function of selection?

B. Selection

The function of selection in Britain cannot be considered apart from the structure of the educational system. There are two important factors to be borne in mind. Firstly there is the division into the private and State sectors. There is also the present division in the State sector between, on the one hand a comprehensive primary system that caters for all children of whatever measured ability up to the age of eleven, apart from certain special cases such as the educationally subnormal, and, on the other hand, the secondary schools that are rapidly differentiating into new types of school, but on the whole are still based on the tripartite system of the grammar, technical and modern schools. The roots of this system can be traced back into British educational history, but it would certainly seem to have been the intention of the new Ministry of Education in the early part of the post-war era that the 1944 Act should be interpreted in this way by the local authorities responsible for its local implementation. It is within this structure and under the influence of its connections with other social institutions, more particularly with the economy and the social class system, that the function of selection is carried out.

1. *The Private System*

Before examining the State system brief mention must be made of the private sector, which for many is characterized by the public schools, though schools other than these are included within the private system. The important part that the public schools still play in providing political leaders has already been described, and in the next chapter it will be found that these schools play a somewhat similar role in the provision of leaders for the economy. Therefore, although in the early 1960's only about 5·5 per cent of all children at school were in independent schools, these schools or rather that number known as the public schools have a social significance far outweighing their numerical importance in the total educational system.

One of the main institutional reasons for this significance is the special relationship of the public schools with the universities. In fact, this is almost inevitable. Because of the way the British educational system has grown the proportion of sixth form places provided by these schools has always been very high. In 1962 32·3 per cent of all boys in sixth forms were in those independent schools recognized by the Ministry of Education as efficient and, if direct-grant schools are included with the independent schools, the proportion rises to 49 per cent. For girls the proportions are lower, namely 19·2 per cent for independent and 34 per cent for direct-grant and independent schools.[1] In the years between 1918 and 1939 boys and girls from independent schools had just over twice the chance of going to a university that children from maintained grammar schools had and, more surprisingly, the chances seem to have moved against the children from the State system during this period. In 1960–61 there was still a greater chance that a boy or girl leaving an independent school would go to university than one from a maintained grammar school, since 45 per cent of leavers from independent schools and only 31 per cent from maintained grammar schools went to universities; if the direct-grant schools, many of which rank as public schools, were included, the proportion would rise from 45 per cent to nearly 47 per cent.[2]

Although many children attend the State primary schools up to the age of eight or nine before going on to private preparatory schools, it is possible for a child to complete his education without ever entering a State school. Providing his parents can afford to send him through the private system the question of selection scarcely seems relevant. There is an examination, the Common Entrance Examination, at around thirteen years of age on passing from the preparatory to the public school. This would seem to operate more as an attainments test than as a selection mechanism, though all children do not enter their first choice of school. The majority do, and those who are not accepted at once appear to find places elsewhere in the private system.[3] Ironically for many of these children the first State-aided institution which they attend is a university.

Undoubtedly there are many very able children in the private system, and without entering the field of political polemics only two valid points may be made. As long as the private system exists, and there are valid arguments of a philosophic nature that it should continue to exist,

[1] *Ministry of Education Annual Statistics*, Vol I, 1962.
[2] See Crowther, Vol. I, p. 200, J. E. Floud in D. V. Glass (ed.) *Social Mobility in Britain*, London, 1954, pp. 114 and 136, and Robbins, Appendix I, p. 229.
[3] J. C. Dancy, op cit., p. 39.

parents who can afford it have a chance of opting out of the State system to buy for their children the prestige which is still perhaps conferred by these schools on their former pupils, whether they have capability or not. Again the children who attend these schools for one reason or another still seem to have a disproportionate chance of entering higher education and, as long as children of the same measured ability do not have the same chance of developing it, the educational system is not carrying out the selection function with the maximum efficiency. Resources of teaching power are being used in one part of the system which from the viewpoint of the system as a whole might be deployed to greater purpose elsewhere. Capability is lost to the country and inequality of opportunity exists.

2. *The State System*

When examining selection it is to the State system that most consideration must be given. This is the way by which the majority of our children gain their education. Despite the changes that are being made in procedures for allocating children to secondary schools, most still sit an examination at about eleven years old as a result of which they are placed in secondary schools. The school to which they go will in most cases determine the type of occupation that they can take up as an adult. Certain educational qualifications lead to certain jobs, and the majority of the higher level jobs demand qualifications that are usually gained in the grammar school, technical college or university. It has already been seen that the British educational system is not organized so that it makes the most of the capability available in this country. We must now try to discover where it is within the system that dysfunction occurs. The most convenient way to do this will be to take each of the stages in the educational system in turn paying particular attention to the points of transfer between the different institutions involved.

(i) *Primary Schools.* When children first go to school at five years of age they enter the infant school. Here the classes are not divided by ability level. There may be parallel classes in the larger schools in order to divide the children into groups of a teachable size. The children remain in such unstreamed classes until they go to the junior school at seven. In many of these schools the children are divided into streams by ability some time between the ages of seven and nine. This is the first selection process in our educational system. The arguments used to justify organization of the junior school in this way are that the brighter children will be given the chance to develop more fully and more quickly, whilst the less able children will have all the advantages of proceeding at the rate most suited to their ability. Admittedly there are innate differences in the potential capability of children that can sometimes be discovered by this age, and certainly by eight many of the effects of social class learning have influenced the development of children's intelligence. But if it can be shown that the I Q scores of the children in the upper streams improve whilst those in the lower streams deteriorate between the ages of eight and eleven, that period when the children are in the junior school streams, much of the basis for streaming would be removed. In fact, it could then be said that streaming acts as a self-fulfilling prophecy, bringing about what it predicts.

It is just this that seems to be shown by the recent work of J. W. B. Douglas (1964). He found that there was a big overlap between the I Q scores of the children in his sample who were in the upper and in the lower streams of junior schools. Yet at all levels of measured intelligence children in the upper streams gained points of I Q between the ages of eight and eleven, whilst children in the lower streams lost I Q points. To give examples, children in upper streams with I Qs between 87·5 and 92·5 gained 8·6 points, whilst children of the same measured ability in lower streams lost 1·5 I Q points. For the I Q range 98·5 to 101·5 the upper stream gained 6·7 points against a loss of 2·4 points by the children in the lower streams. In the range from 107·5 to 110·5 the upper stream gained 3·4 points compared with a loss of 2·9 points by the children in the lower stream. It must be noted in addition that it is the less able children in the upper streams who at every level improve more than the abler children in the same streams, whilst in the lower streams the range of ability remains more or less the same throughout the time spent in the junior school.

The difficulty of interpreting these figures is that many of the un-streamed schools are in rural areas or are schools with poor records of past academic success, but until the results of a planned experiment especially designed to investigate the effects of streaming in the junior school are published[1] this evidence is at least suggestive that apart from any reinforcing of social class learning streaming would appear to bring about some loss of capability. Further it would seem that the results of

[1] This is at present being undertaken by the National Foundation for Educational Research, and results of their long-term survey may be expected in 1967. See also B. Jackson, *Streaming: An Educational System in Miniature*, London, 1964.

the much publicized selection process at eleven have already been pre-judged by the silent selection at about eight. The case that capability is lost due to streaming in these schools is strengthened by evidence from schools with a policy of non-streaming. J. C. Daniels (1961) has shown that the average I Q of children in these schools is significantly greater than that of children in streamed junior schools by about 3 points of I Q, though it is still not clear whether the abler children are held back some-what by the less able and do not develop as high an I Q as they might in streamed classes.

(ii) *Entry to Secondary School*. The methods used to allocate children to the different types of secondary school vary very much from one local education authority to another. Most, however, still incorporate some form of test of measured intelligence. It was found in Middlesbrough and South-west Hertfordshire (J. E. Floud and others, 1956) that more or less all the children of equal measured intelligence regardless of their social class reached grammar school, though when S.W. Hertfordshire dropped the use of an I Q test, a bias in favour of the middle class appeared (J. E. Floud and A. H. Halsey, 1957). Allowing for regional differences in the rate of provision social class chances of entry to the grammar school throughout Britain today are probably not grossly unfair using measured intelligence as the criterion. Even to state this points to the fact that with secondary education organized on the tripartite system the country's use of capability varies according to the way that the num-ber of grammar school places is adjusted to meet changes in local demo-graphic conditions.

In addition because of the influence of social class learning and the differences in parental attitudes towards education chances of entering the grammar school still vary greatly for children of equal measured intelligence, but of different social class. Thus Douglas (1964) found that, whereas 40·1 per cent of upper middle-class children with an I Q of 106 or less were in grammar schools, only 7·9 per cent of lower working-class children of the same measured intelligence gained entry to these schools. What is more, once children reached the grammar school, their average I Q score seemed to change as compared with that of those children in the secondary modern school in much the same way as happened in the streams of the junior school. The average scores of those who went to a grammar school rose, and the average scores of those at the secondary modern school fell. The decline was most pronounced for children from the manual working class with the highest test scores; those in the range 112–15 IQ points lost about 6 IQ points by the age of fifteen.[1]

Some children are, therefore, placed in secondary modern schools whose achievement could be higher in the ethos of a different type of school. It may well be that it is not only the development of intelligence that is crucial in this selection process, but that different levels of aspiration are internalized in the different types of schools. Studies of the vocational aspirations of children in modern schools show them to be realistic and to accord well with the measured intelligence of the children concerned. In a survey in Ealing in 1951 it seemed that children tended to aim at the highest level available in the group to which they belonged.[2] Another and a more recent investigation made in 1956 (T. Veness, 1962) found that boys and girls in secondary modern schools were less preoccupied with their future work than were children in other types of school. Such motivation or lack of it could partly govern the academic attainments of a child and thereby determine whether or not the child had the experience necessary to develop fully his intelligence. If the children of slightly above average or average intelligence are educated apart from other children of their intelligence, but together with children of below average intelligence, they may well come to hold the lower aspirations of those who form the majority of their school fellows. These 'more realistic' hopes may be inappropriate to the more able pupils in a secondary modern school or to children of a slightly higher level of ability in those areas where provision of grammar school places is low.

For some children who are placed in a secondary modern school at eleven there is a second chance for selection, either for transfer to grammar school usually by thirteen or for entry at the same age to a secondary technical school. These possibilities do allow for a recovery of some of the capability lost at eleven, and it should be said that the use of the best available selection methods at present may involve errors in the allocation of approximately 10 per cent of the candidates or in the late '50's of about 60,000 children.[3] Moves to the grammar school are not common; often the presence in the curriculum of such subjects as French or algebra make transfer impossible. Moves are more possible to

[1] Robbins, Appendix I, p. 50 quoting as yet unpublished results of J. W. B. Douglas's long-term survey.

[2] M. D. Wilson, 'The Vocational Preferences of Secondary Modern School-children', *British Journal of Educational Psychology*, June and November 1953.

[3] A. Yates and D. A. Pidgeon, *Admission to Grammar School*, London, 1957, p. 192.

grammar school sixth forms for pupils who do well in 'O' level in secondary modern schools.

The other possibility is a place at the secondary technical school. Courses in these schools often begin at thirteen, and many parents or children consider this to be a second chance for selection for an education which can lead to a job of relatively high status and perhaps a chance of upward social mobility. Since the recruitment to these schools has in the main become part of the selection mechanism rather than dependent upon the desire for a particular type of education, it could be that the practical occupations served by these schools will be deprived of people of high measured intelligence, and this could affect the cultural and political unity of the country. It is perhaps unfortunate that the secondary technical school which could be so well fitted to give an education suited to a technological world should have come to be considered the school that gives the second chance to many after the intellectual cream has been skimmed off at eleven.

(iii) *Leaving at Fifteen*. At the present time the minimum legal leaving age is fifteen, though in 1970 this is to be raised to sixteen. The main weight of leaving at this age is from the secondary modern school, but there are some children who leave the grammar school at this age. Early leaving is once again a selective process. Fifteen per cent of children with an I Q of 113 or more in Douglas's (1964) sample had left full-time education by the time they were sixteen and, as might have been expected, almost four-fifths of these leavers were working-class children. At a higher level of measured intelligence more than 6 per cent of children with an I Q of 120 had left; it is from people of this level of intelligence that potential university students must be recruited.

Though few parents today think, as George Orwell put it in the 1930's, that 'the notion of staying at school till you are nearly grown-up seems merely contemptible and unmanly',[1] many children still leave as soon as they legally can because their parents press them to go to work; a common reason is the need to start earning thereby relieving the economic pressure on the family. Other children leave because they see their friends going from school, and they go too almost in sympathy regardless of contrary advice from the school. These social forces are very great, particularly in areas that lack social variety. Thus in 1951 in Dagenham, an area characterized by great housing estates, and a preponderance of working-class families, the rate for children leaving school under fifteen,

[1] G. Orwell, *The Road to Wigan Pier*, London, 1937 (Penguin edition), p. 104.

as was then possible, was the third highest out of 157 British towns, and the proportion of its population between fifteen and twenty-four in full-time education was the lowest, being 3·8 per cent. The reasons for leaving were partly economic, but in an interview the local headmaster laid great stress on the pressures to conformity.[1] To stay at school when the majority of one's contemporaries have left or to have intellectual or cultural interests means that the adolescent boy or girl has to be different from his peers, and this demands unusual qualities. In this case social attitudes increase the wastage of capability.

(iv) *Entry to the Sixth Form*. Even amongst those who stay on beyond the legal minimum leaving age there are able children who leave grammar school at around sixteen, namely at the point of entry to the sixth form, the start of the course that is almost essential for any higher education beyond eighteen. There will always be some children who either on their own initiative or on the advice of their parents wish to leave school at this age to enter employment. A good example is the case of a boy taking up a technical, as opposed to a craft, apprenticeship. His 'O' level passes together with a practical training should make him into a good technician. As long as facilities are available for the further education of such able children this cannot be called a loss of capability or unfair selection. Whether there are adequate facilities for the further education of this type of leaver will be considered later.

It has been said (W. D. Furneux, 1961) that even in the public schools there is some selection at entry to the sixth form. In these schools this is done 'by discouraging the further attendance of those who do not measure up to a rather "upper-class" archetype of "a good type of boy"'. However, in the maintained grammar school such leaving was found in the 1950's to be connected with the economic circumstances as well as the attitudes and lack of knowledge of parents (Early Leaving, 1954). It has occurred amongst working-class children in spite of the fact that the children have realized to the full the connection between success in the grammar school and their chances of upward social mobility (H. T. Himmelweit, 1954). There is a new, and as yet unmeasured, form of premature leaving at this point. Both boys and girls are leaving grammar schools and transferring to local technical colleges to do the equivalent of a sixth-form course. They do so because they consider themselves to be treated as old children in the sixth forms of grammar schools, whereas at the local technical college they are treated as the young adults that they

[1] P. Willmott, *The Evolution of a Community*, London, 1963, pp. 115–17.

consider themselves to be. This transfer, brought about by the different atmospheres of the two institutions, does not constitute a loss of capability, but it may indicate an unnecessary duplication of courses and thereby use resources in an inefficient manner in that, for example, there may be two half-filled science courses with the same curriculum in the same area.

The proportion of children staying at school after sixteen having the same level of measured intelligence but coming from different social classes varies in the expected direction. In the sample investigated by the Robbins Committee it was found that amongst children with an I Q of 107·5 or more 92 per cent of the children of the upper non-manual class, but only 60 per cent of children from the lower non-manual class was still at school by this age; for children with an I Q of 94 or less the percentages were 27 and 3 respectively. This difference in proportion leads to a social class differential in success at 'O' level. In fact this is greater than might be expected allowing for the social class distribution of I Q. The important level of success here is five 'O' levels, as this is the usual requirement for entry to the sixth form. In 1961 the proportions of children at maintained grammar schools who gained five or more 'O' levels were as follows – for the children of the professional and managerial class 72 per cent, clerical 60 per cent, skilled manual 55 per cent and semi-skilled or unskilled 37 per cent. Further, the proportion of candidates with five or more 'O' levels from professional and managerial homes who were in the bottom third of the intake to grammar school at eleven was higher than the proportion from working-class homes who were in the top third of the eleven-plus intake. In addition the proportions with this level of success from all social classes have risen through the 1950's in such a way that it would seem as if there has been little narrowing in the social class differential.[1]

It can therefore be seen that there are great differences in the social class chances of entry to the sixth form and that it is here as well as at eleven that unfairness and loss of capability occurs due to the way the selection process works. The effect is that the proportion of working-class children who stay through the sixth form to the age of eighteen, at which 'A' level is normally taken, is lower than the proportion of middle-class children who actually achieve two or more passes at 'A' level. Yet it must be stressed that once in the sixth form there is no significant difference in the achievement at 'A' level of children from

[1] Robbins, Appendix I, pp. 51–53.

working-class homes, whether they come from the upper, middle or lower third of the ability range admitted to grammar school at eleven.[1] The selective effect of the handicaps that operate up to sixteen including the difficulties caused by homework conditions and by attitudes within the family that are unhelpful to education seem to cease to operate once the sixth form is reached (W. D. Furneaux, 1961); it would seem that if the child is unusual enough to overcome these hurdles before sixteen, he will have no difficulty in continuing to do so up to eighteen.

(v) *Entry to Higher Education.* The higher one passes up the educational system, the more complex becomes exact analysis of the selection process, since there are more alternatives open to the student. He may, for example, wish to go to university, teacher-training college, or one of various types of technical college. In addition there are many eighteen-year-olds who want, and by any criterion ought, to leave the full-time educational system to enter their chosen vocation whether this is industry, commerce or the armed forces. There is a legal compulsion upon local authorities to supply education to all those who are within the ages when a child must be at school, but after fifteen the position becomes less clear and certainly in Britain the State has never undertaken to provide higher education to all who want it. As the provision of secondary education has grown in this century, so the proportion of first-generation grammar school parents has risen; they in their turn have swelled the demand for more education for their children. So in the 1950's the supply of places in universities never met the demand from qualified applicants. In fact in the late 1950's the chances of reaching university possibly moved against children with the necessary qualifications, so great was the demand.[2]

This increase in the competition for higher education led to multiple applications to universities and teacher-training colleges or to combinations of the two. It also led to a rise in the supply of higher education by such institutions as technical colleges, for some of whom this title almost became inappropriate so great was the weight of their work of a non-technical nature. Clearly rigidities in the supply of places of various types in higher education has resulted in students modifying their vocations or their demands for a particular type of higher education. It seems that unsuccessful applicants to university have entered teacher training

[1] Robbins, Appendix I, pp. 45–46.
[2] A. Little and J. Westergaard, 'The Trend of Class Differentials in Educational Opportunity in England and Wales', *British Journal of Sociology*, December 1964, pp. 310–11.

and further education. In the latter case they have been easily absorbed, but in teacher training, despite a great rise in provision, the standard of entry has had to rise to ration out the scarce places.[1]

Some indication of how the selection process has worked by this level is given by the following figures which relate to a sample of twenty-one-year-olds born in 1940–41. Of those with an IQ of 130 or more at eleven whose parents were in non-manual occupations 41 per cent were in full-time higher education compared with 30 per cent of the children of parents in manual occupations. The gap in attendance became greater with lower measured intelligence; for the IQ range 115–29 the percentages were 34 and 15, and for the range 100–14 they were 17 and 6 respectively.[2] Yet, as in the case of the sixth form, once at the university students seem to achieve equally well regardless of social class.[3]

(vi) 'The Second Way'. This is the name given in Germany to the route by which intelligent adults or adolescents can achieve higher education despite their lack of the equivalent of a grammar school education. Is this concept relevant to Britain? Mention has been made twice above of the need for adequate facilities for the further education of those who leave school early to go into industry or commerce. It has been traditional in Britain for children who either failed to achieve their full capability through the usual educational channels or for those who were not even granted this opportunity to use the facilities provided by further education as their second way. There are very adequate facilities of this nature in Britain, and they have proved very flexible in the face of the varied needs put on them by the country's rising demand for education of all types. Their flexibility has partly offset the rigidity of other institutions.[4] But it must be stressed that this second way is a long, arduous and even inefficient route.

The evidence collected by the Crowther Committee showed that of all the students who start the course for a National Certificate without prior exemption, which is usually gained by passing 'O' or 'A' level examinations beforehand, only 26 per cent eventually gain an Ordinary National Certificate and only 10 per cent a Higher National Certificate.

[1] Robbins, Appendix I, pp. 125–6.
[2] Robbins, Appendix I, p. 42.
[3] See J. G. H. Newfield, 'The Academic Performance of British University Students', p. 120 and R. R. Dale, 'Reflections on the Influence of Social Class on Student Performance at the University', both in *The Sociological Review: Monograph No. 7*, Keele, 1963.
[4] See S. Cotgrove, *Technical Education and Social Change*, London, 1958.

The former examination is at technician, and the latter at technologist level. For those who are exempt from the first year of the course the proportions of successes rise to 51 per cent and 26 per cent at the respective levels. At the lower level of the craftsman the City and Guild five-year courses are relevant. Here in a sample of five courses in the field of engineering 28 per cent passed the examination that marks the end of the third year and a mere 6 per cent that at the end of the fifth year. However, many of the students in both sets of examinations took longer than the minimum periods to succeed. Many of those whose attendance was unsuccessful, if judged by the criterion of passing the examination, must have learnt much of a useful and educative nature. Yet these failure rates are very high. The main reasons for failure were found to be weakness in mathematics and having to rely on evening classes only, a very real strain on an adolescent. In fact, the two reasons are to an extent interconnected. Students who leave school at fifteen cannot achieve a high standard of mathematics, a subject which demands more time, regular practice and individual tuition than can be given to it in the compressed type of course necessarily prevalent in part-time education. The selective effect of these courses can be seen from figures relating to students on National Certificate courses in 1956 and 1958. Not only did many fail, but the farther along this route students went, the more difficult it became for students from the lower social classes to succeed. Thus between the first and fifth year of the course for the Higher National Certificate the proportion of students with fathers in administrative and professional occupations doubled, rising from 10·6 per cent to 20 ·3 per cent, whilst that for students whose fathers were in skilled work dropped from 31·5 per cent to 25·4 per cent, and for those with fathers in semi-skilled work from 18 per cent to 13 per cent.[1]

(vii) *Summary*. It would seem to be inevitable that at some point in any educational system selection must take place in order that the training may begin of those who are to fill the positions of responsibility in a society that needs a high level of education in its potential leaders. However, it is apparent that in Britain the organization of the educational system is such that selection begins in the primary school and goes on up to the point of entry to the sixth form. The initial selection in the primary school into streams hinders the full development of capability. The next selection at eleven divides children into successes and failures,

---

[1] *15 to 18*, Vol. I, Chapters 30 and 31.

many of whom regardless of their measured intelligence come to think of themselves and their future in the light of this allocation. This results in a greater loss of capability than would be expected because of the overlap in I Q scores of the children in the different types of secondary schools. This overlap is due to the very different rates of provision of grammar school places throughout the country, which can also be regarded as due to institutional rigidity. The existence of a second way does not seem to recover much of the capability already lost. This selection process, albeit unintentionally, works against certain social classes so that there is a social class bias in the proportion of those undergoing education beyond sixteen. This is a dysfunction which is largely inherent in the present organization of the educational system, and it must cause a considerable loss of capability.

3. *Conclusion*

Before concluding this chapter there is one possibility that must be considered, though for Britain it is as yet a hypothetical one. It is possible that the increase in educational opportunity may be so great that aspirations for upward social mobility are generated in excess of the number of high positions that are available to the population of the country. In this case it is no longer a case of selecting the most able out of all those qualified to go on to higher education; all will go anyway. Nor is it so necessary to develop the potential capability of the country; this is being done. The function of selection is replaced by that of 'cooling out'[1] those with excess mobility aspirations. There is one area in the world where this has become the problem, namely the state of California in the USA. Here more than half the population continues in education beyond the age of eighteen. A large proportion of these students go to junior colleges. An important part is played in these colleges by the counselling department. As soon as is possible, those students are discovered who have reached their highest academic attainment level and who are not capable of going on to take a university course. These students are counselled towards courses that end at junior college. This is done in such a way that the minimum possible psychological disturbance is caused.

This is a problem that is only marginal to Britain, since the main form in which it is met is amongst some of those wrongly selected for grammar school. Such children have been placed in an ethos that leads them to

[1] Burton R. Clark, in *The Reader*.

hold aspirations that are higher than their capabilities will bear. Of this problem little is known, though a somewhat similar and possibly more important dysfunction of the grammar school has recently been described (F. Musgrove, 1963). The educational system selects with some efficiency the type of child who can succeed in the grammar school. This school has become the recognized avenue of upward social mobility, particularly in that it leads to the higher levels of the labour force. Yet there is some evidence that the type of child that can succeed in the grammar school may not necessarily be the type with the psychological qualities that are needed for undertaking a career in the jobs to which the grammar school now leads. It is almost as if the educational system is now organized to select the children who will succeed in tasks that the grammar school has evolved autonomously, but which have no necessary connection with the future of its pupils.

This problem is typical of the many possible conflicts between education in its individual and social contexts. We have been examining the selection function and this is to view education in its social context. It is clear that the position in Britain is complicated by the private system. However, a consideration of the way the educational system undertakes selection shows firstly that, looked at in various ways, there is a pool of capability which is not at the moment fully used. Secondly, given the present structure of education, which is predominantly the tripartite system, we may ask, are the most capable children selected? It seems that the rigid form of organization makes it difficult to meet demographic change and hence brings about a loss of capability. Within the system children of lower social class still appear to be at a disadvantage, though this is not so gross as formerly. But one can ask a deeper question. Once the children are segregated, even assuming absolutely 'fair' initial selection, is such segregation in itself dysfunctional? The answer, based on studies of the results of streaming, seems to be that it is so. The cumulative nature of both processes may be summed up by repeating some figures quoted in Chapter 5: when the sample of children born in 1940–41 investigated by the Robbins Committee had reached the age of twenty-one, those who were children of fathers in non-manual occupations had greater chances of academic achievement than those who were children of fathers in manual occupations at each IQ level and at each stage of the educational system. The one exception was for the most able at the end of their course in the fifth form. The ratios were a follows:

I.Q.	Degree Level Courses	At least two 'A' levels	At least five 'O' levels
130 and over	2·06	1·43	0·97
115–29	2·12	1·64	1·24
100–14	3·00	1·50	1·68

(Robbins, Appendix I, p. 43.)

Segregation at primary and secondary levels hinders development of capability and leads to low aspirations. The selection process fulfils the prophecy upon which the system is founded, but equally surely it lessens the capability available to this country.

BIBLIOGRAPHY

(i) *The Pool of Capability*

A. H. Halsey (ed.), *Ability and Educational Opportunity*, OEEC, 1961 (especially Chapters 2, 5 and 6).

P. E. Vernon, 'The Pool of Ability', in *The Sociological Review: Monograph No. 7*, 'Sociological Studies in British University Education', Keele, 1963.

15 to 18 (Crowther Report), Vol. II, 1960.

Higher Education (Robbins Report), App. I, 1963 (especially Part Three).

(ii) *Selection*

J. C. Daniels, 'The Effects of Streaming in the Primary School', *British Journal of Educational Psychology*, February and June 1961.

J. W. B. Douglas, *The Home and the School*, London, 1964.

J. E. Floud, A. H. Halsey and F. M. Martin, *Social Class and Educational Opportunity*, London, 1956.

J. E. Floud and A. H. Halsey, 'Intelligence Tests, Social Class, and Selection for Secondary Schools' in *The Reader*.

W. D. Furneaux, *The Chosen Few*, London, 1961.

H. T. Himmelweit, 'Social Status and Secondary Education since the 1944 Act', in D. V. Glass (ed.) op. cit., 1954.

F. Musgrove, *The Migratory Élite*, London, 1963.

T. Veness, *School Leavers*, London, 1962.

Early Leaving, 1954.

15 to 18 (Crowther Report), Vol. I, 1959 (especially Part Six).

M

12

The Economic Function

By this stage the importance of the connection between education and the economy has been made very clear. In the light of this knowledge we must examine in some detail the way in which the educational system helps to maintain the economy. Despite difficulties of exact measurement the economists have shown that education plays an important part in the rate at which productivity rises. Very briefly the economic function of the educational system is to provide the labour force with manpower that matches the needs of the economy and to give future consumers the knowledge that they will require. Manpower needs can be studied in terms of both quantity and of quality. For example, a certain number of physicists or barristers are wanted each year with knowledge or training in certain specified fields. Quantity and quality are not independent of each other, since the quality, or level of skill, of the bulk of the labour force will be one of the determinants of the quantity of supervisory staff, for instance, the number of foremen, that are necessary. Thus in the USA more highly qualified supervisory staff seem to be needed than in Germany, where the proportion of well-trained craftsmen in the labour force is greater.[1] However, for simplicity of analysis we shall consider the qualitative and quantitative aspects separately here.

A. Qualitative Considerations

In an advanced industrial society such as Britain we tend to take for granted the fact that we have an efficient labour force. We forget that in the eighteenth and nineteenth centuries men and women had to be recruited to industry, and we overlook that in many countries this process had to be achieved by force. Once in industrial employment workers must be committed to this way of life and perhaps to one occupation or

[1] F. H. Harbison and others, 'Steel Management on Two Continents" *Management Science*, October 1955.

even one employer for a period of time. The 'here today, gone tomorrow' attitude found among workers in some under-developed countries is a considerable handicap to efficiency in industry. Workers at all levels of the labour force must have the skills and the knowledge appropriate to contemporary techniques, and they must be willing to use these attainments to the utmost if the economy is to prosper. This willingness can come only from a strong desire to work hard and to produce. Such a desire is fostered by the conscious or unconscious attachment to a set of commonly held assumptions. The labour force of an industrial country must be both skilled and 'committed' (C. Kerr and others, 1962).

1. *Skills*

In the first place, then, the educational system must play its part in laying the foundations upon which industrial skills can be built. In the field of technical education the industrial skills themselves will very often be taught. An example is typewriting. Can we go as far as to say that the connections between the economy and the educational system must be so arranged that what is taught at school matches what industry requires? Many would argue that education should be directed to an end such as 'the good life' and not harnessed to the needs of industry. However, once the ultimate end is given, it is true to say that the educational system can be organized so that it gives more or less attention to the requirements of the economy.

There is no conflict between the present needs of the economy and the broader aims of education over much of the curriculum. Both demand the thorough teaching of the elementary techniques of the 'three R's' together with some knowledge of the social subjects such as history and geography. When work may be trivial and leisure long, the place of the aesthetic subjects is important in answering the need for men to live a richer life (G. H. Bantock, 1963). Without any attempt at cynicism it may be observed that, if such an education forms the basis for future happiness, then contented men will make better workmen.

We have already noted many recent developments in education that are helpful to the economy. Such are the tendency to stay longer at school, the development of technical education and the rising proportion of adolescents granted day release. New institutions have grown up outside the educational system. In many large firms youths are taught by instructors who are experienced craftsmen and who also have often had training in the imparting of technical skills. A new type of school has been born with its own hierarchy of headteacher (the education officer) and assistant teachers (craft instructors). There are similar developments at managerial level, usually at industry rather than company level (industrial public schools ?). The passing of the Industrial Training Act in 1964 should eventually spread these improved practices to much British industry and help to systematize the place of industrial education within the national structure of education. The Act has put financial responsibility in the main on industry itself.

Changes within school subjects themselves can be of importance. An obvious example is the revolution in the teaching of mathematics in both primary and secondary schools. Any improvement in mathematical competency has a direct relevance for future members of a modern labour force. Here we shall consider in rather more detail two instances of the way the present teaching of school subjects can have indirect economic consequences. The first will be functional for the economy and the second dysfunctional.

Earlier we isolated a part of the curriculum to which we gave the name education for consumption. This attempts to teach children to discriminate between the many choices open to them. Discrimination in consumption ensures that the economy uses resources efficiently. The schools have come to play an important part in fulfilling the need for education for consumption. A seminal work was published as long ago as 1933, *Culture and Environment*, by F. R. Leavis and D. Thompson. The authors aimed to apply the methods developed in the practical criticism of English literature to a criticism of the whole environment surrounding the individual.[1] The influence of this book has been great, and today secondary schools run courses that aim to teach children to examine advertisements for the use of emotive language and question-begging statements. Leavis and Thompson wrote mainly for sixth forms, but teachers are giving lessons with the same aim to fifteen-year-olds in secondary modern schools. A syllabus for the CSE in Commerce contains a section on 'Buying Wisely', which includes 'The Comparison of Price, Quality and Value', 'The use of Advertisement', and a section on 'Protection of the Consumer'.[2] This is an example of teaching that is often pursued with a frankly moral aim, but which has economic conse-

[1] For a recent study of education in this context see Raymond Williams, *Communications*, London, 1962 (Penguin), pp. 100–111.
[2] *L.C.C. Secondary Schools Certificate Examination, Regulations and Syllabuses* (1961?), p. 7.

quences. In as much as children become more discriminating consumers, the schools are contributing to the efficient running of a *laissez-faire* economy.

A recent survey by the Oxford University Department of Education (1963) indicates that the attitudes conveyed unconsciously through the present teaching of science may have effects for the economy of the opposite nature. Firstly, the academic attainments and vocational aspirations of 1,459 sixth-form boys were investigated. Secondly, 1,434 sixth-form boys in seventy-six grammar and public schools completed questionnaires; the aim was to find out what opinions the boys held about scientific and technological occupations. From these two sets of data it was hoped to find out what effect school science teaching has on a boy's choice of his future occupation. It was found that a far greater proportion of boys whom their headmasters considered capable of gaining first-class honours degrees chose careers in pure science as opposed to careers in technology. Comparison was then made with certain European countries. In Sweden the most able boys appeared to take courses in applied rather than in pure science; in Holland proportions were more equal; in Western Germany, though more able boys went to pure science courses, the proportion was in no way as great as in Britain. It seems that science teachers who are products of pure science departments in universities perpetuate in their own pupils the attitudes that they had learnt as undergraduates. This can be seen from the second part of the investigation in which the boys were asked to rank in order of prestige nineteen professions, including technological occupations such as civil engineer and metallurgist. Doctors and nuclear physicists were given the highest prestige. No engineers or technologists appeared in the six most chosen occupations. When asked about the kind of scientific career that they wished to pursue the largest proportion gave research as their first choice (35 per cent). To the British sixth-former the image of the white-coated physicist doing research in his laboratory is a force that powerfully affects his occupational choice and the attitudes that govern his approach to his job. Comparisons were made with France and Germany, where the results were by no means as pronounced as in Britain. The German 'sixth-former' gave much prestige to a technological career. The schools would seem to be imparting an attitude that is dysfunctional to the economy in two respects. Firstly, too few able boys are choosing technological employment. Secondly, in Chapter 7 we noted that the proportion of pure scientists in industry was much lower in the UK than in the USA. This must be in large part due to the attitudes transmitted in the schools about science and its uses.

The economic function of the educational system is not restricted to teaching skills and to matters of the curriculum, though these are the easiest to understand and, providing the means of communication between education and the economy are good, the solution of problems should be easy. Of far more importance are the attitudes that the schools often transmit unconsciously. There are in addition those assumptions that all must hold if the economy is to work smoothly. We must pass now to the question of how the educational system can help to provide a 'committed' labour force.

2. Commitment of the Labour Force

Any consideration of the values that the members of the labour force of a country must hold if they are to be wholly committed to industry must take into account the type of the economic system and the stage of its development. In a traditional society such as medieval Europe or Japan before the 1860's a conservative approach to the economy was necessary; an apprentice or a peasant in the fifteenth century learnt how to conserve tradition not how to forge it anew. We have seen that a capitalist country in the early stages of industrialization probably needs a different set of values from one that is more fully developed. Britain today has an economy of a mixed nature characterized by rather more *laissez-faire* than Government intervention, but also marked by large productive units. There seem to be three important sets of values that are relevant to the smooth working of a semi-capitalist economy. These are the value attributed to a successful life, more particularly as measured by whether or not high wages or salary are earned, the value given to equality of opportunity so that the able can 'get on', and, finally, the value put on change (E. Ginzberg, 1956). We shall examine each of these values in turn to find out what part the educational system plays in transmitting them.

(i) *Success in life*. Theoretically the mainspring of a *laissez-faire* economy is the attempt by all to buy as cheaply as possible and to sell as dearly as possible. It is assumed that a man will try to earn as high a wage or salary as he can; allowance must be made for any advantageous conditions of work such as great security in the job or good chances of promotion. In theory the various wage-rates direct labour to the highest return and ensure efficiency, since the employer will only pay what a man is worth to him. In fact the wage system does not work as smoothly as this, but what matters here is whether the labour force strives primarily after monetary rewards or gives the wage a low priority as part of its total reward.

In the USA children are imbued with the money-making spirit from an early age. The family plays a large part in the child's early years in encouraging him to work for money on every possible occasion. In the school each generation is inspired with the model of the self-made man. It is not without significance that many Americans work their way through university, whilst British undergraduates receive grants at one of the highest rates in the world. In the 1950's about 60 per cent of graduates in the USA came from what the British would call the working classes, a much higher proportion than in Britain. Much of this educated manpower goes into industry where rewards are high. The economy of the USA may base its efficiency on great natural advantages, but its industry makes the most of this competitive position by ensuring that its management is capable and committed to its economic assumptions.

European management has different attitudes towards money-making. Financial achievement is seen as only a part of the satisfactions yielded by the job; the true essence is considered to be doing the job itself.[1] The place of the school in the initial formation of such values can be vital. To most teachers in grammar schools any emphasis on money-seeking is unpleasant and conflicts with many of the ideals that they wish to impart, particularly that of service. There is a tradition in the public schools, which can be traced back to Arnold of Rugby, that the occupation into which a young man ought to go should be marked by the giving of service to the community; such a choice of occupation was truly a vocation and often did not lead to the highest monetary reward consonant with the capability of the man entering the vocation. The connection established by these schools with the learned professions rather than with industry pays tribute to this tradition. The grammar school inherited this ideal in some measure, though a spirit of competition and thrust may replace the ideal of service as the modern grammar school comes to be seen more as a way into the higher levels of industry. Since the grammar school educates the majority of secondary modern teachers, it has transmitted some of the same tradition of service into this new

[1] A. A Lauterbach, 'European Managerial Attitude', *American Economic Review*, May 1955.

form of school. A recent development in these schools has been the growth of schemes such as the Duke of Edinburgh's Award; here again unpaid service to the community is rated highly. In the secondary modern school the relative material poverty of the working class meets the ideal of service fostered by part of the middle class; this conflict of aims further heightens the clash of cultures already described in these schools.

Many of the values taught either consciously or unconsciously in the secondary modern schools do not match the needs of a semi-capitalist system. Carter (1962) found that among secondary modern school leavers in Sheffield the values taught at school had always seemed irrelevant to life as it was actually lived. Beauty and the things of the spirit were insisted on at school, whilst the children often met ugliness and materialism at home and later at work. Teachers advised their pupils to show enthusiasm and loyalty in their future work, but the children found that their workmates scorned these qualities. So the children tended to ignore the advice of the schools, both before leaving school and after starting work. This is a good example of the strains that are possible between education and social institutions. Here the schools are not helping the economy, but they can claim that they aim to redress what is bad in a materialist world.

In the upper levels of the labour force the ideal of service has directed many capable men from industry into the Colonial and Civil Services, and into the professions and politics. A case can be made that until recently industry has been somewhat starved of capable men. Service and security of employment were put before money and risk. As well as an ideal of service the public schools inculcated a strong corporate spirit that continues into adult life and is symbolized by 'the old school tie'. The connections encouraged by this spirit are used for finding jobs and placing business deals. It would make an interesting study to find out how much of the inefficiency in the British economy is due to such circumstances as the giving of a job to an old school friend who is not quite the best man available or the award of a contract to a school acquaintance without its being put out to tender. There also exists a strong corporate feeling in the British working class. This is not a consequence of education, but was born in the industrial struggles of the last hundred years and is symbolized by loyalty to the trade unions.

In the last chapter we saw that the British working class is early conditioned to failure in school examinations and more particularly in the eleven-plus. Selection to the secondary modern school acts as vocational guidance. The aspirations of the children not selected for grammar school are formed in a climate of opinion that limits their horizon. However, conditions vary very much by locality; the types of employment available to school leavers are very different. How do strictly local economic circumstances alter ambitions ? It seems likely that in an area where one industry is predominant, as is often the case in the older industrial areas of the north of this country, the choice of ways of earning a living, and indeed the level of wages, that is open may not meet the varied choices of school leavers. In Carter's survey in Sheffield, a city where employment is predominantly in engineering or the iron and steel industry, 20 per cent of the boys first chose jobs in the city's main industries, but 40 per cent actually obtained their first jobs in these industries. After a year 27 per cent were still in this category. In the case of the girls the proportions choosing, entering and remaining in either office or shop work were more or less constant, but many who wanted to do other work ended up in factories or warehouses; only 7 per cent chose this work, but 21 per cent found themselves doing it after a year. Where a wider range of occupations is available, a match between choices and vacant jobs is more likely. In one such case, namely Ealing, the Youth Employment Service could place 61·4 per cent of boys and 78·5 per cent of girls in their chosen occupations.[1] Vacancies within broad industrial categories more or less matched choices, though within each category there were difficulties. For example, within the occupations categorized as building too many boys wanted to be carpenters.

All these children, therefore, had been placed in a school where their ambitions were aimed towards a range of occupations that could have been below that of which many were capable. Some were unable to do what they wished, a situation hard to avoid under modern conditions. But what is of particular relevance here is that, when asked what were their reasons for their choice of vocation, only 7·6 per cent of the boys and 6·4 per cent of the girls mentioned good pay. Evidence collected in the late 1940's showed that amongst a sample of 300 men aged eighteen and nineteen attitudes towards job incentives varied with measured intelligence. Those with below average I Qs looked to the immediate satisfaction of the job itself; though they rated pay high, the most important incentive to them was the satisfaction found in the job itself, and they were willing to sacrifice pay to be with good workmates. Men

[1] M. D. Wilson, op. cit.

with higher IQs were more individualistic and looked to longer-term incentives, such as promotion prospects, but they in fact ranked pay lower than did those of lower intelligence.[1]

In theory the school could inculcate excess economic ambition into a child in the same way that excess aspirations for social mobility may be generated. This dysfunction would not appear to have occurred in Britain. However, there is evidence of a not dissimilar one. Aspirations may be inculcated that lead capable men to seek reward in a direction dysfunctional to the economy. In the case described above where the schools, particularly the nineteenth-century public schools, encouraged entry to Government, it can be argued that the British Empire of the time demanded able men in those posts, but there is little doubt that the recent stress on science as mediated by British secondary schools has had dysfunctional results. The public and grammar schools have encouraged able boys to study science in the hope of following a scientific career; the boys and their parents have felt the pull of high earnings in the relevant occupations. But the unconscious bias in the teaching of science seems to have diverted too many able young men into pure rather than applied science.

The ideals taught in schools can influence both the choice of vocation and the spirit in which a man will do his life work. It would seem that money-making is not rated highly in Britain and that ambition may be squashed. Whether this is morally right or wrong is not here in question, but it is clear that the higher the value put on making money and 'getting on', the more efficiently will a *laissez-faire* economy run. What the schools teach may or may not match the contemporary moral ethos of the country, but they certainly do not seem to be stressing one of the values needed by our present economic system.

(ii) *Equality of Opportunity*. Very closely allied with much of what has just been said is the value given to equality of opportunity. Again a comparison can be made between the USA and Britain. In the USA there is a belief that anyone can improve himself by his own efforts. There is difference of opinion as to whether there is, in fact, more upward social mobility in the USA than in Britain. One recent major survey (S. M. Lipset and R. Bendix, 1960) found the rates to be about the same in the two countries. But the really important thing is that men believe that they can rise easily up the social ladder. It is probably true to say

[1] L. T. Wilkins, 'Incentives and the Young Worker', *Occupational Psychology*, October 1949.

that this belief is more strongly held in the USA than in Britain, though more now see a chance to rise in Britain as a result of the reforms implicit in the 1944 Education Act.

Formal educational qualifications provide the entrée to the various levels of the labour force, and therefore the educational system has come to be seen as the key to equality of economic opportunity. Formerly the way to improve one's social position was by founding a small business and making a success of it, often with the help of one's family. Now that the size of economic unit has grown this is less often seen as the way. Today the ambitious youth enters a large corporation with the hope of working his way up the hierarchy of management. Large companies must, therefore, select their potential managers with care, and the stress has come to be laid on education as well as on qualities of personality. The chance to rise is still there, but has come to be centred on education. From which schools do our economic leaders come?

In the mid 1950's Rosemary Stewart (1956) [1] carried out a survey of the managers of fifty-one of the sixty-five British companies that had 10,000 or more employees and were not nationalized. Managers were defined as all those above the rank of foreman. Half of all managers had been educated at either a grammar or a public school. However, a greater proportion of senior managers had been at these secondary schools; a third went to public schools and a third to grammar schools. It seems that boys from such schools had more chance of achieving high positions in management than those who came up through the ranks.[2] In fact, the trend seems to be moving further in this direction, as might be expected in view of the greater stress on selecting recruits to management who have formal qualifications. More than a fifth of those aged from thirty-five to thirty-nine, that is the more recent recruits, went to public school as compared with only a tenth of those between fifty-five and fifty-nine. For the same age groups one in four of the younger group had university degrees, whereas only one in ten of the older men had. In Britain those below managerial rank rarely have formal qualifications.[3] In smaller companies there is less stress on educational qualifications, but even

[1] An abridgement of this book has been published as *Managers for Tomorrow*, DSIR, London, 1957.

[2] See T. Lupton and C. S. Wilson, 'The Social Background and Connections of Top Decision Makers', *Manchester School*, January 1959, for the education of London bankers and financiers.

[3] In a survey carried out in two large British iron and steel companies in 1961 the author found that only 1 out of 365 foremen had a degree, 4 had HNC, 6 ONC, and 9 City and Guilds.

here at technician level emphasis is growing. It is by founding such companies that self-made men can make their start, and among such men formal educational qualifications may be rarer. We saw that in these smaller companies nepotism can perhaps occur more easily than in large public limited companies. Both these reasons work against stress on educational qualifications in the management of many small companies.

Nevertheless the trend is towards an emphasis on education by industry and commerce. Equality of educational opportunity has, therefore, become linked with equality of economic opportunity. It has already been shown in the last chapter that in this country there are very much more restricted opportunities for higher education than in the USA. The universities of this country have an intense care for their academic standards. It could be that this leads to a restriction of the places available. A similar attitude will help to limit places in selective secondary schools. A wider educational avenue of the American pattern could lead to greater opportunity; standards might, but need not, fall if the narrow British road were widened. The connection between management and the selective secondary schools is growing closer, and therefore the bias inherent in the present selection of these schools which was described in the last chapter stands in the way of equality of economic opportunity.

(iii) *Acceptance of Change.* The part of the population that is trained in the universities is of great importance, since it contains most of those who will create and mould the new industrial society. It is the graduates of our universities who will make up a large part of those who formulate new ideas, sweep away old organizations and achieve consensus in the midst of change. An easy acceptance of change by workers and management alike is a basic need of a modern industrial society.

It is not only that new techniques must be accepted, but those who produce are also consumers of goods and to keep a modern high consumption economy running consumers must be willing to accept new products at regular intervals. Knowledge about consumers' attitudes towards new products is usually collected by commercial market research rather than academic research, which has tended to concentrate on the problems involved in changes in industrial techniques. Even in this field little exact knowledge exists. Technical innovation brings into being new occupations and may even demand that workers move to another part of the country. Occupational and geographical mobility are as important for full employment as social mobility is for industrial efficiency. Has the educational system as vital a part to play here as it has in the social sphere?

In a traditional economy a son followed his father's occupation and often learnt it from him. Though there is still a tendency in the professions for sons to follow fathers, it is on the whole rare in an industrial society.[1] This is particularly true since the nature of most occupations changes rapidly as new techniques are introduced. The job most young managers or workers are doing today will in all probability no longer exist when their children enter the labour market and, even if it is still called by the same name, the actual work done will be very different (Crowther, 1959). Little is known about the connection between education and attitudes towards economic change. In a survey of a large British iron and steel company the higher levels of the labour force, namely those with a longer education, seem to have been less hostile to technical change. Managers approved of change more than workers. Even at the same level of the labour force those with a higher educational level were more sympathetic towards change; maintenance men, mainly skilled craftsmen, favoured change more than production operatives of the same status.[2] It may well be that just as longer experience of education increases political tolerance, a similar tendency operates in the case of tolerance of economic change. Under full employment the problem is eased somewhat, as a new job should soon be available to replace the old, but the human stresses inherent in such changes make it important to create an easy acceptance of them.

The grammar school seems to act as an avenue of geographical as well as social mobility. The growing concentration of industry in certain areas particularly in the South-east, and growth in the size of production unit demand that many move to other regions to seek their first job. Rural grammar schools channel the more highly educated from the country to the towns, but there is also a high rate of interchange between cities based on educational qualifications gained in grammar schools. Grammar school pupils seem significantly more 'migratory-minded' than those from secondary modern schools. This process affects both sexes, though it seems particularly strong in the case of girls from grammar schools in medium-sized towns, where

[1] R. K. Kelsall, 'Self Recruitment in Four Professions', in D. V. Glass (ed.), op. cit.

[2] W. H. Scott and others, *Technical Change and Industrial Relations*, Liverpool, 1956; see especially pp. 251–3. An abridgement of this book has been published as *Men, Steel, and Technical Change*, DSIR, London, 1957.

sufficient jobs do not exist to match their qualifications (F. Musgrove, 1963).

The exact way that education works towards adaptability is not understood. Certainly in Britain it is not explicit educational policy that an attitude favourable to change should be cultivated in schools, but this need not be so. In Prussia before 1914 a definite policy of the educational system was to make a pliant population. The basic aim was political, but an additional and welcomed result was that the labour force accepted economic change without question. This was a great economic advantage at a time when Prussia was industrializing rapidly. Docility replaced adaptability. Undoubtedly the political price of such a policy would be too high for modern Britain to pay.

As has been made clear, in the light of our present knowledge the main explicit way in which the educational system can help to meet the needs of a rapidly changing economy is by giving its pupils a long and general education. In this way they may excercise what choice they have over their first occupation as wisely as possible and may have a firm educational foundation upon which they may build the various specialisms that they will have to learn throughout their working lives.

This demand on the educational system raises important questions of policy. To what age should young people stay at school ? Purely from an economic point of view does the country require both boys and girls to be educated up to this age ? Who will pay for this policy ? In considering such political issues it must be remembered that education may depend upon the economy to find the resources of men and materials to keep it going, but the economy, as has been shown, very clearly relies upon education to provide it with a labour force that is committed to a modern industrial system, eager to use its capabilities in the economy, and willing to accept rapid change.

B. Quantitative Considerations

Technical innovation very often changes the education required in the labour force of an industry. The invention of nylon and of the other artificial fibres resulted in a need for many more chemists in the textile industries. Innovation can be met in two ways. Firstly, at the point of entry new recruits with the necessary qualifications can be taken direct from the educational system. Secondly, the existing labour force may be retrained; this can put demands on the facilities available for technical

education, and the technical colleges of this country run a wide variety of
ad hoc courses to meet the needs of innovation. A good example is the
large number of courses organized since the late 1950's in the techniques
of automation.

Any consideration of the way the output of the schools and universities
relates to the needs of the labour force is complicated by the fact that
identical qualifications are demanded by different industries. It is very
rare for a qualification to be specific to one industry. The teacher's
certificate is nearly so. Young people with academic qualifications such as
two 'A' or five 'O' level passes may enter a variety of commercial and
industrial occupations. Even in the case of a qualification so apparently
specific as a first degree in metallurgy 80 per cent of those qualifying in
1961–2 went into the engineering and allied industries, a very heterogeneous category.[1] This lack of specificity may be a blessing in disguise
in that it could be a reflection of the need for a sound general education
upon which specialisms can be built. It may, however, be a sign that the
educational system is slow to respond to the more exact needs of the
economy. If, for example, more physicists are required from the universities it will take at least three years to educate them providing that
laboratory space is available and that sufficient youths with the necessary
prior schooling are leaving secondary schools. If the last two conditions
are not fulfilled, an even longer time will be necessary. The gestation
period for educational investment is long. There will still be some at work
in Britain who left school before the 1902 Education Act was passed.[2]
Yet, in theory at least, there is an optimal labour force for any set of
technical and economic conditions. When the educational system has
adjusted to produce the manpower with the qualifications and in the
numbers that meets the needs of the economy, then equilibrium has been
reached.

1. *Equilibrium*

This position is naturally never reached. The educational system tends
towards it as successive changes occur. The quicker the reaction, the
better will education serve the economy. However, strains are possible.
The chronic shortage of scientists and mathematicians since 1945 is an
example. The educational system has two responsibilities. It must make
good the losses from the labour force due to normal retirement and to

[1] *First Employment of University Graduates, 1961–2*, 1963.
[2] For a brief detailed consideration of this point see J. R. Hicks, op. cit., p. 152.

death; these are largely predictable. But it also has to meet the needs of unforeseen innovations. There are two other difficulties. There is free vocational choice in Britain; a school may advise a career, but no one can compel a young person to enter any occupation. In addition, full employment complicates the task; before 1939 there was a pool of unemployed at all levels, and it is possible that men and women changed their vocations in their search for work.

In the period of full employment since 1945 there has been constant talk of the shortage of highly educated and skilled manpower. It is well to be clear in what sense the word 'shortage' is being used. In the strict economic sense shortage implies that the supply of a given grade of labour falls short of the demand for it. This results in a rise in price; in the case of labour the wage or salary rises to ration out the supply. In view of the tones of urgency used in many recent discussions of these shortages a considerable rise in the level of salaries might be expected, especially in the case of scientists and mathematicians. Certainly in Britain for various reasons this has not always been so. Teachers of science and mathematics are in very short supply, but their salaries have risen little more than those of teachers of other subjects who are in far less short supply. 'Shortage' has been used in a second and not strictly economic sense to describe a state where not only the supply, but the demand, is too low. This condition may be caused by a lack of knowledge of what qualifications are actually required in a job or by dysfunctional attitudes towards the relevant branch of knowledge. Both of these forces have probably influenced the long neglect of science by British industry. This type of shortage has been called 'an unmet need'.[1] The criterion here may be comparison with the proportions of a type of labour with a given level of education employed in another industry or even in another country, or it may be based on some measurement of economic returns. In all these cases there are formidable statistical problems of calculation.

Can equilibrium be reached more quickly with or without Government intervention? In the nineteenth century many in Britain believed that 'the invisible hand' of the *laissez-faire* economists would force the schools to meet the needs of the economy. Only rarely have attempts been made in the twentieth century to interfere with the flow of labour from the educational system to the economy, and these have usually been as a result of war. Since 1945, however, the problem of shortages has grown

[1] J. Jewkes, 'How Much Science?' *Economic Journal*, March 1960.

so acute that Government intervention has become politically possible. Action has taken three main forms. Educational institutions have been given aid on condition that it will be used for a specific purpose; universities have received financial assistance to build laboratories. The Government has also given great publicity to deficiencies of manpower; the prominence given to scientific and technical education since 1956 may be quoted and a particular care has been the drive to recruit more teachers. Lastly, there have been regular attempts to forecast the future demands for manpower so that educational institutions, particularly at the highest level, may try to match the expected needs, thereby easing the way to equilibrium between supply and demand.

2. Forecasting

At the national level the Government has issued several White Papers attempting to forecast the future needs of labour in the economy.[1] Some large firms make estimates of their future needs of managers and craftsmen, in which case analysis will be purely at a local level, though the same difficulties underlie forecasts by companies as those by the Government. The Government's estimates have been carefully compiled with the help of the industries concerned. Yet they have gone awry within the brief period of three years.

The reasons for this failure are both economic and educational. At a time of rapid technical change the educational system takes time to answer to the new needs of the economy even where its institutions are very adaptable. But apart from any educational consideration assumptions of an economic nature underlie any attempt to foresee the needs for trained manpower. An industry that expresses a demand for a particular type of educated and skilled man may find that by the time the educational system has trained him he is no longer required. This may be due to the introduction of a new technique or to a change in the competitive strength of the industry in overseas markets. Again a basic assumption is that the wage structure will remain unaltered. An industry may offer a salary that influences a school leaver to start a sandwich course at a College of Advanced Technology, but by the time he qualifies some four years later the salary in another industry may tempt the graduate away from the industry that he originally intended to enter. Lastly, it is not

---

[1] e.g. *Advisory Council on Scientific Policy, Committee of Scientific Manpower, Scientific and Engineering Manpower in Great Britain*, 1956 and 1959; *The Long-Term Demand for Scientific Manpower*, 1961; and *Manpower Studies*, No. 1, 1964.

possible to say whether or not the forecast itself will affect the future supply of labour. Probably the most valuable effect of forecasts so far has been to give publicity to the shortage of trained manpower in certain fields, thereby influencing the direction of recruitment to the labour force. The need for scientists has been stimulated in industry and the knowledge of openings has been transmitted to the educational system. The 'unmet need' is converted into a true shortage. Despite this result forecasts do not yet appear to have been very successful tools of economic planning.[1] It must be made clear that a fully planned economy will have much the same economic and educational problems in matching the supply of and the demand for labour. There is one major difference, namely that in many planned economies direction of labour replaces free choice of occupations.

The achieving of an equilibrium position between the supply of and the demand for labour is made more difficult by the gradual realization that an 'unmet need' exists. Over the last century in Britain an escalator effect has been at work; when plans for educational expansion have been made to meet one level of needs, a deeper level has been discovered leading to further needs. There seem to be two influences apart from that of technical change at work here to raise the demand for education. There is the natural tendency for education to create a desire for more education. But there are also various economic tendencies; for instance the growing proportion of the labour force in maintenance work and in the tertiary sector perpetuate the rising demand for educated manpower with specific qualifications. If forecasting is almost impossible except in broad terms, we are again forced to take up the position that education can best help the economy not by attending to the exact numbers that are following a specific type of education, but by concentrating on giving a broad general education that meets the needs of a technological age.

3. *The Pool of Capability and the Labour Force*
Before deciding that the educational system is carrying out this part of its economic function well, further consideration must be given to the pool of capability. In the last chapter this pool was analysed purely in terms of social selection; here its connection with the labour force will be examined. There is an upper limit to the numbers possessing a given

[1] For some comments on the whole problem of forecasting manpower needs see *Scientific and Technical Manpower (1962)*, 1963, pp. 18–19; Robbins Report 1963, pp. 71–73 and op. cit., Appendix 4, p. 95.

level of capability in any country. The question arises whether the educational system is organized in such a way that manpower needs are met as nearly as the available supply of different levels of capability allows. There is no measure of 'capability' in the sense that the word is used here. The only possibility is to state the argument in terms of measured intelligence, whilst realizing that the case is open to criticism.[1] It can be argued that, if the factor of capability could be isolated, its attributes would be very similar to those of measured intelligence. More particularly its distribution throughout the population would follow the same law as that for IQ. Each level of the labour force requires a minimum IQ. A manager must have a higher IQ than an operative in order to do his work. It seems that the minimum IQ's required by the respective levels of the labour force are approximately as follows: senior executives 130; technologists, such as professional engineers, 120; technicians, such as junior laboratory workers, 110; skilled craftsmen 100; semi-skilled and unskilled operatives less than 100. It is true that these are minimum IQ's and a worker may decide to do a job which demands a lower IQ than he possesses.

The distribution of measured intelligence amongst the population falls along the curve of normal error and therefore is of the shape shown in Fig. I.

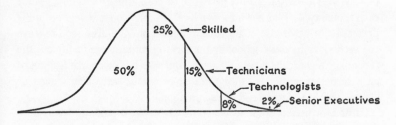

FIG. I

In each of the IQ ranges shown only a certain proportion of the population falls, and therefore there is a limit to the actual numbers capable of working at each of the levels of the labour force.

In an analysis of the possible effects of automation on education J. F. Coales (1958) has pointed out that, where an educational system is

[1] See a letter by Prof. P. E. Vernon in *British Journal of Educational Studies*, November 1958.

selective and where each level of the educational system is strongly associated with a given level of the labour force, the cut-off points for selection for the different types of secondary school may be such that the supply of educated manpower does not match the needs of the economy. Using realistic assumptions Coales calculated that this may well be the case by 1975 for one important range of occupations. The level necessary to become a technician is that now provided in the main by the grammar school for which the minimum I Q is about 113, though there are large regional differences which bear little relation to the needs of the labour force. But it would appear that, unless the same education is given to those with an I Q of 110 and above, there is likely to be a shortage of those capable of becoming qualified technicians, the I Q range 113 to 120 not being large enough to fill the probable needs of industry. This type of analysis raises the whole problem of the relationship between the different types of secondary school and the labour force.

4. *The Structure of Secondary Education and the Labour Force*
Secondary schools can be thought of as graded series of take-off ramps into the labour force (J. E. Floud and A. H. Halsey, 1956). Each type of secondary school aims towards a definite range of occupations. This can be seen very clearly from the existence of predominant leaving ages for each school type. This age implies a level of education and very often the possession or otherwise of a formal qualification. Children tend to leave the secondary modern school at the legal minimum age of fifteen, the secondary technical school at sixteen after a five-year course leading to an external examination, the grammar or public school at sixteen or eighteen after a higher level of examination.

Although there is some overlapping each school tends to lead into a definite level of the labour force. The public school historically has served the professions and the needs of the Government at home and overseas. Particularly since 1945 it has come to have stronger connections with top management in commerce and industry; perhaps this new emphasis offsets the lack of openings in the former Empire to which young men from these schools might have expected to go. The grammar school has come to feed the lower levels of management; almost never do grammar school boys become foremen, which in Britain, unlike the USA, is not a career grade, but the highest level to which a capable and ambitious operative can aspire. The secondary technical school tends to prepare technicians and skilled craftsmen; some of the latter may hope to rise to junior managerial level. The secondary modern school is strongly associated with the operative and craftsmen level.

Prior to the 1944 Education Act many children of less wealthy parents could hope to rise up the labour force, certainly to the level of foreman, if not beyond, although they had left school at the legal minimum age. Now these more capable youths are selected at eleven-plus for a grammar school education and therefore tend to enter the higher levels of the labour force. The process ensures a fuller use of the pool of capability, but it raises questions about the intellectual quality of the lower levels of the labour force. One important issue is what will be the future source from which foremen are to be recruited. Management may have to re-assess the position of foreman and start to feed back ex-grammar school boys into the labour force at this level as junior supervisors with the chance of promotion.

If there is a shortage of educated manpower at any level of the labour force, then clearly the structure of the educational system must be arranged so that it gives the maximum of help or the minimum of hindrance to the economy. The schools must be organized so that they do all they can to develop capability and so that no one shall have his aspirations limited, as far as they are realistic. But, as Coales has pointed out, by 1975 this country may well be short of technicians because the secondary schools associated with this level of the labour force select only those with an I Q of 113 and above, whereas the work can be done by those with an I Q of around 110 and above. Those in the range from 110 to 113 are channelled off into the secondary modern schools and into a lower level of employment.

5. *Vocational Guidance*

The actual transition from school to job is vital, since it is at this point that the new recruits, as opposed to re-trained adults, enter the labour force. Changes in the direction of recruitment in answer to new tech-niques can be made here. It is important to consider at what stage and by what means children are shown the occupational opportunities open to them. Vocational guidance now exists at all levels. In the universities there are Appointments Boards that link higher education to the economy. The public and grammar schools now frequently have Careers Masters who specialize in giving advice on jobs. Finally, there is the

Youth Employment Service, a Government-sponsored organization, that operates particularly for secondary modern, but also for grammar, school leavers. This service was established by legislation whereby local authorities are permitted to incorporate the vocational guidance service into their educational service, if they wish. Where a local authority does not opt to do so, the Ministry of Labour is responsible. Therefore the service is not uniform in organization throughout the country. It is not therefore surprising to find that the Youth Employment Service does not wield great influence.

In a survey of Lancashire engineering and cotton towns made in 1950[1] it was found that Youth Employment Officers only placed between 30 and 50 per cent of secondary modern school leavers in their first job. In Sheffield, Carter (1962) found that in 1959 just under two-thirds of the boys in his sample entered the jobs recommended by the Youth Employment Officers; as a result of job changes the proportion fell to a half. In the case of girls the proportion was still about three-quarters after a year, probably because of the rather narrower range of occupations available. Contact with the youths starts during their last year at school. Most young people have made their decision of occupation before the Youth Employment Officer speaks to them and these choices are respected, although these decisions seem to be made in a very haphazard fashion. There is no guarantee that the chosen job suits the youth concerned. Many youths are influenced by parents, relations or school friends, whose detailed knowledge about occupations has been found to be scanty and unreliable.

There has been one attempt to set forth a general theory of occupational choice. This was made by the American Eli Ginzberg and his associates.[2] Choice is seen as a process that passes through three stages. First the child makes a fantasy choice; this is the stage when a boy wants to be a fireman or a spaceman. Gradually he adjusts to reality and reaches the second stage of making a tentative choice in which probabilities, are recognized. Finally a realistic choice must be made in which compromise is usually necessary to meet the prevailing economic conditions. The aim of the Youth Employment Service is to help the child pass from the second to the third stages in such a way that as few youths as possible

[1] G. Jahoda, 'Job Attitudes and Job Choice among Secondary Modern School Leavers', *Occupational Psychology*, April and November 1952.

[2] See E. Ginzberg and others, *Occupational Choice: An Approach to a General Theory*, New York, 1951. For a brief account see T. Caplow, *The Sociology of Work*, New York, 1954, pp. 226–8.

become 'flounderers', who attain their ultimate occupation by a series of short trials in jobs for which they are unsuitable.[1]

It must be added that in Britain most workers are placed in jobs at all levels of the labour force by interview and without the help of any psychological testing. In the interviews personality as well as educational attainment is assessed. The interview is known to be a fickle tool and social background can unconsciously influence decisions. The aim of many interviewers is consciously to assess social factors. A public school education may be considered important for an industrial appointment on social rather than educational grounds. Social background can influence the work of the Youth Employment Officer in that he may consciously place secondary modern school leavers in jobs that match their family background. In both these cases the placings can be defended as matching the needs of the workers and the companies. However, it is clear that there is need for the closer integration of this service into the educational system, so that children can be helped to a wise choice by learning accurate details as early as possible.

3. *Conclusion*

In its economic function the educational system has to observe both quantitative and qualitative criteria. Schools inculcate ideals that can help or hinder the economy, but the curriculum best suited to the rapidly changing needs of a modern economy seems to be that preferred by most teachers on strictly educational grounds, namely a broad general education ensuring both literacy and numeracy pursued to as late an age as possible. To organize schooling in this way would also seem to assist the economy by inculcating an attitude favourable to change. The fundamental difficulties in accurately forecasting the needs of the labour force leads to the same conclusion. Therefore on the criteria of both quality and quantity the same type of curriculum is needed. However, the actual structure of the educational system has also to be considered. This may be dysfunctional in that the pool of capability may not be developed in the way that matches the needs of the economy, as mediated by the labour force. The situation can be made worse by institutions which are ancillary to the educational system, but which are not usually considered in Britain to be a part of it; such are apprenticeship and the method of giving vocational guidance.

[1] E. M. and M. Eppel, 'Young Workers at a County College', *British Journal of Educational Psychology*, February 1953, report that half of their sample of 380 had held more than one job even at fifteen years of age.

It is apparent that there may be conflict between the ideals needed for a smoothly working economy and those inculcated by the ethos of the schools. A *laissez-faire* economy requires on the production side a positive attitude towards money-making and 'getting on' and on the consumption side there must be an eagerness to 'keep up with the Joneses'. These attitudes have not been greatly favoured by British teachers. Such conflicts may be, as is probably true in this case, due to autonomous developments rather than to policy decisions. It is none the less true that, if dysfunctional these tensions must be discovered so that they may be resolved in the light of what the country wants as its educational aim.

It is fitting to end the functional analysis of the educational system contained in this Part by indicating that political decisions in pursuit of aims involving one function that education can serve may lead to dysfunction in another sphere. This may happen fortuitously or because there was insufficient thought before the political decision was taken. In this chapter an example has been given. In the 1944 Act the main political aim was the provision of equality of educational opportunity, and the stress was laid on the function of selection. Undoubtedly this helped the economy by developing capability, but very little thought has ever been given to the way that the quality of the lower levels of the labour force will be altered. Yet in its economic function the educational system is responsible for the schooling of all levels of the labour force. One more example must suffice. In a previous chapter it was indicated that an examination system which can in many ways help in the function of selection may hinder the development of the creativity that is so essential if the educational system is to fulfil its innovatory function.

Functional analysis of social institutions, carried out in as neutral a way as possible, can bring such conflicts to light. This can be done for social institutions in their existing forms, but it can also precede political decisions to alter institutions. This should help to prevent the creation of social institutions that are structured to produce conflict. Such an analysis will also show where conflict may emerge and thereby force a clear decision on political priorities. The functions of education are complex and closely inter-related. To change the educational system sets off a re-structuring of these relationships. The tools needed for the functional analysis of the educational system have been provided in the second part of this book. It would give a clearer picture of the problems

involved in such political decisions as the re-organization of the secondary school system, if the argument were to be carried as far as possible in
these terms, before the final political decisions were made.

BIBLIOGRAPHY

(i) *Qualitative Considerations*

G. H. Bantock, *Education in an Industrial Society*, London, 1963.

M. P. Carter, *Home, School and Work*, Oxford, 1962 (especially Chapters
5, 6 and 13).

E. Ginzberg, 'Education and National Efficiency in the USA, *The
Yearbook of Education*, 1956.*

S. M. Lipset and R. Bendix, *Social Mobility in an Industrial Society*,
London, 1959.

C. Kerr, J. T. Dunlop, F. H. Harbison, and C. A. Myers, *Industrialization and Industrial Man*, London, 1962.

F. Musgrove, Oxford University Department of Education, *Technology
and the Sixth Form Boy*, Oxford, 1963.

R. Stewart, *Management Succession*, London, 1956.

15 *to* 18, (Crowther Report), Vol. I, London, 1959 (especially Chapter 5).*

(ii) *Quantative Considerations*

J. F. Coales, 'Education for Automation', *British Journal of Educational
Studies*, May 1958.

J. E. Floud and A. H. Halsey, 'Education, Social Mobility and the
Labour Market, *The Yearbook of Education*, 1956.*

K. Liepmann, *Apprenticeship*, London, 1960.

G. L. Payne, *Britain's Scientific and Technological Manpower*, London,
1960.

* Also in *The Reader*.

PART III

The Sociology of Teaching

13

The Teacher in a Profession

An immense amount of work has been done in several fields of the sociology of education. As we have seen, sociologists have given much thought, for instance, to the relationships between the social class system and education, and also to the effect of social environment on school attainment. If one field has suffered comparative neglect, it is the sociology of teaching. Waller (1933) wrote the major text on this subject, but, though it is full of insight and in many ways still relevant, he wrote over thirty years ago and almost entirely of teaching in the U S A. In the final part of this book we shall look at the same field and shall start by examining the teacher's position as a member of a profession, pass to two chapters analyzing respectively the teacher in the school and in the classroom and conclude by considering the personal role of the teacher.

In the present chapter we must first establish what sociologists mean when they speak of a 'profession'. In doing this we shall try to answer the question of whether there is 'a teaching profession'; this will demand reference to the historical growth of teaching as an occupation since the early nineteenth century (A. Tropp, 1957). Finally, we shall look at the determinants of the status of the individual teacher within his 'profession'.

A. The Teaching Profession?

There is a group of occupations which the general public usually refer to as the professions. In the nineteenth century doctors, lawyers and the clergy were included in this category. During the last hundred years there has been a 'flight into professionalism' (R. Lewis and A. Maude, 1952). In the main this has been a result of the rising proportion of occupations that have required a high standard of education. Many of these newer occupations have aspired to professional status. This tendency can be seen in the Census returns. In the 1901 Census 1·12 per cent of occupied males were classified as belonging to the major professions; by 1951 the figure has risen to 2·36 per cent. Over the same period the so-called lesser professions rose from 0·50 per cent to 2·23 per cent of occupied males and the teaching profession from 0·30 per cent to 0·57 per cent. Teaching rose less proportionately than either the major or lesser professions.

About 5 per cent of occupied males are, therefore, classified as members of professions. This is a large proportion of the labour force, and it forms an important group in view of the responsible nature of the work undertaken. Is this group of occupations merely a statistical category? Or has the term 'profession' entered modern usage because it proved a useful analytical tool to nineteenth-century social historians? Or are the professions what Durkheim called 'a social fact', namely a social phenomenon with a firm foundation that careful examination will reveal?

The practice of the professions that were recognized as such in the last century is based on a close personal relationship between the practitioner and his client (T. H. Marshall, 1950). The layman who is sick consults his doctor since he is ignorant of the nature of his illness, whilst the doctor is assumed to know how to cure it. In the same way the lawyer can help his clients because of his knowledge of the complexities of the law. Therefore the professional situation is characterized by the expert practitioner in consultation with the ignorant client who has absolute trust in the advice tendered to him. The practitioner does not use his knowledge except to benefit his clients. This basic situation is that upon which the social fact of 'the professions' rests, and we must judge the more recent claimants to the title, including teaching, against this yard-stick. From the essential relationship there follows a number of characteristics common to all professions. We shall examine these characteristics and in each case see whether teachers as an occupational group have in the past shown or do today display these particular characteristics. In this way we shall be able to come to a conclusion as to whether teaching is a profession or not. It must be said in advance that this is a controversial question and that there is no clear-cut answer.

1. *Knowledge*
The ignorance of the client is fundamental to the need to consult the practitioner. Therefore a member of any of those occupations that are normally called professional must have a command over a very definite

field of knowledge, much of which will be particular to one profession. There would seem to be an 'optimal base of knowledge' for any profession. If the knowledge needed is too broad, the field can be split up and new jobs will be created. If, on the other hand, it is too narrow, too many can learn the knowledge easily, and the ignorance that forces the layman to approach the practitioner will largely disappear.[1] The mastery of such a core of relevant knowledge requires high intelligence and some training. Law and medicine provide clear examples, since considerable training is necessary and in both cases the nature and the complexity of the knowledge demands a high level of intelligence. There is even a certain mystique about the practice of professions. Here the church provides an example. In this context teaching is relevant, since it is often claimed that training is not enough to make a good teacher; there is some other undefinable quality that marks out the real teacher.

Under modern conditions the mass media and advertising have shown that they can sometimes teach better than many teachers. In the schools children have for some time now learnt from the radio and films. More recently any claim to a mystique of teaching has been further undermined by the introduction of programmed textbooks and teaching machines. Teaching grows to be less of an art and more of a science as research reveals more about the process of learning and the best way to communicate information. Yet it is still true that to practise as a teacher assumes a core of specialized knowledge and that a relatively high level of intelligence is needed to be a teacher.

2. *Control of Entry*

The knowledge and training essential for any profession can be specified so that control of entry to the profession is possible. The medical profession was the first to achieve control of entry in its modern form. In 1858 the Medical Act established the General Medical Council whose main function is to keep a register of practitioners and to make certain that only those fit to practise are on this register. The academic qualification and length of training necessary for admission to the register are laid down in detail. This ensures that all medical practitioners are professionally qualified and thereby guarantees to the general public that professional advice is sound. The newer professions have established similar systems. For example, certain examinations and periods of

---

[1] H. L. Wilensky, 'The Professionalization of Everyone?', *American Journal of Sociology*, September 1964, pp. 148–9.

practical training lead to membership of the Institute of Mechanical Engineers and thereby to the status of a qualified professional engineer.

The struggle by the teachers to establish a similar register has been a long one.[1] In 1912 a Teachers' Registration Council was established, but it lapsed in 1949. It was never possible throughout this period to make the Register of significance, since unregistered teachers were permitted to practise. In the 1900's anyone who was over eighteen, had been vaccinated and was satisfactory in the eyes of a member of Her Majesty's Inspectorate (an HMI) was allowed by Article 68 of the Regulations to teach. Unqualified teachers are still permitted to teach for short periods under certain regulations of the Department. Furthermore, any graduate can claim the status of qualified teacher regardless of whether he has had any training in teaching or not. That untrained teachers may still practise may be due to the shortage of teachers, but their continued existence makes very clear that control of entry to the occupation of teaching is lax compared with the medical and most other professions, old or new.

In addition, teachers are not themselves responsible for control of entry, since the system is operated by the Department through administrative regulations. The Department can both grant and withdraw the teacher's certificate. However, the teachers have had sufficient power through their professional associations, and more particularly the National Union of Teachers (NUT), to prevent the quality of the 'teaching profession' from falling through the appointment of a large number of untrained assistants. Many have suggested this course as one way to meet the desperate need for teachers. But to a sociologist much of the discussion over qualifications that takes place in the present shortage of teachers appears as the defence of an assumed professional status.

In the inter-war years A. M. Carr-Saunders and P. A. Wilson (1933) wrote a well-known book on the professions. They saw 'the application of an intellectual technique to the ordinary business of life, acquired as the result of prolonged and specialized training, as the chief distinguishing characteristic of the professions'.[2] Because of this emphasis they thought formal qualifications to be of prime importance to the future development of professionalism. Qualifications must have a major place in any analysis of the professions since they guarantee competence, but

---

[1] G. Baron, 'The Teachers' Registration Movement', *British Journal of Educational Studies*, May 1954.

[2] Op. cit., p. 49.

in the case of teaching control of entry has to some extent been divorced from the question of formal qualifications. Unqualified practitioners, including the untrained graduates, can practise as teachers. Moreover, it is in those subjects where graduate teachers are in shortest supply, namely in mathematics and the sciences, that young graduates appear to enter the schools very often without any training. Yet research in the teaching of these subjects shows that here perhaps more than anywhere else is training necessary in order to teach competently.

3. Code of Professional Conduct

A professional man must not only be of proved competence, but he must be trustworthy. The client assumes that his ignorance will not be exploited and that the practitioner is of a good character. We usually judge personality by behaviour or by what others tell us of a man. In the case of the professions we can rarely know the practitioner well and must refer to others to gain knowledge of his personality. Written references are commonly used as a means of guaranteeing a man's character. Teachers usually cannot apply for posts without supplying some references of their character. Many questions of fairness are raised by this system which is certainly less objective than most formal examinations.

The client trusts the practitioner to behave in a well-defined way. The older professions have ethical codes of long standing. There is the Hippocratic oath for the doctors, the inviolability of the confessional for the priest, and the devotion of the lawyer to his clients' interests. In some cases the code can conflict with the interests of the State or of other citizens. A clear example is the case of the lawyer who is defending a murderer. The fundamentally personal nature of the relationship between client and practitioner is at the root of professional morality. A code of conduct guarantees that the doctor does not misuse the trust that his patient puts in him. The prohibition of the advertising of professional services prevents practitioners from behaving unethically with regard to others in the same profession and from influencing the public's judgement of their capabilities and suitability. Were we not considering the claim of teaching to be a profession, we might pause here to examine whether or not advertising is a profession.

Some of the teachers' associations have published codes to govern the behaviour of their members in relation to their clients – the children, to outsiders – the parents, and to their colleagues. One of the most important

o

ideas implicit in the ethical codes of all professions is that the work is a thing of importance in itself. It has been said that the professional man does not work in order to be paid, but is paid in order that he may work. Yet, ironically, since we must trust a professional man, we feel that he must be of high status and this implies that he must be paid well. However, we tend to assume that a member of the professions will have a high sense of vocation. A doctor will turn out in the middle of the night to help a sick person; a lawyer will take work home at night, if necessary, without a thought of charging overtime; a clergyman will not refuse to preach because his pay is low. One of the most difficult questions of all for teachers has always been whether they ought to strike. This is more than a moral issue. It has a sociological importance. Teachers have a calling to help their clients, the children. A strike would damage the children's interest and would, therefore, be seen by the general public as unprofessional conduct, contravening the ethical code expected in any profession. Despite their relatively low earnings teachers have rarely struck.

4. Freedom to Practise the Profession

There are sanctions on the actions of any profession. An ethical code controls behaviour and only suitably qualified persons may call themselves practitioners. In return for these restrictions the profession expects absolute freedom to practise its calling as the members think fit. We assume that the doctor is competent and of good character; he in his turn assumes that we shall permit him to advise his patient in the way that he feels best and that we shall not interfere with his practice. There is a tension in this position, since where the State gives protection it may also wish to interfere.

Under modern conditions the State is coming to employ more and more professional men. Some professions are wholly employed by the state, for example, the colliery managers. In some cases almost all the profession works for the State; examples are the doctors and the teachers. Very few professions are totally outside State employment; instances could be the actors and the journalists. Two dangers stem from this tendency. Firstly, professional men often find themselves subject to laymen as they do their work. Gone is the absolute authority implicit in the phrase 'Doctor's orders'; the Medical Officer of Health is perhaps more a salaried adviser than a professional practitioner. In addition once the State has decided that it wants a job done, it can lay down the necessary qualifications and conditions of service. Ironically the professions as a whole, and particularly the teachers, have helped this process of increasing dependence to come about. When a group employed in one occupation has bid for professional status, they have put great stress on formal educational qualifications and thereby on longer education. Since the State now pays for much of this extra education, it has naturally felt that it has the right to a greater control of the use of such education. In the case of teaching the State pays for the greatest part of the education provided in this country. It therefore wishes to exercise some control of educational expenditure. Though the HMI has several functions, at the heart of his work is the need to prevent the wasteful use of public money. This entails inspecting the work of teachers. In this respect there are few other occupations which are in the same position as teaching. An HMI can walk into a classroom and criticize a teacher's work at any time. Certainly doctors and lawyers, even when employed by the State, are not subject to such interference.

One of the main problems of the professions today is how to maintain their right to practise as they think best, when the contemporary tendency is for a larger proportion of their members to be employed by the State. When the majority of professional men were in private practice, the private practitioner set the standard for those who were employed elsewhere. The fewer there are in private practice, the less influence they can have, although there may be a time-lag before the State assumes the major or complete control. When the State employs the whole of any profession, it can call the tune and there is an arguable case that the profession in this situation has ceased to be a profession and has become a body of expert officials.

The teachers have a difficult position to hold. Very few of their number are privately employed and therefore interference could be easy. Furthermore the very nature of their work raises difficult questions of principle. The case of whether known Communists should be allowed to teach children in Britain illustrates the problem. Since 1950 there has been a ban on the employment of Communists as headteachers in Middlesex. On the one hand there is a strong argument that in this case the local authority are guarding the children from a probable source of propaganda. Yet on the other this interference is preventing an absolutely free practice of the calling. These alternatives are implicit in any control of professions that are assumed to be free, even though the aim of intervention is that of safeguarding the general public. The work of the professional associations entails a constant watch that the freedom to practise the calling is not eroded by State interventions.

5. Professional Organizations

We have already seen that the professions have formed associations to whom they have delegated some important functions. It is usual, for example, for the professional association to control the register of practitioners. Professional associations are, therefore, normally in a monopoly position and could use their power of control of entry to raise the educational threshold of membership. This course would lower the supply of qualified practitioners and tend to increase the level of remuneration to those in the profession. The US medical profession has been accused of behaving in this way.[1] This was the policy of the trade unions with regard to apprentices. An association that follows such a course endangers the position of the profession, because it is fundamental that professional men are not seeking their own selfish or material ends. The profession is a vocation and has a duty to its clients. A trade union acts out of self-interest. A professional association works for advancement of the profession only so that it may more completely fulfil its social duty.

The association helps to build the framework within which its members practise. It provides the sanctions so that members undertake their obligations and responsibilities to society. Thus, in essence, it is disciplinary. The association ensures that its new members are able to provide the best possible service to their clients. When a practitioner fails in his obligations by acting in an incompetent or unethical way, that is unprofessionally, the association guards the public by withdrawing the right to practise from that member. The General Medical Council and the Law Society are responsible for both admitting members to and striking them off their respective registers.

Associations cannot call strikes in the way that trade unions do. The NUT has never called a national strike. In recent years there has from time to time been great pressure to do so over the question of salaries, but professional duty towards the children has overcome the desire to use unprofessional conduct. In the early part of the century the NUT did organize strikes on a local basis mainly with the aim of gaining a national salary structure and uniform conditions of service. In 1907 teachers were

[1] M. Friedman and S. Kuznets, *Income from Independent Professional Practice*, New York, 1945.

withdrawn from schools in West Ham, and in 1914 the NUT forced the closure of more than sixty schools in Herefordshire. The clash of interests here is very difficult to resolve. The NUT, as representative of teachers, can maintain that without a higher salary scale recruits to the occupation will not be well enough qualified to do the job required. Yet, as has been indicated, the strike undoubtedly is unprofessional in that it harms the interests of the children.

The NUT, like other associations, takes as one of its most important functions political action of another type. It carefully watches the professional interests of teachers in Parliament at question time and during the passage of any major legislation that has even a remote connection with education. There has been a series of famous teacher Members of Parliament. Two of the best known have been Yoxall, who had an influence on the 1902 Education Act, and Chuter Ede, who was Parliamentary Secretary to the President of the Board of Education, during the passing of the 1944 Education Act. Such political action is legitimate for a professional association in that it is not based on any selfish motive but helps to provide a more adequate framework within which the profession can help its clients.

There is some danger in activity, particularly of a political nature, by professional associations, since the image that the public has of the profession may be changed by such action. The NUT followed a very forceful policy between 1870 and 1895. At the beginning of this period the school teacher was seen as a docile, lower middle-class, useful citizen; by 1895 many thought him to be a politically-minded, ambitious pusher. A professional association that wishes to assist its members has to avoid appearing to follow self-interest. Once the public thinks that the profession is behaving in a selfish way, the trust between the profession and its clients has been broken. Even policies that will ensure a more efficient fulfilling of that trust will be misconstrued by the general public.

On the whole since 1945 the NUT has followed high professional standards in its activities. In one particular instance it set the very highest example possible between 1950 and 1952. The local authority in County Durham tried to impose a 'closed shop' on all the teachers whom it employed; all had to belong to one union. The NUT, despite obvious advantages to itself, successfully opposed the authority on grounds of professional freedom. During the period 1954–5, however, the NUT was pressed by many of its members to follow a policy of militancy in a fight with the Government over changes in the statutory superannuation scheme that were disadvantageous to teachers. In this struggle the NUT acted more like a trade union, though actual strike action was avoided. Yet the NUT has largely retained the image of a professional association, and this is clearly symbolized in the defeat of the several attempts that have been made to secure a vote in favour of joining the Trade Union Congress. Such a move would have political connotations unwelcome to any professional body.[1]

6. *Conditions of Service*
A field in which professional associations have always been very active is that covering conditions of service. They have been eager to secure adequate pensions, good tenure of office, the chance of promotion and a minimum of extraneous duties for their members. This has been more especially true of those professions whose members are employed by the State or industry rather than in private practice, since by control of conditions of service the State may interfere with the freedom of a profession to practise its calling.

The teachers' associations, especially the NUT, have paid considerable attention to conditions of service since their foundation. This has been so for two main reasons. Firstly, conditions were very bad for teachers in the early and mid-nineteenth century, and this reflected the low status of teachers. Secondly, the associations wanted to raise the status of their members and saw that by gaining adequate conditions they were promoting respectability. They hoped that in time this would lead to higher status. The battle for adequate pensions has been waged since 1846, and Fisher's Superannuation Act in 1918 was a landmark in the struggle, since it founded a scheme of pensions backed by the State. Security of tenure was gained by 1902, although dismissal is still not in the hands of teachers themselves, but under the control of the State or its representatives; this is very different from the position in the old professions, where a court of one's peers strikes one off the register. One of the ways in which teachers fought for adequate promotion possibilities was by requesting the admission of elementary teachers to the inspectorate; this was achieved by the late nineteenth century.

A major problem for teachers has always been the demand that they carry out duties extraneous to teaching. In the middle of the last century

[1] N. N. Roy, 'Membership Participation in the NUT', *British Journal of Industrial Relations*, July 1964.

many teachers knew that they would only be appointed if, for example, they played the church organ on Sundays. As late as 1891 the NUT found that 400 out of 1,200 of the teachers in four areas were in the position that their appointment depended on their doing extraneous duties. The nature of these duties has changed considerably. The growth of what may be called welfare services in the schools has led to the need for teachers to collect dinner money and supervise meals. Many teachers regard such tasks as unprofessional. The achieving of a satisfactory position with regard to conditions of service gives stability and respectability to a profession. Yet it is true to say that for a member of the old professions in private practice the problem did not arise. The new concern with conditions of service is due to the greater proportion of professionals who are not in private practice and to the increased number of occupations of rather a different nature from the old professions, that are now considered as professions.

7. Recognition by the Public

At the beginning of this examination of what is meant by the term 'profession' we found that there was a factor common to the old professions. This was the nature of the relationship between practitioner and client. Yet by the end of the last paragraph we are admitting that the principle of the self-fulfilling prophecy may work in the case of professions. Thus, the majority of teachers consider themselves to be members of a profession; on the whole the public and the authorities treat them as a profession. Therefore, teaching is a profession. Is this true? Does professionalism merely depend upon a consensus of opinion?

The occupation of teaching is based on a personal relationship between, on the one hand, children who are ignorant of knowledge and their parents who, even if they actually know this specialized knowledge, do not know how to impart it, and, on the other, a teacher, who is usually trained and who is guaranteed to be of good character. Despite the possibility of inspection the teacher is trusted to have almost complete freedom in his classroom to practise his vocation. As in all the professions the exact balance between the teacher's duty to children and parents and his own interest is difficult to assess. The main differences between the teacher and the typical professional are two. The teacher practises on more than one client simultaneously; however, this can be claimed to be a difference of degree rather than of kind. Secondly, the teachers have far less control over their own occupation; in this respect the State seems to exercise its powers of control according to the best professional standards.

Thus far the teacher can on the whole claim to be a member of a profession.[1] Yet historically teachers have had a status rather lower than those occupations admitted to be professions. Therefore much of the work done by their associations has been much more akin to that done by trade unions than that of professional associations. Typical of such work were the strikes to ensure uniform conditions of service referred to above. By the 1960's the status of teaching has risen. This may be due to the work of the professional associations or to the fact that education has come to have a higher status in Britain, but certainly teaching is now often included in those occupations called professions. Many of the other new professions are comparable with teaching in that they are not of the 'pure' nineteenth-century type, since so many of their members are employed by the State in one capacity or another. For the most part these new professions stick to the standards of conduct implicit in the personal relationship fundamental to the 'pure' professions. This is also the case for teaching.

So far the case for considering teaching to be a profession has been built on a definite functional relationship between clients and practitioners. Recently an attempt has been made to outline a natural history of professionalism.[2] The development of eighteen American professions was analysed, and on the whole each seemed to pass through an identical series of stages. First the occupation must have become a full-time job, as teaching had done in Britain well before 1800. Next a training system must be established; this took place after 1839 for elementary teachers, though its development for graduates is not entirely complete even now. Thirdly, a professional association is founded, as occurred in Britain in the case of elementary teachers in the 1870's and of secondary teachers around the turn of the century. In some professions these associations achieved legal recognition, but this does not appear to be an integral part of the process of becoming a profession. Finally, a code of ethics is evolved; this also has taken place in the case of teaching in Britain. Teaching would seem to have passed through all the stages deemed necessary in the American situation for developing into a profession. This reinforces the conclusion already reached that there is an arguable

[1] For a somewhat different summing up see The Editor's article, *The Yearbook of Education*, London, 1953, pp. 27–30.
[2] H. L. Wilensky, op. cit., pp. 142–6.

case for saying that there is a teaching profession. This case is mainly based on the theoretical grounds that a particular relationship exists between teachers and taught, but has been reinforced by indicating briefly that in its history teaching has evolved in much the same way as the more widely recognized professions have done.

There is one final point. Who are the members of the teaching profession? Should all those employed today in the field of education be considered as members of the profession? Those administering education are in a very different sociological relationship, since they are far removed from the profession's clients, the children. The administrators are much nearer to experts and hence should be excluded. There are also teachers who are in a professional situation in other educational institutions, for example, the universities. Their position is hard to assess until we have examined what determines the status of individual teachers within the profession as a whole. The differences in status between teachers may be so great that teaching may not be a unitary profession.

B. The Status of the Individual Teacher

A recent High Master of Manchester Grammar School was created a life peer. Headteachers of primary schools who appear in the Honours Lists are awarded the MBE. This is one indication of the very wide range of status that exists within the occupation of teaching. We shall here consider four main determinants of the status of individual teachers (The Editors, *The Yearbook*, 1953).

1. *Sex*

In the nineteenth century there was no doubt that women had a lower status than men in the world of teaching. The struggle for emancipation for women and the subsequent fight for equal pay for women in many occupations affected the position of women teachers. In the years since the war women teachers have been granted equal pay, so that today there is the same salary scale for both sexes in teaching. But, since there are more men in the more highly paid posts of head teacher or of head of department, the average earnings of women teachers are lower than in the case of men.

This is a common situation throughout the labour market and has a real basis in the fact that few women today expect to follow a career unbroken by motherhood. They therefore in effect lose their position on the scale of seniority and normally expect to forfeit their chances of promotion. In recent years the position has been complicated by the growing number of part-time married women teachers whose status appears to be considered lower than full-time married teachers.[1] Women teachers may be on the same salary scale as men, but they do not seem to have the same status in the schools.

2. *The Status and Age of the Pupils Taught*

There is an immense range of status of schools from independent schools such as Eton to maintained schools in slum areas. The status of the pupils attending these schools covers an equally wide range and to a great extent the status of the pupils affects the status of those who teach them. Up till 1944 this difference was enshrined in two terms in common usage – 'the teacher' and 'the schoolmaster'. The latter was applied to those who taught in grammar or private schools, whilst the former was given to the lower status elementary school. The schoolmaster was usually a graduate of a university, whilst the teacher had been to a training college. A degree has always had higher status than the teacher's certificate. As late as 1949, when the term 'elementary' had officially been abolished, those running the London School of Economics survey of social mobility found that 'elementary teacher' was the term that the general public most readily understood when considering teachers. The sample ranked the elementary teacher as having equal socio-economic status with a news reporter, a commercial traveller, and a jobbing master builder, and of higher status than an insurance agent, but of lower status than a nonconformist minister.[2]

Since the 1944 Act we can speak of primary and secondary teachers. It is doubtful whether the general public can or does distinguish amongst teachers in general. The only differentiation seems to be that they still use the term 'schoolmaster' in the case of those who teach in grammar and private schools. W. Taylor (1963) clearly showed that a difference in status between the two main types of secondary school does exist. The grammar school has higher status than the secondary modern school. This difference is based on the fact that the modern school recruits its pupils from low status parents and channels them into jobs that are of

[1] M. Collins, *Women Graduates and the Teaching Profession*, Manchester, 1964, p. 52.
[2] D. V. Glass (ed.), op. cit., p. 34.

low status. The average earnings of those who teach these low status pupils reflect this difference.

Despite the common salary scale such differences occur not only between those teaching pupils of different status, but also between those teaching children of different ages. Those who teach the younger children in the primary schools earn less on average than those in secondary schools. This seems to be a measure of a difference in status, which is partly connected with two other facts. There are far more women than men teaching in the primary schools. In 1962 out of the 141,878 teachers in these schools 106,026 (or 74·7 per cent) were women. Furthermore, only 3·7 per cent of all teachers in primary schools were graduates.

Such internal differences in status are important, since they may act to prevent structural change in the educational system. Some teachers realize that they cannot claim individual status from the profession as a whole; they therefore cling to the status of the institution to which they belong. Today grammar school teachers may, at least unconsciously, oppose the change to a comprehensive system of secondary education because they believe that this will lower their own status.

3. *Subject Taught*

In the nineteenth century the place given to science in the public schools was very low and those who taught science were often considered to be of a lower status than those who taught the classics. Today the situation has changed radically. There is still, however, an academic pecking order in some universities with classics and the pure sciences high, whilst the social sciences, especially education, and applied science are put low.

To some extent qualifications have come to be tied up with the status of subjects. In primary schools teachers tend to be general practitioners, most of whom have the same qualification, the teacher's certificate, and therefore status cannot be accorded by the subject taught. But in secondary schools specialists are the rule. The growth in the number of graduates in the old elementary schools did help to raise the status of these schools. Graduates are not uncommon in the secondary modern school today; in 1962 20·2 per cent of men and 13·0 per cent of women teachers in such schools were graduates, and this may have made the modern school more acceptable to many. But there are some subjects in which graduates are almost unknown. The clearest examples are handwork and physical education in the case of both boys and girls. Despite the important part played by games in British schools the P E teacher seems not to have the same status as other teachers, and this is particularly true in the grammar school where he is often one of the few non-graduates.[1]

4. *The Social Origin of the Teacher*

In the last century teaching was a common route for upward mobility. In a sample of 8,516 teachers taken in 1955 J. E. Floud and W. Scott (1956) found that almost half came from working-class grandfathers whose sons showed a more than average likelihood of rising up the social scale when compared with the rest of their class. Perhaps rather oddly, six or seven times as many as might be expected were descended from grand-fathers who were farmers. However, trends in recruitment since the war seem to indicate that this pull on working-class children to enter teaching is no longer effective. Whether due to the greater security provided by industrial employment today or because of changes in salary differentials teaching is no longer so attractive an occupation and proportionally more middle-class youths are entering teaching.

If this trend continues, there will be a slow change in the social background of teachers. In 1955 about half of all teachers of both sexes came from lower middle-class families. During the last century very many teachers came from a lower social class than was usually associated with the old professions. This rubbed off on the status of the occupation as a whole. Hence they often aspired to higher status. Today the status of teaching and the social background of teachers appear to have risen, and are on the whole on a par with the new professions. There is no longer the same need to aspire to professional status. Though this may be true of the profession as a whole, it may be different for individuals.

The proportions of teachers from various social classes does vary by type of school. The position in the case of men in grant-earning schools in 1955 was as follows (' %s):

Father's Occupation when Teacher left School	Primary	Modern	Technical	Maintained Grammar	Direct-Grant Grammar
Professional, Administrative	6·0	7·5	6·0	12·5	19·8
Intermediate	48·3	45·9	51·0	55·1	61·5
Manual	45·7	46·6	43·0	32·4	18·7

(J. E. Floud and W. Scott, op. cit., p. 540.)

[1] See Charmion Cannon, 'Some Variations on the Teacher's Role', *Education for Teaching*, May 1964, especially pp. 32–36 for the role of the PE teacher in girls' selective secondary schools.

The trend in the case of women was much the same. The proportions of teachers from working-class homes was higher where the status of the school was lower and, conversely, the proportions of teachers from parents of higher social status rose as one went from the lower to the higher status schools.

This pattern matches what we should expect from our discussion on the relationship between the status and age of pupils and the status of their teachers. The differing status of these schools is much more likely to be a result of the age and status of the pupils in the schools than the social origins of the teachers concerned. In a society that has a relatively high rate of social mobility the social status of any occupational group tends to be given to all its members whatever their social origins. This is the more likely where geographical mobility is high, since in most cases no one will know the kin of any individual and status will be given according to the socio-economic position that is achieved. Many teachers move to obtain new posts and this may be an additional force in obscuring the influence of social origins on the status of the individual teacher.

C. Conclusion

In the first part of this chapter we saw that there are grounds for calling teaching a profession, but we now see that there is a range of status amongst teachers. There is a similar range within the medical and legal professions. We may compare the surgeon or specialist with the general medical practitioner and notice that there is a difference in status. Despite this both are members of the medical profession. Teaching then is not disqualified on these grounds. There are differences in status, but teachers are sufficiently near in status to be grouped as a profession with perhaps the exception already noted of the difficult case of those who teach in universities. We may finally speak, as we have so far on the whole avoided doing, of 'the teaching profession'.

Historically the profession was born in 1833 when the State intervened to raise the standards of training amongst elementary teachers, who soon founded associations to watch their professional interest, more particularly after the 1870 Education Act. In 1902 the State stepped in to organize secondary education; at about this time the secondary teachers formed their own association. The aim of the 1944 Act was a unified educational system. Symptomatic of the failure of this aim is the fact that the teaching profession is still not a unified one, since the teachers in selective secondary schools tend to stand apart from the rest.

There may be a sociological argument for speaking of the teaching profession. The case is based on the relationship between teacher and taught. Teachers are, however, in danger of becoming a group of experts employed by the State rather than a profession. This is a danger common to the majority of the professions today, but as the last paragraph indicated, teaching is and for the last one hundred and fifty years has been extremely dependent upon the State. If teachers wish to remain professionals, they must hold fast to the code of conduct implicit in any professional relationship. Professional status implies a contract to serve society over and above any specific duty to client or employer in return for the privileges and protections given by society to the profession. Private practitioners in all professions set the standard. Private schools may set teachers the best example of their code of behaviour. Teaching will not remain a profession if teachers only work from nine to four or if, without extreme provocation, they go on strike.

BIBLIOGRAPHY

A. M. Carr-Saunders and P. A. Wilson, *The Professions*, London, 1933.
The Editors, 'The Social Position of Teachers' in *The Yearbook of Education*, 1953.
J. E. Floud and W. Scott, 'Recruitment to Teaching in England and Wales', 1956 in *The Reader*.
R. Lewis and A. Maude, *Professional People*, London, 1952.
T. H. Marshall, 'The Recent History of Professionalism in Relation to Social Structure and Social Policy', in *Citizenship and Social Class*, London, 1950.
W. Taylor, *The Secondary Modern School*, London, 1963 (especially Chapters 3 and 4).
A. Tropp, *The Schoolteachers*, London, 1957.

14

The Teacher in the School

We can consider any teacher in a school to be at the centre of a web of forces that act upon him, some more strongly than others, but all influencing his professional behaviour. These forces may come from outside the school, but can nevertheless have a big effect on the quality of his work. This type of force will be termed external; examples are the influence of the State, the governing body of the school and the parents of the pupils. Other forces can be called internal since they originate within the school, as for example, the influence of the head of the school, the other members of the staff, and the children themselves. A third group of forces are those that affect the teacher from outside the school, but over which he himself can exert some control. An example of this reciprocal type of force is the examination system. We shall examine each of these three groups in turn later in this chapter.

The educational system is a complex of institutions, some of which are old and some new (T. Burgess, 1964). When once an institution has been established, values and patterns of behaviour develop autonomously within it. Teachers do their work in such living institutions, each of which is different, but the majority of which have certain important common features. If the latter can be isolated, we shall distinguish one major influence on the teacher in the school. Those aspects of the schools in any country that are common to all are the outward signs of that nation's idea of what a school shall be. In Britain these common features indicate the British idea of a school.[1] This idea will define much of a teacher's work. In this chapter we shall first examine what the British idea of school is and then consider how the three groups of forces described above play upon the teacher as he teaches his class within a British school.

[1] The next section owes much to Dr G. Baron of the Institute of Education, University of London.

A. The British Idea of a School

The range of school types in Britain is immense. On the one hand there is the public school and on the other the primary school. There are also historical differences between the school systems of the constituent countries of Britain though they are today of less importance than they were even fifty years ago. It seems almost impossible to say that there is one idea of a school in Britain. The position taken here is that the following four assumptions underlie most British people's idea of what a school is:

(1) A school should have independence and individuality.
(2) A school should be small enough to have a common purpose and be under one head.
(3) A school should mould character.
(4) and therefore should transmit a definite set of values.

Each of these assumptions will be examined in turn.

1. *Independence and Individuality*

The care given to ensure that all schools have the independence necessary to develop their own individuality can best be seen in the attention paid in legislation to the establishing of governing bodies for schools. During the latter part of the nineteenth century the independent schools felt the need to defend themselves, more particularly by founding professional associations, against the possibility of State Intervention. At the time of the 1902 Education Act those who had political power and those who advised them were men reared in this tradition of independence, and they therefore felt that they should write specific provision into the Act that was to found the new maintained grammar school. So as to guarantee a degree of autonomy all secondary schools by statute had to have a board of governors. In the 1944 Act similar arrangements were made and the new primary schools were given boards of managers. These provisions, certainly at secondary level, have ensured the wide diversity of internal organization and curriculum in British schools that is remarkable to any foreigner who examines our educational system. Another sign of the same desire for individuality and independence is that nine different examining bodies organize the General Certificate of Education. In Britain the educational unit tends to be the school, whilst the administrative unit is the local authority. This is not always so clearly the case in other countries, nor need it logically be so. Paradoxically, one common feature of British schools is that they all may be different.

2. *A Community that is Small and under one Head*

(i) *Community*. Education need not necessarily take place in a community that is set apart. One of the oldest of European educational institutions is the apprenticeship system, whereby individuals are educated and trained not in a school but at their place of work. Similarly in higher technical education there has been a growth since 1945 in the number of so-called 'sandwich courses' in which the student undertakes a part of the course in an educational institution and part in the factory. However, the influence of the British boarding-school has been great in this respect as in others. During the nineteenth century these schools grew by recruiting their pupils from a wide geographical area. This tended to limit their contacts with the immediate locality. More recently many of these schools have moved somewhat in the other direction and have encouraged their pupils to go out into the community around the school to undertake social service in various forms. Yet the emphasis remains the same; the school, either consciously or unconsciously, is the educative community. This leads to a stress on communal activities. Meals together and school games have a higher importance than, for example, in Germany or France.

(ii) *Size*. To most British parents and teachers a school must be small so that each individual child may be known well to his teachers. It has often been said that no school should be so big that the Head does not know each child as an individual. The claim that large schools would be more economic to run has usually given way in the interests of the individual child. The fact that some of the most famous British boarding- and day-schools have a thousand or more pupils is conveniently overlooked. These schools have developed the house system so as to guarantee that despite their large size someone is responsible for knowing each child well enough to watch his growth. Many have opposed the comprehensive school on the grounds that they are too big to cater for the child as an individual. Invariably these new schools have bowed to the British tradition and have organized elaborate house systems in order to gain the advantages of the small school whilst remaining large.

(iii) *The Headmaster* (G. Baron, 1956). In the mid-nineteenth century the headmasters of the public schools who felt that they must fight for their independence did so often by stressing their own authority. In addition to this the *laissez-faire* economic ideas of the time helped to ensure that interference was rare. By 1909 a famous headmaster, Sir Cyril Norwood of Harrow, could write that the headmaster in this

P

country was 'an autocrat of autocrats'. Between 1828 and 1842 Thomas Arnold of Rugby had built the model that was to be imitated by most later heads. He was the leader of a community who was also a clergyman, and therefore the idea evolved easily that the head had a pastoral care for his pupils.[1] Such a headmaster would do all in his power to identify his pupils with the aim of the school as determined by himself. All these characteristics of the British idea of a headmaster as it developed in the late nineteenth century tended to force schools to be small. The shepherd's flock could not be too large if he were to tend them properly. Yet it must not be thought that this was an inevitable result. Even by 1850 the position of the headmaster was not as stable as it was to be. In schools in both England and Scotland it was not unusual for the masters to take turns to act as head. The problem of how to organize a school larger than was normal at the start of the last century had still not been solved.

Today a similar problem faces the comprehensive school. The tradition of what a British head should be is opposed to an administrative non-teaching headmaster, to what an American head of a large high school once called 'a four-ulcer man doing an eight-ulcer job'. The Arnold tradition passed into the State secondary system after 1902, since so many of the first heads of the new maintained grammar schools were educated and had taught in public schools. From grammar schools this idea of a head has passed into the other types of secondary school and also into the primary schools. Everywhere the head is thought of as a man with power who moulds his school as he wishes.

3. Character Training

It follows from the British idea of a head that a school must care for all aspects of the child's development, for his character as well as his academic attainments. In Europe character formation is left to the home, the church and the youth organizations. In the USA the school tries to adapt the child to the community's, and not its own idea of good character. But in Britain the school tends to lay down the way in which children are to behave and it holds itself responsible for enforcing this code. The school also takes a protective attitude towards the effects of the rest of the environment on the child; for example, the school must defend the children against the damage that the mass-media, television or the cinema, may do. Therefore, the school concerns itself with how its

---

[1] Matthew Arnold's poem 'Rugby Chapel' (1857) can be read as a gloss on this sentence.

pupils spend their leisure time and organizes games and societies in order to inculcate the approved virtues and interests. Again, this is not normal in European schools.

4. Values

This stress on the formation of character assumes an agreed standard of values by which personality may be evaluated. In fact the teacher in Britain has become an agent by which the attempt is made to transmit the typical middle-class values. Since the educational system did not grow from the community, but was imposed from above, it is the values of those in positions of higher status that were considered, usually unconsciously, as worth inculcating. No moral judgement is here being passed on this set of values, but the result has been that many teachers see the schools as a rescue operation to save the children from their parents and their social class.

Schools in Britain vary enormously, but these four assumptions are common to the majority. Comparison with other countries shows that such assumptions are not universal. In the future mass literacy may bring change, but at the moment this is the idea of a school that influences the way in which administrators, teachers and parents see schools and therefore this idea governs much of what a teacher considers he ought to do as he practises his vocation.

B. The Forces at work on the Teacher

1. External Forces

(i) *The State*. In this country the finance of education comes from two main sources. The treasury provides funds through the Department of Education and Science; initially this money has come from national taxation. In addition certain local authorities find further money from rates. Since both national and local authorities jointly hold the purse-strings, both are in a position to influence the schools and thereby the teacher.

(a) *The Department of Education and Science*. About 55 per cent of the funds for current expenditure on education is supplied by the central Government through the Department. The largest part of once and for all capital expenditure is financed centrally. Thus the Department is in the position of being able to lay down the regulations that govern how this money is spent. As was indicated in the last chapter it is a major part of the Inspectorate's work to see that the regulations are observed. The influence of these regulations is far reaching, since they cover staffing ratios, the dimensions of classrooms, the scale of equipment for laboratories and gymnasia, and a multitude of minor features that matter much to the practising teacher. The sheer detail is immense, but, unless a new school meets the present standards of the Department, expenditure will not be authorized and, if old buildings are not up to present standards, criticism may be expected. This system governs the immediate material surroundings within which the teacher carries out his work.

The financing of British Education was organized purposely so that both the central Government and the local authorities played a major part. The intention was that local interests should come to bear in a democratic manner on the provision of the local educational system (G. Baron and A. Tropp, 1961). But this seemingly admirable aim has within it the possibility of conflict, since there is always the chance that the two financing authorities may wish to pursue opposite or different policies. Since both Government and local council are democratically elected, their respective majorities may represent different political parties. In Britain since 1945 local government, particularly in the large cities, has often been dominated by the Labour Party, whilst the Conservatives for much of this period formed the central Government. Since the 1950's the educational policies of the two parties have grown more unlike. There is therefore the chance of head-on collision. An example may be given; in 1955 the Manchester council wished to establish two new comprehensive schools in line with the policy of its Labour dominated council. The Ministry (as it was then called) refused permission, since Conservative policy was only to allow expenditure on such schools on certain conditions that did not apply in this particular case. The conflict went to the point that the Ministry threatened to withdraw Manchester's financial grant, a step that would have brought the city's school system to a halt. This sanction forced Manchester to abandon its scheme.

This is a very striking case of what is always possible, but rarely happens. The Department has greater power to push through its own policy and prevent local schemes with which it does not agree. Hence its power over the teacher in the school is greater than is often realized. However, the Government's power is not absolute, and once again the case of the comprehensive school is relevant.[1] In 1945 the Ministry in its

[1] See A. V. Judges, 'Tradition and the Comprehensive School', *British Journal of Educational Studies*, November 1953, especially pp. 11-14, for a brief account of the early growth of the comprehensive school.

pamphlet, 'The Nation's Schools', indicated that its policy was a tripartite secondary system of grammar, technical and modern schools. During 1946 the local authorities began to submit their development schemes to meet the needs of the 1944 Act, and the Government realized that local feeling demanded a change in policy towards the provision of more comprehensive schools. In 1947 the pamphlet, 'The New Secondary Education', took notice of this and envisaged a greater variety of type of secondary school. Despite the power of the State democratic pressures, in education as in other fields of Government expenditure, can bring change to Government policy. To the individual teacher, however, the possibility of his influencing policy seems so remote that the Department remains a powerful, if indirect, external force.

(b) *The Local Authority*. The local authority both acts as the channel for expenditure of State funds and spends on education from its own rates. It therefore stands between the Department and the school and appears to the teacher to be the main direct external force that influences his work. Though the whole council is responsible for all local government, there are committees responsible for each major field of expenditure. The Education Committee consists of democratically elected members – councillors or aldermen, members co-opted to this committee, and paid officials of the council, such as the Director of Education, who give advice as experts on the matters under discussion.

The political complexion of the council will normally decide the composition of this committee and, as local politics have become more a party matter, so policies on education have tended to be judged on national political, rather than local educational, criteria. However, the position of the Director of Education can be very influential. He is a former teacher and in close touch with his teachers in the schools. In theory he may be purely an expert who tenders his advice, but often because he alone has the necessary knowledge amongst a committee mainly consisting of laymen, he has great power. Major policy decisions may stem from his advice. Thus the Cambridgeshire Village College system owes its existence to Henry Morris, the pre-war Director for that area.

Local authorities have great power over their schools and the teachers within them. Often teachers are appointed to the authority rather than to the individual school. But the power of the local authority varies according to the type of school. The authority has most influence on fully maintained schools, since it provides either directly from rates or indirectly from the Treasury the whole of the finance needed to run such schools. In addition there are the various types of voluntary schools – the aided, the controlled and the special agreement schools. The factor that differentiates these three school types is the amount of State finance received in each case. The more money given to the school, the greater influence the local authority can claim over it. This control is symbolized in the proportion of the governors or managers that the local authority may nominate to the school's governing body. The more finance the authority finds, the more governors it appoints and hence the more power it can exercise over the workings of the school. This will affect the appointment of the head and staff, and to some extent the activities of the teachers in the school. The intention of this complicated system is to safeguard the interests of the mainly religious bodies who since the nineteenth century have provided so many British schools.

The schools that are least influenced by local authorities are the direct-grant schools, whose finance comes directly from the Department, but who by law have to provide some places for children from maintained schools. The local authorities have some interest in these schools since they pay the fees of a substantial proportion of the children in such schools and, therefore, they will wish to ensure that ratepayers' money is not spent on poor education. However, direct-grant schools are in many ways more akin to the independent schools which must now be considered.

(c) *Independent Schools.* There are a large number of schools that are independent of the Department. They may be run on a profit-making basis or as charitable foundations. These schools include the famous public schools, the so-called 'progressive' schools, and many privately run kindergartens. By Part III of the 1944 Act, which came into operation in 1957, all independent schools must apply for registration by the Department. They are liable to inspection and must on the whole conform to the Department's regulations. These regulations are not rigorously imposed. If they were, the experiments of progressive schools might be curbed, but the philosophy of the 1944 Act is that, although parents should be permitted to choose their children's school, the State should safeguard the public by preventing the setting up of poor schools.

Since the independent schools are liable to inspection, they must be influenced by the regulations that set the Department's standards. However, in many respects, especially in the case of the public schools, standards are higher than in maintained schools. The strongest influence on the teacher will be either the proprietor or the governing body of the school. Teachers in these schools need rarely worry about the influence of the Department or any local authority.

(ii) *Governing Bodies.* As has already been indicated, since the 1944 Act all maintained schools by law shall have some form of governing body so that they may retain some independence. In fact very little is known about what these boards do or even to what extent or in what form they exist.[1] In the case of secondary, particularly grammar, schools their influence appears greater, since they usually play a major part in selecting a new head of the school; in many cases all staff appointments receive their approval.

The governing bodies of the independent schools are extremely influential and can form the model for analysing the position in other schools. The governors of such schools provide a strong and continuing influence. Headmasters may come and go, but the governing body remains, though its membership may change. It is the guardian of the school's traditions. In many schools and also in colleges a legal trust lays down what interests shall be represented on the governing body and thereby perpetuates the intention of the institution's founder. Many independent schools have religious foundations, and provisions of this nature ensure that the school continues in the spirit in which it was started. The governors guard their trust in two main ways. They personally appoint the headmaster, choosing, as far as they can, the man who seems best fitted to continue the tradition entrusted to their keeping. They also control the financial affairs of the school. Since the school finds all its own funds and none come from the State, the governing body has a big influence on the life of the school. Decisions concerning changes to the fabric of the school, such as a new laboratory or gymnasium, are ultimately in their hands.

In maintained schools the governing bodies are much less powerful, since they are not in a position of financial independence. They can play a part in choosing the head and can watch the interests of the school in local affairs. Governors have been known to fight for their school's survival when the local authority wished to close it down. It would, however, be of interest to know who serve as managers or governors. Are they councillors, local businessmen, and old boys of the school ? Whose

[1] Research on this topic is now being carried out at the University of London Institute of Education.

interest do they serve beside that of the school? Are the old boys a conservative influence? We do not know the answers to these questions and, therefore, are not able to see clearly in what way governing bodies influence maintained schools.

(iii) *Parents*. Parents can influence a teacher indirectly through their children, but here we are thinking of their direct influence. In a small village or town the teacher may well live in or near to the school. Most of the parents of the children that he teaches will meet him in the street and can easily talk to him about the school and their children. In the contemporary large urban area this is not often the case. Teachers do not want to live in the middle of a slum area or even in a city. They prefer to travel long distances to their schools. Under these conditions that are typical for the majority of schools and relations between parents and teachers must be structured. It is because of this that in some schools today Parent-Teacher Associations have been established.

Teachers and parents alike are dedicated to the interests of the children. In theory therefore disagreement is impossible. In practice, however, it is very likely since in this country the parents' wishes are usually held to be subordinate to the teacher's idea of what is good for the child. The teacher assumes that he knows better than the parent, and thus few heads in this country have established any form of parents' association, since this would allow the parents a direct influence on the running of their schools (J. B. Mays, 1962).

The contact between parents and teachers is closest with younger children. This may be exemplified if one calls to mind the picture of parents clustered about the doors of an infant school around 3.30 p.m. during term time; the junior school next door has a much smaller group. In secondary schools far less contact is observed; in grammar schools fear or shyness may prevent visits by parents, particularly amongst parents who did not themselves attend such schools.[1] But at any age the chance of conflict between parents and teacher is great. Values may differ between the middle-class teacher and the working-class parent; methods have changed since father was at school. Yet there is usually no machinery to resolve these differences.

In the case of the independent schools the position appears simple. The parent is a customer who is buying education for his child. If he ceases to be satisfied with the service provided, he may withdraw his custom. In fact, though organized ways in which parents may approach

[1] B. Jackson and D. Marsden, op. cit., pp. 205–9.

the school are rare, there is a long tradition that the headmaster or the housemaster is in close touch with the parents of their pupils.

In the USA the situation is very different. When a new school is established, the local parents can have a very strong influence on the type of school built and on the choosing of the head teacher. One author goes so far as writing of the American school as 'belonging' to parents and family. Social pressure is great enough to ensure that a high proportion of American parents belong to Parent–Teachers' Associations. In one area 40 per cent of middle-class parents were members, though the working-class proportion was somewhat lower. But a survey in England revealed that only 3 per cent of all the parents in a comparable area were members.[1]

The relationship between parents and teachers in Britain is summed up by the feeling so often expressed in staffrooms that 'we could do so much better a job if only the parents would not interfere'. The contact that is necessary at the infant stage, because the child is young, can create a partnership between parent and teacher in the education of the child. But the teacher of the older children will rarely meet their parents unless there is an organized channel for this purpose. In this country Parent Teacher Associations are rare, though any increase in the real interest in education might bring about a change. It seems odd that 'the office', the symbol of the State and the local authority, should have so much more influence on a teacher than the parents of the children that he teaches.

2. *Internal Forces*

(i) *The Headteacher*. The forces which play upon the teacher's position from outside the school are in the main impersonal or corporate. We have only so far mentioned the influence of one individual, the Director of Education. But as soon as we turn to those within the school who influence the teacher we are in the world of individuals, all of whom have their own characteristics. The first person to be considered in any school is the head. In Britain the tradition is that the head is all powerful in his school. Once appointed he has very great freedom to influence the development of the school for which he is responsible.[2] For instance he

[1] H. E. Bracey, *Neighbours*, London, 1964, pp. 125–9. See also W. H. Whyte, *The Organization Man*, London, 1957 (Penguin), Chapter 28 for an account of parents' influence over the establishing of a new school in the USA.

[2] See W. R. Niblett, 'Administrators and Independence', *British Journal of Educational Studies*, November 1958.

decides the curriculum and the broad allocation of time to each subject. This decision in itself deeply affects the work of all his staff.

Teachers tend to speak of 'strong' and 'weak' heads, as though the former determines the ethos of the school, whilst under the latter things just drift. This may be so, but many of the 'weak' heads intend to act in this way in order to create a spirit of tolerance and democracy. If they achieve this, it is as much due to their influence as any effect of a 'strong' head. The point that must be appreciated is that whatever the personality of the head he can act to establish the atmosphere that embodies his values whatever they are, and this will affect his teachers. Or, if he is inefficient, he will do nothing and in this case the teachers will be influenced in that they will have to exert the leadership that has not been given by the official leader.

One of the main ways by which a head maintains or creates the ethos of a school is by his choice of staff. In as much as he makes or influences appointments he can try to pick teachers who appear to meet his needs, though he may be limited by shortages of particular types of teachers. The limiting case of the public school shows very clearly how the head goes about choosing his staff. If the school stresses games, he will want to find 'Blues' for his vacancies; if, however, the school has an academic tradition, the head will look for 'Firsts'. The average headteacher has an average policy and so there is a big range of indeterminancy within which his choice of staff may fall. The average teacher will suit him.

Bad choices are possible. The head may choose wrongly or the teacher may allow himself, consciously or unconsciously, to be appointed to a post for which he is not suitable. In these cases the teacher may realize the mistake and move to another post. The head, however, can influence him to apply elsewhere by hints or by making his life unpleasant. In such moves, as in all changes in school staffing, the question of references is relevant. One of the most powerful, if hidden, sanctions by which a head can maintain a conformity to his wishes amongst his staff is the fact that the majority of applications for posts elsewhere must be backed by a written reference from him. If this reference is not forthcoming, questions will be asked as to why the applicant left his last post. This is no doubt an extreme example, but it is in just such cases that we can see how much influence the head can ultimately have on his staff.

(ii) *The Staff*. Once the teacher is in his classroom with his children he has very great freedom in Britain. How and what he teaches is very largely his own affair, though he may receive suggestions from visiting inspectors. His classroom is his own territory, rarely, if ever, visited by his colleagues. Yet he cannot be entirely independent of the rest of the school staff. In most secondary schools there will be a head of department who is responsible for the work in a major area of the curriculum. He will influence, even if only by consultation, the subject matter that is taught. He may be responsible for spending the department's allowance for books or equipment and in this way influence what or how the teachers in his department can teach. In primary schools teachers will have to co-operate with those in the classes a year ahead or behind their own so that continuity is ensured for the children who are passing through the school. All these relationships involve individual personalities.

In all schools there are some activities that cut right across the normal work of the school. Duty lists for school dinners or for the playground must be fixed, and this demands co-operation amongst the staff. Some teachers organize out-of-school games or clubs, the timing of which may force consultation amongst the whole staff. There are great personal problems involved in the need to do things about which some teachers may be keen, others apathetic and to which some may even be opposed. A teacher's work depends for its success not only on his skill with children, but on the way in which he handles his relationships with his colleagues. Philosophical issues of means and ends are involved here. On the one hand is the scheming, but charming teacher who is out for his own interest; on the other is the teacher who furthers the interest of the children for whom he is responsible by co-operation with other teachers. It is to the latter way of handling personal relationships that attention is here being drawn.[1]

(iii) *The Children.* In the next chapter the way that the teacher and his pupils interact in the classroom will be examined at some length. Here the intention is merely to establish the point that the children can influence the way the teacher runs his class. This is not merely a question of the poor disciplinarian whose class takes over. It will be remembered that in the discussion of the sub-cultures within a school Coleman's work in the USA was quoted. The fun culture in the US high school attracted many adolescents away from the values and ways of behaviour that the teachers wished to instil in these pupils. Similarly in Britain there are many teachers in secondary modern schools who know that their approach to the fourth-year leavers, aged around fifteen, is partly influenced by these children and is not entirely controlled by themselves.

[1] A useful text here is Josephine Klein, *Working With Groups*, London, 1961.

In girls' grammar schools the dress that may be worn by sixth formers is often not controlled by the school and may be of a type that does not meet the full approval of the teachers.

There is a clear example of this process in higher education. The ideal of the university that the newer British universities on the whole tried to imitate was that of a group of teachers and learners meeting together to pursue a life of scholarship and discussion. Today many university students study from nine to five and return daily to the suburban life from which they came. No residential facilities or organized societies will change their habits. The university and its teachers must alter and not the students.[1] It would appear that this power of the pupils to influence the teacher is a matter of age. In the primary school children are still very much under the influence of their parents and lack sufficient knowledge or confidence to challenge their teachers. But the older the pupils, the more they can become an independent force determining the actions of their teachers.

3. *Reciprocal Forces*

There are channels through which influence can be brought to bear on the teacher, but through which he in his turn can bring pressure on those who are trying to change or determine his course of action. This final section will deal briefly with three such channels.

(i) *Syllabuses.* The broad outline of what a school will teach is decided by its head, but within this framework heads of departments and class teachers have a wide choice. Often, however, the teacher has to prepare his pupils for an external examination. In this case he may feel himself to be very much at the mercy of the examining body that sets his syllabus. Yet teachers can influence examining bodies, since there is machinery available to ensure that the teacher's voice may be heard. Professional associations annually collect comments on GCE papers from the schools and, if there are any complaints, bring their influence to bear on those setting the papers. A panel of university and school teachers set the examinations, though university members predominate; a larger, but similar, panel mark the scripts, though in this case school teachers form the majority. Therefore, teachers have some chance of influencing the setting and marking of this examination, though their attitudes may

---

[1] See B. R. Wilson, 'The Needs of Students' in M. Reeves (ed.), *Eighteen Plus*', London, 1965.

coincide with those from the universities, since they were educated there. Finally, few teachers apparently realize that, if they want it, examining bodies will arrange to set special papers for individual schools. The teacher who feels really strongly can almost completely control the syllabus and examination papers of his pupils, though the examining board must approve the standards of these special papers.

This picture of the GCE may seem idealistic, but it is a description of existing machinery that is little used. The organization of the CSE puts the onus of running the examination entirely upon the teachers. The boards in each local area that are responsible for drawing up syllabuses and setting examination papers are made up almost entirely of teachers. Only after pressure from their association were lecturers from training colleges invited to sit as observers on the panels responsible for the examination papers in the various subjects. Here the secondary school teacher has the fullest opportunity to teach a syllabus set entirely in accordance with the wishes of himself and his colleagues. He can, if he wants, escape the influence of those examining bodies who have so long been accused of hampering the schools' work.

One syllabus is less open to influence from the schools than most, namely that in religious instruction. Voluntary schools have the freedom of teaching religion according to their trust deeds; syllabuses will meet the needs of the denominations that are responsible for each particular school. But by the 1944 Act maintained schools must follow an agreed syllabus. This is drawn up by the representatives of local religious interests, of teachers and of the local authority. Agreed syllabuses are rarely revised, and some local authorities have adopted the syllabus of another authority. In all these cases the teacher has far less influence than in other school subjects, and his freedom to teach as he wishes is diminished in a way that offends the English tradition. This position is the price of the compromise between the various denominations and the State that was needed to ensure the passage of the 1944 Act.

(ii) *The General Public.* Public opinion influences the school and hence the teacher by the normal democratic process. The policies of the various political parties, both nationally and locally, are brought to bear on the provision of education in the same way as on the supplying of the other services maintained by the State. But teachers in their turn can influence the parties and the public. This is done in several ways, though the place of the professional associations is important. Local branches watch local educational problems, whilst at the national level headquarters is in close touch with the Department and also lobbies Members of Parliament. In the case of deciding pay these associations are also represented on the committees that propose the various salary scales.

Professional associations operate in all the sections of the educational system. Thus, the NUT guards the interests of teachers in the schools; there are associations of teachers in training colleges and universities that fulfil the same function for their members. These bodies use many methods, as do their local branches. The officers and secretaries of professional associations make radio and television broadcasts in order to work on public opinion. They form delegations to call upon the Minister or Members of Parliament so as to influence administration or legislation. Letters may be written to national and local newspapers on specific issues as they arise. Lastly, perhaps rarely but certainly to great effect, teachers' associations submit evidence to committees or Royal Commissions. The democratic dialogue is no less real in education than in any other field, and teachers can in this way influence the way the educational system is run.

(iii) *The Central Advisory Councils.* One of the major political institutions that Britain has invented is the office of the Leader of the Opposition, who is paid by the State to stand by to form a Government if the present majority party loses the support of the country. In the field of education a rather similar institution has been created. The 1944 Act laid down that there should be two permanent Central Advisory Councils, one for England and the other for Wales; the ancestry of these bodies dates back to the 1902 Education Act. Similar machinery exists for Scotland. Representatives of the wide range of educational institutions and also informed outsiders are members of these Councils. The Minister remits to them topics that are central to the educational problems of the time. The Councils deliberate for as long as they feel necessary, examine any witnesses or evidence that they feel fitting and issue a report. The Government pays all the expenses. In the past the Councils have always interpreted their function as being to make constructive criticisms of the educational system in the light of the best contemporary knowledge, and they have tended to be progressive rather than *avant-garde*. Here is an institution that ensures that criticism is built into the educational system. There is a demand for ideas to come into the open, to influence opinion and to assist the Government of the day to form policy. Teachers are represented on it; they, as individuals and through their associations, can and do change the course of the Councils' reports by their evidence.

4. Conclusion

All teachers are members of institutions and do their work of helping children within an administrative framework. Very often they feel lost and incapable of determining the direction in which the educational system as a whole is moving. Teachers can only hope to influence this system if they have some knowledge of the administrative machinery within which they are operating and of its historical background at national and local level. Only in this way can they know the forces at work that have brought the system to its present position. If they understand the strengths and weaknesses of today's situation as created by the past, they have a greater chance of changing things in the direction that they feel necessary. In a country where evolutionary change is the rule, a successful revolutionary must work for his purpose in this way. The external forces that were described earlier in this present chapter form the more permanent forces at work within the contemporary educational system; they provide the elements of stability and the framework within which manœuvre can take place.

The teacher must deal with many people as he plays his role of teacher. R. K. Merton has referred to the complement of roles organized round any particular role as its 'role-set'.[1] In this chapter we have studied many of the roles that impinge on the teacher both from outside and from within the school; in other words we have examined the role-set of the teacher. The exact nature of the complementary roles has often been influenced by their historical development. It was partly for this reason that a brief historical account of the British idea of a school was necessary.

One of the problems of any role-set is how the central role, here the teacher, manages to play his role effectively when influenced by so many other roles that often act upon him in contrary directions. The position of the teacher in Britain is eased in several ways. The law creates a number of checks and balances to control some of the influences on the teacher. The composition of governing bodies and their position between the local authority and the teacher is one example. Another is the way that the local authority exists as a buffer between the Department and the school. The traditions that the school is independent and that the teacher is king in his own classroom help further to lessen the influence

---

[1] R. K. Merton, 'The Role-Set: Problems in Sociological Theory', *British Journal of Sociology*, June 1956. This extremely important article uses the role of the teacher as an example on several occasions.

of the role-set, since in both cases the actions of the teacher are insulated from the outside world. Membership of a professional association enables the teacher to face the role-set from a position of greater strength and no longer as a mere individual. Finally, the teacher, and more particularly the head, takes steps to abridge the role-set by failing to establish adequate channels of communication with parents. It is in such ways that a teacher can cope with the pressures put upon his position in a school.

Role-sets consist of individuals who have different personalities. The incidence of any one type of person, strong or weak, is quite unpredictable, but it is through the personal relationships between individuals of very different characters that change can come within the educational system, as in any other institutional framework. Teachers, who wish to follow their vocation of teaching children in some way that is even slightly different from the generally agreed methods must know how to work with their colleagues to gain their legitimate end. To do this successfully they must study the forces at play on their position that come both from outside and from within the school, and they must know what channels they can use to influence those who make the decisions that govern the educational system

BIBLIOGRAPHY

G. Baron, 'Some Aspects of the Headmaster Tradition', *University of Leeds Institute of Education, Researches and Studies*, June 1956.
G. Baron and A. Tropp, 'Teachers in England and America', 1961, in *The Reader*.
T. Burgess, *A Guide to English Schools*, London, 1964 (Pelican).
J. B. Mays, *Education and the Urban Child*, Liverpool, 1962 (Chapter 6).

15

The Teacher in the Classroom

The school class is a group that consists of a teacher and a varying number of children. Like any other social system the class can be divided into its constituent parts in order to see what function each part is playing in the whole. It should also be possible to see how the various parts interact with each other in fulfilling their functions. In this chapter we shall first examine the school class as a social system and secondly describe a technique, namely sociometry, that has been devised to study the inter-relationships within such small groups as the school class.

A. The School Class as a Social System

The complex functions of the educational system that were outlined in Part II can be expressed in brief terms under two main headings. The school assists the family in developing the personality of the growing child or, to use the sociological term, contributes to the socializing of the child, and it helps to allocate the child when he has grown up to the most fitting niche in adult society. In any school the major part of these tasks is done in the classrooms. Talcott Parsons (1959) has advanced the thesis that the school class as now organized will always differentiate the children in it by their achievement. This, if true, will make the process of allocation much simpler. Parsons examined schools in the USA, but his method of analysis can be applied to British schools and yields somewhat similar results.

The great majority of school classes have certain common conditions that govern their organization. It is usual today for all the children in any one school class to be of approximately the same age. This was not the case in Britain in the early nineteenth century nor is it always so in the under-developed countries today. Often in addition the children are of the same social class. This is particularly the case for smaller schools with homogeneous catchment areas as is true for many primary schools. The children in the big secondary modern schools of large urban areas tend also to come from more or less the same, mainly the working, class. Independent schools mainly consist of middle-class children, and only two British school types can be guaranteed to contain a mixed social class composition, namely the selective grammar school and the non-selective comprehensive school. Thus in very many British classrooms the children are equalized for both age and social class. To this relatively homogeneous group the teacher usually gives a common undifferentiated task. This is obvious at secondary level, where all the children will do the same set of sums or the identical questions to test their comprehension of a passage of prose. Much the same pattern is true of the top forms of the junior school; even in the lower forms and in the infant school for much of the time the teacher will split the class into small groups that will each have their own individual common task. When all the children are doing the same, comparison becomes easy, and, since variations in age and social class are often absent, the standard of performance in the work that all are doing seems to the children the obvious and main measuring rod of any differences between themselves.

This stress on academic achievement is somewhat offset in British schools by the tradition that the school shall play an important part in moulding the child's personality. Many teachers make a point of giving as much individual attention to the children in their class as possible. This both helps the children's academic achievement and enables the teacher to know the quirks of character of each individual child. Although this emphasis is true at all stages of education, it is particularly true in the infant school where academic education is not stressed so much. Yet the teacher who moulds character assesses his results in terms of good and bad. The children soon know the standards and can compare their own behaviour or 'moral achievement' in much the same way as they compare their academic results. There are also a number of progressive schools in which the emphasis is on co-operation rather than competition and on personality rather than achievement. Yet, even in these schools, the children often work in small groups in much the same way as in the junior schools; attainment determines the membership of these groups and comparison of achievement is still possible. Therefore, despite these apparent exceptions, Parsons's analysis seems to hold. The organization of the contemporary school class is such that the children are bound to stress comparative achievement, whether it is moral or academic.

A closer examination of the school class will reveal that it is in addition performing other functions of a very different nature. Although it was set up to socialize and to allocate, it has autonomously come to do other things as well. An obvious way to see what is happening in the classroom is to divide the social system into its main parts, namely the teacher and the children, and to see how each undertakes the two main functions. Finally, we shall put the two parts together again as a school class and see how they interact. Throughout we must note what additional functions this social system as a whole fulfils.

1. The Teacher

In one respect the teacher is in a unique social position. He has been formed by the social system to which he returns to form others. He can very easily transmit the values that he has picked up himself as he passed through the educational system. The 'teacher' in a secondary modern school who went through a maintained grammar school and a training college will have learnt a different set of values from the 'schoolmaster' in a public school who attended an independent school and Oxford or Cambridge. Despite such differences due to the inbreeding of values all teachers have the two main functions described above in common, namely of teaching the three R's and of moulding personality, although in the latter case the 'teacher' may aim for a different ideal from the 'schoolmaster'.

The stress on achievement is considerably strengthened because of the nature of the relationship of teacher and child. The teacher is an adult who is usually much older than his pupils and therefore appears as the judge of what they do. As the only adult amongst a group of children this seems almost inevitable, but the fact that most British schools have highly developed assessment systems makes the emphasis on achievement certain. There are many complex arrangements that force the children to compare their achievements with those of their classmates. Even in infant schools ticks and stars on sums correctly done lead to comparisons. Beginning in the junior school, but especially at secondary level, marks on individual pieces of work, tests and examination results are publicly displayed in form lists so that all, often including parents, can see. The measurement of moral achievement is often institutionalized. One of the benefits of playing games is supposedly that it builds character. The winners of house matches gain points and at secondary level, sometimes even at younger ages, competitions between houses are common. Thus the children can compare their toughness and determination as well as their English and arithmetic.

As the British educational system is now organized the stress on doing well in academic work grows on entry to the junior school and increases the nearer the children come to taking the eleven-plus examination that determines whether or not they will go to a selective secondary school. Up till eleven years of age the majority of children will come under this influence from the teacher or their parents or both, but after eleven there is a difference since some will have been selected for grammar school and the majority will have failed at this hurdle. Those who are in the grammar school have been chosen for education for the *élite*. They have been 'sponsored' either for upward mobility or for remaining in their present middle-class position. Those who have gone to the secondary modern school have at an early age to adjust to failure in the competition for social status, since transfer to grammar school after eleven is rare. The teachers in these schools play a part in helping the children to re-adjust their aspirations. In the comprehensive school a situation more akin to the US high school is found, since here the final choice for the *élite* has not yet been made. The teacher can put stress on competition in school achievement until at least the minimum legal leaving age. In this new type of secondary school the avenue to the *élite* is competitive rather than sponsored as in the more usual grammar–modern system.[1]

If the teacher is to fulfil his functions he must influence his class by providing the leadership that is usually referred to as discipline in discussion of this topic in schools. There are purely legal sanctions on the teacher to maintain discipline since a chaotic classroom cannot provide the education envisaged in the 1944 Act. There are several types of leadership and each ensures a different atmosphere in the classroom. The problem is to discover whether any one type will enable the teacher to do what he wants more efficiently.

In 1939–40 three American sociologists undertook a famous series of experiments that is relevant at this point. This work was very sophisticated and can only be described in the briefest outline here. Lippitt, Lewin and White (R. Lippitt and R. K. White, 1940) arranged for three groups of adolescents to have three different types of leader for the

[1] See R. H. Turner, 'Sponsored and Contest Mobility in the School System', *American Sociological Review*, December 1960 for some comments on the way in which ideas of mobility influence education in the USA and Britain. This article is also in *The Reader*.

activities that they undertook in a youth club. There were authoritarian leaders (the reader should throughout mentally substitute 'teacher' for 'leader' so that he may catch the full relevance of this experiment), who gave orders without reasons, accepted no questions as to aim or method, distributed blame or praise without any objective explanation, and remained aloof from their groups. There were *laissez-faire* leaders, who allowed their groups to do what they wanted, made no suggestions, and were neither critical nor helpful; these leaders were merely adults who were present. Finally, there were democratic leaders, who gave suggestions without forcing them on their groups, gave constructive and objective criticism and praise, did not interfere excessively, and tried to be positive without being masterful. Each type of leadership was found to create a totally different atmosphere in a group. Authoritarian leadership resulted in a lack of co-operation amongst the adolescents who stressed 'me' rather than 'us'; there was an air of either rebellion or repression. The *laissez-faire* leader's group were unable to work together, as they found no common aim and so merely drifted. The democratic group decided what was to be done, co-operated well and enjoyed what they did together. It would seem that a teacher who creates a democratic atmosphere by the leadership that he gives in Britain as in America can hope for good results and a happy class. Democracy can be viewed as an end in itself, but here it is seen to be a method of leadership in a classroom that results in the children imposing a discipline upon themselves so that they accomplish the work that their teacher feels necessary.

Another investigation that was carried out in the USA in the 1940's reinforces this conclusion.[1] It was found that teachers' behaviour in the classroom was dominated by two opposing aims. The desires to dominate and to achieve social integration were both present in all the teachers observed, but the relative amounts varied in each teacher even within any one day and also through a school term. However, the children reacted differently according as to whether dominance or social integration was the predominant aim. Where social integration was the major element, the children were less restless, contributed more to the lesson and showed more initiative than where dominance was shown. The pattern of behaviour shown by the teachers did not seem to be influenced by different groups of children, since they were observed a year later with their new classes and exhibited the same patterns. There was little

[1] Work of H. H. Anderson quoted in K. M. Evans, *Sociometry and Education*, London, 1961, pp. 102–4.

doubt that the teachers were influencing the children and not vice versa.

The importance of these findings has been indicated by work in Salford in 1951. Here Wiseman found that progressiveness in the teachers was a factor that could be separated out as a statistically significant influence on children's success in school. More especially progressive teachers had considerable effect on the attainment of children in reading and writing.[1] Activity methods are seen by many teachers as a philosophy rather than as a means to more efficient education. A teacher's philosophy will govern his attitudes. It is known that parents' attitudes to education can influence their children's success at school, so it should be no surprise to find that teachers' attitudes can influence the achievement of the children whom they are teaching, even if only by adopting a curriculum or method that grasps the attention of their pupils.

2. *The School Class*
Sociologists refer to a group all the members of which are of the same age as a peer group. The school class is one such group that plays an important part in socializing its members. Teachers are often so immersed in fulfilling their functions of teaching the three R's and of moulding character that they forget that membership in a peer group itself plays a large part in educating children. The process of education in such a group is unconscious but none the less real.

As has been indicated the family is too simple a social system to provide all the needs of the growing child. For many purposes the best way to view the socialization of the child is to consider the family and school and peer group as one social system. The child goes out from the family into the primary school where he is a member of a peer group, the school class. In this group he tests out the personality that he has learnt in the family and, if he cannot survive with that set of traits, he must modify his personality, adapting to meet the world at large outside his family. The child who bosses his young brother around at home learns to be bossed around at school as he undoubtedly will be in adult life. The new learning is achieved with the security of the family as a support upon which he may fall back.

The school class is one of several peer groups of which British children are members and which may include the scout troop and the street gang, but it is the group to which the child must belong by law and in which he

[1] S. Wiseman, op. cit., pp. 158–61.

must participate very regularly for about ten years. Hence it is of great importance. In the school class the child moves in an egalitarian group; this is not the case in the family which is hierarchical by its structure. The child must learn to move amongst his peers and gain non-adult approval. This is a preparation for mixing with others in the way in which he will commonly have to do as an adult. Very soon the selfish child must learn to adapt to the wishes of the rest of the class in the play-ground or else suffer unpopularity and rejection by his peers. The child must experiment with personal relationships. The friendship groups in the younger age ranges change rapidly as the children learn whom they can trust and in what way they must behave towards their contemporaries. Parents are used to a child coming home from school and saying 'John's not my friend any more' of the classmate who was his inseparable companion till yesterday. The school class is an important testing ground for experience and in it the child will be valued by his peers as a whole personality, not just on his school work or on his 'good' character as judged by the teacher's criteria.

All small groups such as the school class quickly create particular patterns and standards of behaviour to which their members must adapt. The group will provide models of behaviour either from its own member-ship or in the form of a hero, for example a cowboy or a spaceman, to which its members will look. An important additional function of the school class is that minority groups begin to be differentiated out from the group as a whole even as early as the junior school. Despite the efforts of the teacher and some enlightened parents children come to realize that our culture on the whole treats Jews and those with darker skins in a somewhat different way from other people. Children will try to live up to these standards much more readily than those provided by the family or the teacher, since the authority or power within the peer group is of a very different and usually more acceptable nature.

At the kindergarten stage school classes consist of children of both sexes and play groups cut across sex boundaries. Although the junior school is still organized on a co-educational basis, the play groups at this stage tend to be single sex groups and remain so until adolescence.[1] During this period the child is learning the sex role ascribed him or her by the society in which he or she is living. In the main this process takes place in the school class. In this way boys become boys and girls become

[1] W. A. L. Blyth, 'The Sociometric Study of Children's Groups in English Schools', *British Journal of Educational Studies*, May 1960, pp. 138–9.

girls. After children pass the age of puberty they start to enlarge their
sex roles as they learn to mix with the opposite sex. This is very much
easier in a secondary school that takes both boys and girls. The very need
that adolescents feel to experiment with relationships in this way leads
to some of the main problems that are implicit in the organization of
schools on a co-educational basis.

At the age of about eleven, British children in the State system move
to new schools and this can mean a reshuffle of friendship groups. For
the children who go to selective schools that serve a large catchment area
the school class mainly consists of children who were unknown to them in
their junior schools. For some the range of peer groups is only determined by age, but for others social class can be an influence. The school
class in the secondary modern school will tend more often to consist of a
single social class, but the grammar school includes children from all
social classes. The question can be asked as to whether friendship
cliques in such schools are formed on the basis of social class. If the
results of work done in the early 1950's in four London grammar schools
is typical, this would not appear to be the case; friendship groups are
not bound up with the socio-economic status of the family as seems to
happen in the USA.[1]

The influence of the school class on vocational aspirations is important. A group who have either failed the eleven-plus or never taken it and
now find themselves considered out of the competitive race for high
status will together re-adjust their ideas of the jobs for which they wish
to aim. The group who have passed into a selective secondary school feel
that they have succeeded in that activity upon which the educational
system puts greatest emphasis, namely academic achievement. The
majority of this latter group will be from the middle class or aspire to it,
often under the pressure of their parents. In this situation the whole
school class will tend to reinforce each other in continuing to stress the
academic work that they know will lead to a chance of success in later
life. This tendency will be stronger, the greater is the proportion of
middle-class children in the school class.[2]

In addition to its function with regard to academic achievement the
school class provides adolescents with opportunities for socialization that

[1] A. N. Oppenheim, 'Social Status and Clique Formation Among Grammar
School Boys', *British Journal of Sociology*, September 1955.

[2] Compare B. Jackson and D. Marsden's (op. cit.) evidence for a high proportion of middle-class children with H. T. Himmelweit's (in D. V. Glass (ed.), op.
cit.) description of the opposite case.

do not occur within the family. They can experiment among their peers in what values they should hold. Is a trade union leader more important than a pop singer ? Furthermore, the sources of prestige within an adolescent group are not the same as amongst adults, and this can both help and hinder the process of socializing the growing child. If the parents are behind the times with their values or the knowledge that adolescents now consider necessary, the school class can often supply the missing need. On the other hand, as children grow older, there is every chance that discontinuity will appear between the values of the parents and teacher, and the peer group. In many countries throughout the world today there is a flourishing youth culture (T. R. Fyvel, 1963). The adolescent learns what is momentarily fashionable in behaviour, speech and clothing. At times the peer group is reinforced or even replaced by 'those formidable peer-surrogates, the mass media'.[1] Today the peer group, an important example of which is the school class, is a major agent in the socialization of the young and by the stage of adolescence in many respects it is often out of the control of both family and school.

3. *The Teacher and School Class as a System*

Where there is not great discontinuity of values between the school class and the teacher, the classroom is a social system in itself that performs certain definite additional functions. The teacher is not merely manipulating the children by providing leadership, but by his very presence he affects the currents of feeling that flow between the members of the group and between the group and himself. To the children in the school class the teacher is a superior adult who is not a member of their families. Before going to school the relationships of most infants with adults have been of an emotional nature. The family have cared about happiness. The teacher, even of young children, puts stress on performance and the older the child grows, the more true does this become. This is an important preparation for life as, when the child leaves school and starts a job, he will meet many who are in a superior position to himself and who will concentrate on his achievements, for instance at work, rather than on his personality as a whole. This process is made easier in the primary school because the teacher is normally a woman and can be seen by the child as like his mother. But the class teacher changes year by year and the child comes to see the difference between the position of teacher and the individual teacher who fills that position. The absence of this idea can

[1] T. Parsons in S. M. Lipset and L. Lowenthal (ed.), *Culture and Social Character*, New York, 1961, p. 91.

be observed when children call their teacher 'Mummy' and its growth when, as sometimes occurs, a child is taught by his parent and in the classroom addresses him as 'Daddy-Sir'.

The whole social system of teacher and school class adjusts through conflict. This is not just a question of children letting off emotional steam. It is most clearly seen when a teacher takes over a school class that is new to him. The children must learn his ways and the teacher must discover the characteristic manner of each child. Each must test the other to learn the limits of behaviour, but this conflict serves a useful function in that it leads not to a position of equilibrium but to a point where tension is reduced to a minimum for this group. When this is achieved, teacher and children know what to expect of each other and the class as a whole can fulfil its functions as efficiently as possible.

As a rider to this it follows that since there must almost always be tension between the teacher and the children, the school class must usually be working below full efficiency. For example the problem of social class learning will show itself early in the primary school and may hinder the academic achievement of some children, and the clash of the teacher's middle-class culture with the values of some of the class may depress the moral achievement of others. In this situation teachers are often hostile to the children and may even act somewhat like a drill sergeant. The school class or a part of it sees the teacher as their enemy, and this helps to define the group as a gang hostile to the school and its values.[1] Such dysfunctional conflict can be very important in the secondary modern schools of slum areas. It is clear that whereas the teacher and the school class will reinforce each other's ends in the selective grammar school where each tend to be working towards the same purpose, in the secondary modern school there is the possibility of the type of conflict that leads to a separate youth culture radically opposed to the school.

B. Sociometry

So far we have analysed what the functions of the teacher and the school class are but have not tried to see what are the exact inter-relationships within the class itself. If the teacher wishes to see the class objectively as it is and not subjectively as he thinks it is, there is available to him the

[1] For an account of such a school see J. Webb, 'The Sociology of a School' *British Journal of Sociology*, September 1962.

technique of sociometry. This is a particular way of measuring social behaviour that leads to the study of the structure and development of groups. J. L. Moreno invented the method in Austria before 1914 whilst doing group therapy with children. Moreno developed his ideas further whilst organizing a refugee camp in the 1914-18 war. In 1925 he went to the USA and gathered a group of disciples in New York. Together they did much research work. Moreno always held the view that his methods could be used to lower social tensions and make the world a happier place.

However, there is no doubt that the tools that Moreno and his co-workers devised can be used to provide an objective and quantitative picture of the relationships within such a group as the school class. The first step is to ask the members of the group individually a series of questions in which they have to choose with whom they would under-take some relevant task (G. Jahoda, 1962). For example, the teacher might ask each child in a junior class with whom he would like to sit to read or with whom he would like to go out to tea. The answers to these two particular questions would give some idea as to whom each would prefer as a work mate in the first case or as a friend in the second. The technique is easy to administer and might be of help to the teacher in two ways. He could in a rather academic way learn more about the children in his class, and this should help his handling of this class. Secondly, he could take specific action. In one experiment in a junior school a socio-metric test showed that a class was split into two groups of boys who did not mix. The groups came from the same social class, but had different intelligence levels, leisure interests and home areas. The teacher did not suspect this cleavage because the children gave no trouble.[1] The teacher here could use this knowledge in order to reorganize the children's seating plan so that they had to mix with each other, if this was what he considered to be good for these children.

The answers to the questions given in sociometric tests can be plotted as a sociogram (K. M. Evans, 1961) that displays in schematic form the relationships within the group. Groups of three persons who choose each other will be represented as a triangle with its apexes joined by lines. Mutual friends who choose each other can easily be seen. A popular figure who is the choice of many will appear in the sociogram as the centre of a star, whilst those who are not chosen at all will be seen as

[1] W. A. L. Blyth, 'Sociometry, prefects, and peaceful coexistence in a junior school', *Sociological Review*, February 1958.

isolates. Such a diagram will reveal to the teacher the social forces at work in his classroom at a moment of time in respect of the particular activity about which he has asked the children. If he wishes to observe whether change is taking place, he can repeat the test after, say, three months.

One of the problems that sociograms can pose is what to do about isolates. To place the child in an existing group may make this child withdraw even further. To put a number of isolates together in one group may prove even worse as the qualities that make them incompatible to the rest of the class may well make them unacceptable to each other. Teachers can, if they are not careful, create isolates by the way that they treat individual children; rejection by the teacher may cause his classmates to isolate this child.

There have been a number of general findings in English sociometric studies (W. A. L. Blyth, 1960). The tendency towards complete division between the sexes has already been mentioned, but in addition girls' groups are smaller and more intimate than those of boys. The pattern of any class changes through the academic year in one of two ways. Either a scatter of mutual choices leads to an aggregate of sub-groups who eventually form a group with a single star or collective leadership at the centre, or there is an initial pattern at the start of the year that changes, but reverts to its original form by the end of the year. It would also seem that where regrouping of the class is undertaken after sociometric analysis, some slight improvement in social adjustment takes place without academic performance falling away, but in all such experimental work there is great difficulty in defining the criteria of measurement.

Sociometric studies have been made of teachers as well as of children.[1] In both the USA and Britain it has been found that different generations like and dislike very similar traits in teachers. For instance, they like a kindly, patient and firm teacher, but not one who is sarcastic, domineering and has favourites. If a teacher knows this and understands that he has a character trait that works to his disadvantage in the classroom, one would presume that by control he could rid himself of it. However, from work done in the USA it seems that teachers build up patterns of behaviour over the years which they use both in and out of the classroom. They can modify teaching techniques but, in as much as their response to their pupils is governed by their personality, change is very difficult. Certainly the main lesson from such studies is that students must learn

[1] See K. M. Evans, op. cit., Chapters VIII and IX.

their disadvantageous habits and traits before these become so deeply ingrained in their patterns of behaviour that change is difficult or almost impossible.

C. Conclusion

Sociometry is a method that a teacher can use in the classroom to see just what is happening amongst the children in his class. He may treat the results of sociometric analysis as a valuable addition to the knowledge upon which he bases his decisions as to how he will handle the whole class or individuals within his class. Moreno used the technique that he invented with the aim of promoting social harmony and social effectiveness. The teacher can use the same methods with caution as one means towards whatever ends he has in view.

Knowledge of the detailed structure of his class may obscure for the teacher the picture of what the whole social system of the class is doing to the children in it. These functions were analysed in the first part of this chapter. In outline they may be represented by the following diagram; in each box an example has been quoted to give an indication of what part that sub-system is playing:

		Sub-system		
Function	Age	Teacher = leader	Class = Peer group	Teacher (Class = Conflict)
Socialization {	Primary	Testing moral attainment	Testing of personality in a group away from family	Contact with mainly one adult (woman) in a non-emotional role
	Secondary	Testing moral attainment	Development of sex roles to opposite sex	Contact with several men filling the role of teacher
Allocation {	Primary	Testing academic attainment	Experiment in values	Start of culture clash
	Secondary: Selective	Educating for sponsored mobility	Group stressing high aspirations	Parts of sub-system reinforcing each other
	Non-selective	Helping readjustment of aspirations	Group adjusting to failure	Definition of the gang (v. the school)

BIBLIOGRAPHY

W. A. L. Blyth, 'The Sociometric Study of Children's Groups in English Schools', *British Journal of Educational Studies*, May 1960.

K. M. Evans, *Sociometry and Education*, London, 1961.

T. R. Fyvel, *The Insecure Offenders*, London, edn. 1963 (Pelican).

G. Jahoda, in G. Humphry and M. Argyle (ed.)., *Social Psychology through Experiment*, London, 1962 (Chapter 6).

R. Lippitt and R. K. White, 'An Experimental Study of Leadership and Group Life', in G. E. Swanson and T. H. Newcomb and others, *Readings in Social Psychology*, rev. edn., New York, 1952.

T. Parsons, 'The School Class as a Social System', 1959, in *The Reader*.

16

The Role of the Teacher

So far in the third part of this book the position of the teacher has been examined from several viewpoints with the intention of building an adequate sociology of teaching. It is clear from Chapter 13 that the teacher is marginally a member of a profession; this defines the status of his role as a teacher. In Chapter 14 the main forces that impinge upon the teacher were described; the complex of complementary roles around the teacher is termed his role-set. Chapter 13 was a brief introduction to the sociology of the school. The aim of this final chapter is to examine the role of the teacher himself and then to see what teaching does to the teacher.

A. The Role of the Teacher

'Role' is a two-way concept. Any role covers the set of values and expectations of a particular position in a social system from the point of view of both the occupant of the position and those with whom he interacts. Implicit in the idea of a role, therefore, is a self-image and a public image. The role of the teacher is organized around the functions that he fulfils, to be more specific, in the main around the transmission of knowledge and values. In different parts of the educational system the weight given to these and to other functions will vary. For this reason the role of the teacher in the infant school will not be the same as that of the secondary teacher. Almost no research has been done directly on this topic in this country and often the findings of workers in other countries will be quoted, not as definitive, but as suggestive. Clearly the role of the teacher in a school system that is characterized by non-selective secondary schools as in the USA will differ in many ways from that of a teacher in a British grammar school.

There is a close connection between the self-image and the public image of any profession. A change in the self-image may affect the public image and hence the prestige of the occupation. This in turn will influence the occupational choice of the next generation. This process is particularly important in the case of teaching, since the supply of new recruits to the profession is below the demand for them. The way in which teachers view themselves will be reflected in the way that the public look at teachers. Furthermore, how teachers are seen by the public will help to determine how many young people take up teaching.

The possibility exists that there may be a difference between the public and the self-image of any occupation. As a result of a survey J. Kob (1963) has shown that this was the case for teachers in secondary schools in Hamburg. Here the public rated teachers higher in respect of social prestige than teachers voted themselves. Nothing is known of the comparative rankings in Britain.

1. *The Public Image of Teaching*

Most people have in their minds a number of imaginary pictures that cover what they consider to be the salient features of any occupational role. Walter Lippmann, the American journalist, christened these pictures 'stereotypes'. If teachers are called to mind, several stereotypes exist. There is, for example, the stern and dignified teacher and there is also the gentle and self-effacing teacher (W. Waller, 1933). Much of our social intercourse is determined by the stereotype of the occupation with which we are at the moment in contact. When we meet our doctor or a clergyman in the street, the stereotype that we have of these occupations governs our behaviour towards that particular doctor or clergyman. Parents are often heard to say of their child's teacher, 'He's a typical teacher', or 'She's not at all like a teacher', and they will adjust their behaviour to this teacher according to the way in which he differs from their stereotype.

A very full investigation of the public image of the teacher has been made by the University of Missouri in Kansas City between 1958 and 1960.[1] This work showed that the most usual stereotype of the American teacher was centred around three points. The first and most important was the relationship between teacher and child; the teacher was expected to show no favouritism and to be interested, helpful and loving towards

[1] B. J. Biddle, H. A. Rosencranz and E. F. Rankin, *General Characteristics of the School Teacher's Role*, Columbia, 1961, especially Vol. II 'Studies in the Role of the Public School Teacher'.

his pupils. The second focus was the manner in which he taught the children; he was expected to stress things, particularly of a verbal nature, to observe the children and to give them tasks to do. Finally, control was important and was seen in terms of order and quietness. The public considered the relationship between teacher and children to be much more important than the other two points. This emphasis on the emotional support of the child at the expense of his instruction is probably one of the main differences between the role of the teacher in Britain and the USA.

A thorough survey was made into the way in which the public expected teachers to behave. Teachers were expected to reflect the general moral values of the community in their behaviour and to set a good example by their high standard of conduct. They were expected to avoid all the interesting sins of our age. If they sinned at all, it was to be by omission rather than by commission. Teachers were seen as conformists and as rather neutral persons who do nothing out of the ordinary. In an investigation in Britain in the early part of the 1939–45 war an absence of an adventurous spirit was noted amongst teachers.[1] This might be expected amongst a conformist group. However, at that time the attitudes of teachers were governed by a very different set of social conditions from today and more particularly by the prolonged mass unemployment suffered by this country during the inter-war years. In such a time timidity at work is more understandable.

The American survey noted that the wide extension of the teacher's role seemed to be coming to an end. Certainly up to 1939 the role of the teacher covered many aspects of his life away from school. He was always a teacher in the eyes of the public. Today in America and in Britain this is not so true. Men teachers need not always dress in a restrained manner, and women teachers may smoke and wear make-up. Yet one suspects that an investigation of the role of the teacher in Britain would reveal a very similar picture to that in America. The public image may not be so all-embracing as formerly, but the teacher is still expected to be a virtuous conformist.

One of the main social functions of the educational system is to assist in social selection, and therefore the teacher's role contains an element concerned with selection. He helps children towards the opportunities

---

[1] W. B. Tudhope, 'Motives for the Choice of the Teaching Profession by Training College Students', *British Journal of Educational Psychology*, November 1944.

for which he feels that they are best fitted, and he acts as a model of the behaviour in the status to which the children are aspiring or to which they are made to aspire. The British teacher stresses both moral and academic attainment in the classroom so that he becomes a model in the field of behaviour as well as in matters of the intellect.

The teacher has often been called 'a social stranger'. This is almost inevitable because of his position. Firstly, the teacher spends much of his life amongst children; to parents he is nearly always known only in connection with their children. His life is built around those things usually associated with childhood such as games, examinations and school rituals. In this respect the teacher is in many ways cut off from the world of adults. But he is also bound to be remote from children because he must keep discipline in his class and usually has at his command a whole arsenal of rewards and punishments. Secondly, the teacher is often culturally (in both senses of the word) apart from the community that he serves. If he lives in it, he is not of it, and, if he travels daily to his school from a distance, geographical as well as cultural separation exists. This cultural aspect is important since it indicates that the role of the teacher is a mediating role; it acts as a bridge, linking present and future. The clergyman links sacred and secular, the psychiatrist sick and well, and the teacher taught and untaught.[1] Those who play mediating roles must try to stand in two worlds and hence tend to belong to neither.

One of the most striking pieces of British empirical research that is relevant at this point is the investigation that W. M. Williams carried out in Gosforth during the early 1950's. In the course of this he asked those living in the area to rank each other according to social position. A hierarchy resulted that was akin to social class. There were upper and lower classes, but in between was an intermediate group, smaller than any of the sub-categories into which the two classes were divided. In this were placed those who were 'neither one thing nor the other' and included the local schoolmaster and a retired teacher who lived locally. The comments of the other classes on the intermediate group make clear the isolation that is here under consideration. The upper working class spoke of 'school teachers and that sort' who were 'in between because of education'.[2]

This tendency to social isolation is reinforced by the fact that teachers

---

[1] K. D. Naegele, 'Clergymen, Teachers and Psychiatrists: A Study in Roles and Socialization', *Canadian Journal of Economics*, February 1956.

[2] W. M. Williams, op. cit., pp. 94–95 and pp. 107–9.

are often transients. The Newsom Report showed that in England and Wales the proportion of teachers who were appointed to secondary modern school staffs in September 1958 and who were still in the same school three years later was 65 per cent for men and 58 per cent for women.[1] Although some movement may be expected this is a very high turnover of staff. Teachers come from outside the community. Children and parents know that they may not stay long. This is particularly true of all young teachers. Young women teachers are expected to marry early and leave school to look after a family. Young men teachers who wish for promotion must have experience in several schools. If movement is assumed to be normal, neither the teacher nor the community will be keen to sink much emotional capital in the other, and isolation will once again tend to be the result.

One of the signs of the isolation of the teaching profession has been the tendency to intermarriage. The proportion of trained women graduate teachers who married teachers remained at around a quarter between 1936 and 1954, but the proportion of certificated teachers who married teachers slowly diminished between 1936 and 1955 from 18 per cent to 14 per cent.[2] This decline and the possibly abridged nature of the role of the teacher described above may perhaps be taken as a measure of the somewhat less isolated nature of the training-college trained teacher.

Despite the lack of British empirical work it would seem that several clear stereotypes of the teacher do exist. Though he is not perhaps so cut off from the world as he used to be, the teacher still tends to be a social stranger by virtue of his very position. He is thought of as a paragon and as a model to be imitated. As a representative of middle-class virtues the teacher is not expected to be too different in any way, and it may well be that as a result teachers tend to be conformists.

2. *The Self Image of the Teacher*
(i) *Men of Knowledge.* Teachers may serve in 'learned schools' or in 'generally educative schools'[3]. In the first type of school social roles may be taught, but knowledge is stressed and in a theoretical or academic form. The British grammar school is obviously a relevant instance. In the generally educative schools the balance is reversed and the emphasis is rather on ensuring the maintenance of the social order, though the

[1] *Half Our Future* (Newsom Report), 1963, p. 245.
[2] *Women and Teaching* (Kelsall Report), 1963, pp. 24–25.
[3] F. Znaniecki, *The Social Role of the Man of Knowledge*, New York, 1940, pp. 153–7.

rise in the educational threshold has led to a greater stress on academic learning in these schools. The secondary modern school is relevant here. Teachers serving in these two types of school will tend to see themselves in very different ways. In the first case the teacher is a graduate and whilst at university he associated with scholars who were working on research. The grammar school teacher will wish to initiate his pupils into this world, whether he is teaching the arts or the sciences, and will tend to see himself as a junior colleague of the university lecturer. In the generally educative schools the stress will tend to fall on personality and behaviour; the teacher will see himself as more committed to the interests of the whole child.

The age of the children taught will influence the view that the teacher has of himself. The younger the children the more diffuse is the teacher's role. Tasks are not usually specific in the primary school. The job of the primary teacher is concerned with both mathematics and morals. The teacher is committed to the child. Unlike many roles today his is not a neutral role. The doctor cares unemotionally for 'cases', the teacher with warmth and understanding for children and often for a much longer period of time than the doctor.[1] It seems clear that there are two types of men of knowledge that match the two types of school. We shall return to this point later.

(ii) *Motive.* Essential to an understanding of how teachers view themselves is a knowledge of why they choose to teach rather than to follow some other occupation. As a result of work in Holland in the post-war period Langeveld (1963) reported that teachers gave many motives for entering teaching. Amongst those mentioned were that the profession seemed a safe and easy one; it was in a sphere well known to them and it carried intellectual prestige; study was familiar to them and the job provided satisfaction to hard workers; idealism, whether moral, religious or intellectual, could find an outlet in this work. In addition some admitted to seeing in teaching a way to exercise power and satisfy ambition. In Britain in the early 1940's Tudhope found very similar motives amongst the 643 training-college students in his sample, though, since 427 were women, it is not surprising that fondness for children was also a predominant motive and was ranked first by the women students.[2]

Since the war two surveys have been made that throw some light on

---

[1] B. R. Wilson, 'The Teacher's Role,' *British Journal of Sociology*, March 1962 and K. D. Naegele, op. cit., pp. 53–54.

[2] W. B. Tudhope, op. cit.

the motives of those taking up teaching in Britain. The first was carried out in Scotland; 296 students at St Andrews and Dundee Training Centres were asked in 1951-2 to rank twenty motives that were most influential in their decision to teach. Fondness for children was ranked first, desire for a profession closely associated with one's favourite studies second, fondness for teaching third, security fourth and ideals fifth. However, within the overall pattern there were differences between the sexes and between graduates and non-graduates. Women and non-graduates both ranked fondness for children first, but men and graduates placed first the desire for a profession associated with their studies. Women and non-graduates put fondness for teaching second, whilst graduates and men placed it fourth and fifth respectively. Graduates put fondness for children second, but men ranked it eighth.[1]

In 1961 a survey was made in sixteen universities in England and Wales of third year women under-graduates who were questioned about their attitudes towards teaching. Forty-nine per cent of the sample put teaching either firmly or tentatively as their first choice of career, only 8 per cent of whom considered their choice as a reluctant acceptance of the inevitable. Eighteen per cent gave teaching as a second choice, 11 per cent of whom were bowing to the inevitable. Of those with teaching as their first choice 47 per cent stressed the holidays as an attractive feature of their chosen profession, 32 per cent work with the young, 22 per cent helping children progress, and 21 per cent mentioned the chance of continuing their academic work. Those who put teaching as their second choice on the whole stressed the intellectual element of the work rather than the contact with children.[2] In the case of the first choices the results compare with the Scottish investigation. The picture is one of women stressing the motive of working with children and of graduates wanting to continue their intellectual work. This impression is reinforced by a small survey reported in 1962. In a sample of 131 teachers and 43 first-year students at training college the graduates were oriented towards teaching their subjects, and those connected with training colleges put stress on the child's need for understanding and sympathy rather than his need to be taught or to learn.[3]

(iii) *Three Ideal Types.* A sociologist uses the term 'ideal type' without

[1] A. F. Skinner, 'Scotland. Part I. Professional Education', *The Yearbook of Education*, London, 1963.

[2] M. Collins, op. cit.

[3] P. H. Taylor, 'Children's Evaluation of the Characteristics of a Good Teacher', *British Journal of Educational Psychology*, November 1962, p. 264.

any connotations of value. The term carries no moral overtones, but is a descriptive model which need not necessarily exist in its pure form in the real world, but which is constructed for analytical purposes as characteristic of the institution or particular social phenomenon under consideration.[1] In this examination of the role of the teacher we have gone far enough to give two ideal types of the way in which teachers view themselves. There is the academic teacher and the child-centred teacher. Later it will be necessary to add a third, the missionary teacher.

The academic teacher is usually in a 'learned school' and is keen on his subject. He sees his role to centre on the stress on knowledge. He was trained at a university and feels himself to be a little lower in status than the majority of graduates who have entered other professions. He therefore tries to seek prestige by taking part in social activities outside the educational world such as the local dramatic society. In Gosforth the upper class thought that the presence of people like teachers in the village was 'handy when you have about a dozen village organizations to see to'.[2] The second type is the child-centred teacher who sees himself as teaching the child and not as teaching any particular subject. He, therefore, puts much more emphasis on the skills of teaching than on any subject matter. For this reason the child-centred teacher tends to be much more of a general practitioner.

The important question for the sociologist to answer is whether there are any particular determinants of these two types (J. Kob, 1958). Training is one of the most important factors to be examined. The teacher from a training college has undergone a professional course that lays great emphasis on the psychological needs of the child. Concurrently he has studied one or more academic subjects. There is every chance that this academic knowledge will be related to the teaching of it to the child in the school, particularly since all the lecturers who teach the academic subjects to him will themselves have been teachers for a period. There may be dangers of inbreeding of methods and attitudes in an ethos that is usually markedly child-centred, but the final result in all probability will be that the young teacher is committed to teaching and to children rather than to any academic subject. The teacher who comes from university has spent three years doing academic work under teachers who rarely, if ever, have taught children. He then may, but need not necessarily, have had a year's vocational training before he begins to

[1] See M. Ginsberg, *On the Diversity of Morals*, London, 1956, pp. 205–7.
[2] W. M. Williams, op. cit., p. 107.

teach, but his subject was studied apart from the need to teach it in schools, and any professional training will take place after the student has become attached to his specialism as a subject. The graduate teacher can be a graduate in exile in the schools who teaches inefficiently what he knows and loves to children whom he does not really understand.

The way that the teacher views himself as a result of his training may be reinforced by his social origins. Teachers in primary schools are mainly from training colleges and a high proportion have come from working-class parents. In 1955 45·7 per cent of the men and 38·9 per cent of the women teachers were children of manual fathers, whilst in the grammar schools the figures were 32·4 per cent of men and 19·1 per cent of women.[1] The teacher from the training college who is aspiring to higher status has firmly chosen teaching as a profession to which to rise and has either forgone or never had academic pretensions. He (in fact the majority of teachers in this category are women) sees himself as a teacher of children, not of subjects and thus fits well into the ethos of the training college. The graduate teacher tends more often to come of middle-class parents and clings to his own connection with the university. Therefore he stresses his own claims to the status of the majority of those with university degrees. This is especially the case of that fair proportion of graduates who take to teaching as a second choice and fully realize that thereby they have lowered their claim to prestige. The graduate is therefore reinforced in seeing himself as a teacher of his subject rather than of children.

The influence of age on how the teacher views his role is difficult to assess. In both Germany and Holland the evidence suggests that the effect of age on the attitudes of the two ideal types can be attributed to the historical circumstances of the period in which the teachers grew up and were educated. The educational theories that were current at the time of their training seemed more powerful influences than any hardening of attitudes as teachers grow older. What little British evidence there is would suggest that there are no significant differences between age groups in the way that teachers view their role.[2]

Sex may be another determinant of the way a teacher views his role. There are more men than women graduate teachers and more women than men teachers from training colleges. The latter, as women, will tend

J. E. Floud and W. Scott, op. cit., p. 540.
[2] J. Kob, 1958, op. cit., pp. 571–3; H. W. F. Stellway in *The Yearbook of Education*, 1963, pp. 427–8; and P. H. Taylor, op. cit., p. 261.

to take more interest in children. In addition a larger proportion of women teachers are marrying and will have less interest in claiming status, since they will take that of their husbands rather than that of their own occupation. The men, even the non-graduates, will put more stress on their status and hence feel insecure. The men graduates will also more readily see themselves as academics in exile.

These determinants seem to reinforce each other and to influence teachers so that they will tend to see their role either as academic or child-centred. There is a third ideal type, whose incidence is more dependent upon personality and, therefore, is far less predictable. This is the teacher who views himself as a missionary. He sees his role as rescuing the child from his environment. In the nineteenth century social conscience stirred many teachers to their work. Some commentators today see a need for teachers who enter the profession not in search of status but to counter those contemporary trends that they consider harmful to society. Thus one American sociologist, David Riesman, views the teacher as exercising countervailing power against the evils of the day. The teacher is the crusader who will fight for intellectual standards against middle-class mediocrity and the missionary who will check falling moral standards.

When such suggestions are made it is apparent that the role of the teacher under contemporary conditions is no longer an adequate one (J. E. Floud, 1963). In a modern industrial society the teacher, particularly in the secondary modern schools serving large urban areas, may find that he has no common language of morality with his pupils. As Spinley pointed out in her work on personality structure to which reference has already been made, slum children do not have a highly developed conscience. These children learn by experience, not by precept, and appeals to principles from a teacher or anyone else mean little to them.[1] Yet mainly because of the needs of the economy children stay at school longer and because of the higher material standard of life they are mature physically at an earlier age than thirty years ago. At a time when the mental gap between the generations is widening and the biological gap is narrowing more tasks are handed to the schools, although the nature of the teacher's authority over the child has greatly changed. The teacher frequently condemns the very conduct that the family will approve. The relationship between home and school becomes strained when the teacher is telling the parents through the child what

[1] B. M. Spinley, op. cit., p. 83.

they should eat for breakfast or how they should dress their family to meet various weather conditions.

Under these circumstances the teacher has little moral authority over the child. Although he may see himself as a missionary, the sanctions that the teacher can use are very different from those that were present when moral consensus existed amongst teachers and parents. Today the only common factor may be the need for education on utilitarian grounds. At the secondary level if the child passes examinations he will gain a better-paid job. In the junior school to pass the eleven-plus will lead to the grammar school and to a chance of rising up the social scale. Under such conditions the ideal types that have been used here for analytical purposes may well prove dysfunctional if they represent common self-images of teachers in the schools. The academic type who loves learning for its own sake and bases his teaching on this idea of his role is unlikely to understand or have great success with pupils whose motives are purely utilitarian. The child-centred teacher may still succeed at primary level, but is unlikely to meet the vocational demands of an adolescent in the secondary school. The missionary teacher will need more than a well-developed social conscience to tackle rebellious youths backed by seemingly amoral parents. If teachers see themselves in ways at all near to these three ideal types, they are hindering their own work by casting themselves in the wrong roles. A critical re-assessment of what they are trying to do in the light of contemporary social conditions is a regular need for all teachers who want to continue to do effective work.

B. The Adjustment to Teaching

If many teachers play the same or nearly the same role, the life that they lead in the practice of their profession may influence the structure of their personalities. The three ideal types mentioned above have certain common features; for example, all teachers are adults amongst children. Because of these identical experiences teachers may undergo 'occupational moulding'; they may be forced to take on the personality of the job. Two other possibilities exist. Firstly, because of its nature the role of the teacher may attract a certain type of personality into the profession thereby ensuring in some respects at least a more or less uniform personality type amongst teachers. Secondly, the teacher under training may learn the responses expected in his particular role as he gradually meets the whole of his role-set. The supposition is that in much the same way

S

as a child becomes Scottish or English through the socialization process, the teacher will take on much the same personality as those already in the teaching world. To test the truth of these three arguments the first step must be an investigation of the psychological traits of teachers. If they are not in some measure the same for all teachers the above arguments cannot be true.

1. The Psychological Traits of Teachers

There have been very few attempts in Britain to discover the traits of teachers (P. E. Vernon, 1953). As long ago as 1931 R. B. Catell undertook an investigation that demonstrated very fully how difficult this task is.[1] His sample numbered 208 and consisted of educational administrators, inspectors, staff of training colleges, and head and assistant teachers. Catell asked them to say what they thought were the traits needed in a teacher. From their answers twenty-two major categories were devised. The really important result of the investigation, however, was that the different groups of informants consistently gave very different stresses to their pictures of what were the necessary traits. Administrators at that time emphasized general culture; inspectors named conservatism, orderliness and precision; training college staff demanded intelligence; also different requirements were desired in each sex; men ought to have energy, initiative, discipline and humour, whilst women needed tact, conscientiousness, insight and idealism. In other words the traits demanded consistently varied with the position in the educational system of the informant.

In the USA personality tests administered to teachers in the inter-war years showed them to have much the same interests as other professional people, though there were perhaps some slight differences between men and women teachers. During the same period Valentine found that British teachers were as liberal in attitude as the members of other professions but more liberal than the general public. Within the teaching profession itself there may be differences in certain of the attitudes held. A survey made in the late 1950's of teachers in secondary modern schools in the London area showed that these teachers could be divided into two main groups that were differentiated by their social philosophy.[2]

---

[1] R. B. Catell, 'The Assessment of Teaching Ability', *British Journal of Educational Psychology*, February 1931, especially pp. 52–55.

[2] M. K. Bacchus, 'A Survey of Secondary Modern School Teachers' Concepts of their Pupils' Interests and Abilities in relation to their Social Philosophy and to the Social Background of their Pupils', unpublished M.A. thesis, University of London, 1959.

One set of teachers were authoritarian and the other democratic in their outlook. The democratic group held views that were more favourable than the authoritarian teachers towards the children's home background. They encouraged social qualities in their pupils, whereas the authoritarian group emphasized moral qualities. Finally, the democratic teachers favoured much less rigid methods of teaching than their authoritarian colleagues. Neither the age nor the social class origin of the teachers appeared to be a determinant of the philosophy held and therefore of these differences in attitude.

This work dealt with a very small area of the attitudes held by teachers, but differences were found. Catell's investigation revealed the difficulties of discovering the psychological traits of teachers and that they appear very differently to various sets of people. The American results showed that teachers held interests that were much the same as other professional people, who have a remarkable diversity of personality type. The conclusion must be that, even though we can envisage teachers as having a definite role, they do not undergo a process of special selection or occupational moulding as a result of playing this role. There does not appear to be a distinct and consistent teaching personality.

2. *The Adjustment to Teaching*

Those who take up teaching are of very diverse personality, but they must all play a somewhat similar role that, by its very nature, is a difficult one. The teacher moves daily from the adult world where his role may be a relatively subsidiary one into a classroom of children where he is dominant, though the equilibrium between himself and his pupils is never stable. In the eyes of the children that he is teaching he moves from friend to judge and back to friend again many times in each day. Each evening the teacher ceases to deal with immature minds and returns to his life as an adult.[1] Some adjustment in personality is needed to cope with what is a demanding task.

Langeveld (1963) has shown that teachers enter the profession for many and different reasons. These motives can be twisted through long service either functionally or dysfunctionally. For instance a teacher who chose this profession because it seemed a safe way of life may easily come to fear life in the world beyond the school; he may tend to limit his experience and become tied to teaching. To an outsider such a teacher may appear to be a dedicated person, whereas in fact he is narrow and

[1] See W. Waller, op. cit., especially pp. 380-92.

therefore unable to give his pupils the full benefit of the degree of devotion that he bestows upon them. Again a teacher who chose his profession because the world of schools was well known to him may become so absorbed in his milieu of school, children, and parents that he grows into a 'Peter Pan' teacher who never becomes a fully grown adult. Or, again, he may turn into an educational climber whose ambitions rest upon diplomas for himself and cups or examination successes for his school. In the first case the children are no longer taught by a mature personality and in the second they have ceased to matter to the teacher as children.

Both these motives may, however, adapt functionally to teaching. The fact that a teacher feels absolutely safe in his work may allow him to put all his energies into fertile uses. This can be true particularly of teachers who are upwardly socially mobile, since they may well be willing to work very hard. In this case the children stand to gain much. Again, the man who chooses to teach since he knows the world of the school well can become a truly devoted teacher to whom his daily work is a labour of love. Once more the motive for teaching has adapted functionally to the test of the classroom.

Throughout this chapter there has been a recurring thread of insecurity in the role of the teacher. Always at the back of his mind is the problem of discipline and under contemporary conditions this is more difficult than formerly when moral authority was greater. The teacher has to keep in mind and adapt to a wide role-set, the membership of which changes frequently; therefore his relationships with, for example, his colleagues alter constantly and are unstable. Many teachers, but especially those who can be included in the academic type, feel insecure in their social status. The teacher still finds himself to be something of a social stranger. He feels that he must be a paragon of virtues as a teacher, but knows himself to be as near falling from grace as the next man. The adjustment to the sum of these threats to his security may be that he emphasizes conformity. His class must behave alike; to differ is dangerous and even unpredictable. He must be unadventurous to escape the notice of those around him; in this way even sins of omission may go unheeded and his isolation becomes less pronounced. Social forces make this one possible adjustment, but the effect of conformity on the children in the teacher's class must be examined. The teacher may crush their creativity and produce children who are trained to think convergently rather than divergently. In this way the teacher's own personal adjustment to his role is dysfunctional to the needs of the children and of contemporary society.

There are other ways in which the teacher's adjustment to his role may hamper his efficiency. Since he is continually on a pedestal before his class he may grow into a pedant and lose contact with the children. This can also happen if the teacher feels joy in using his power over his class. The distance between himself and the children widens. Again the organization of any institution demands some routine. The timetable of the school and the annual pattern of his teaching may encourage a rigidity in a teacher that will not help him to meet new conditions or difficult children who do not fit his preconceived ideas of how they should behave.

Finally, the majority of teachers begin their career with high ideals but they will all fail with some children. If a teacher has not a personality marked by a sense of optimism he may react to the failure to live up to his ideals by a retreat into cynicism. This is an adjustment to the problems of teaching that is particularly harmful to the children in his class. The teacher who has no hope will never engage the full interest of the children. In each of the cases described the teacher has adjusted to the circumstances of his profession in a way that hinders efficient teaching. Teachers have some chance of avoiding this, if they know that these hazards exist, and if they regularly examine themselves to see how they are adjusting to the circumstances of their professional life.

4. Conclusion

To the general public teachers probably seem conformists and isolated from the real world, but there is reason to believe that the role of the teacher is changing and that teachers are coming to be seen as ordinary people who teach rather than as cultured paragons. Teachers see themselves in various ways. Two common self-images are the academic and the child-centred types, neither of which seems to meet the needs of the schools in contemporary Britain. Little is really known about the role of the teacher in this country. What evidence exists has mainly to be drawn from psychological researches in allied fields. It may be that in Britain we are less prone to self-conscious analysis than the Americans, or it may be that we have less money to spend on such work, but there is an importance in more exact knowledge of the role of the teacher. The image of the teacher helps to determine vocational choice and hence the attraction of a profession that is undermanned and seems likely to remain so in the near future.

The traditional stereotype of the teacher with definite traits in his personality, mostly unpleasant, seems to be untrue. Yet forces exist that play upon anyone who teaches and to which an adjustment must be made. The teacher who begins his career with the soundest possible of motives may in time change so that he is no longer helping the children as much as he might. This conclusion emphasizes the need for continual self-assessment by practising teachers to see whether their idea of what they are doing meets the public need. If it does not, the teacher is not having the maximum possible effect on the children.

Throughout this book the public need has been taken as given. The first part was an examination of the place that children had in three important social institutions – the family, social class and the economy. In the second part the social functions of the schools were analysed. Finally the part that teachers play in educational institutions has been described. The aims of education have not been central to the argument. The sociology of education considers how the educational system works with given aims. Whatever the aims are, the same concepts are of use for sociological analysis; they are, in addition, legitimate tools to use on institutions other than education. The ideas of function, role, social mobility and the other concepts that have been introduced here can be applied as easily to a totalitarian as to our more democratic educational system. This book has on the whole dealt with problems of means not ends, though this is no reason for the teacher to study the sociology of education and to ignore its philosophy.

BIBLIOGRAPHY

J. E. Floud, 'Teaching in the Affluent Society', in *The Yearbook of Education*, London, 1963.

J. Kob, 'Definition of the Teacher's Role', 1958 in *The Reader*.

J. Kob, 'The Teacher in Industrial Society', in *The Yearbook of Education*, London, 1963.

M. J. Langeveld, 'The Psychology of Teachers and the Teaching Profession', in *The Yearbook of Education*, London, 1963.

P. E. Vernon, 'The Psychological Traits of Teachers', in *The Yearbook of Education*, London, 1953.

W. Waller, *The Sociology of Teaching*, New York, 1933 (especially Part V).

Index of Authors

Index of Contents